handy homework helper

U.S. History

Writers:
Susan Bloom
Maggie Ronzani

Consultant:
Linda Symcox

Publications International, Ltd.

Susan Bloom is a writer and editor with Creative Services Associates, Inc.

Maggie Ronzani is a writer and editor with Creative Services Associates, Inc. She has more than 25 years experience in educational publishing.

Linda Symcox has consulted and written numerous publications, including *World History The Easy Way, Vol. I*, and *America: Pathways To The Present*. She is a member of the American Historical Association and the National Council for History Education.

Cover Illustration: Dave Garbot.

Contents

About This Book

Homework takes time and a lot of hard work. Many students would say it's their least favorite part of the school day. But it's also one of the most important parts of your school career because it does so much to help you learn. Learning gives you knowledge, and knowledge gives you power.

Homework gives you a chance to review the material you've been studying so you understand it better. It lets you work on your own, which can give you confidence and independence. Doing school work at home also gives your parents a way to find out what you're studying in school.

Everyone has trouble with their homework from time to time, and *Handy Homework Helper: U.S. History* can help you when you run into a problem. This book was prepared with the help of educational specialists. It offers quick, simple explanations of the basic material that you're studying in school. If you get stuck on an idea or have trouble finding some information, *Handy Homework Helper: U.S. History* can help clear it up for you. It can also help your parents help you by giving them a fast refresher course in the subject.

This book is clearly organized by the topics you'll be studying in U.S. History. A quick look at the Table of Contents will tell you which chapter covers the area you're working on. You can probably guess which chapter includes what you need and then flip through the chapter until you find it. For even more help finding what you're looking for, look up key words related to what you're studying in the Index. You might find material faster that way, and you might also find useful information in a place you wouldn't have thought to look.

Remember that different teachers and different schools take different approaches to teaching History. For that reason, we recommend that you talk with your teacher about using this homework guide. You might even let your teacher look through the book so he or she can help you use it in a way that best matches what you're studying at school.

American Beginnings

Prehistory

The United States is a young nation. Yet, people have lived on American lands for more than 20,000 years. Around that time, the earth was going through an ice age. Huge sheets of ice covered most of the northern half of the planet, and the level of the oceans was lower. Land that is now underwater was exposed. Part of the Bering Strait, which is the body of water between Russia and

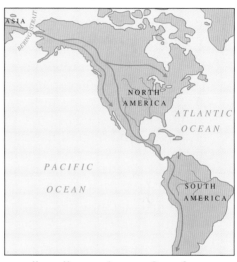

HUMAN MIGRATION ACROSS THE BERING STRAIT

Alaska, was above sea level and formed a bridge between the two lands. Asian hunters following animals crossed the bridge and spread throughout the Americas. They were the first Americans. Eventually, people were living everywhere from the northern regions of North America to the southern tip of South America.

The first Americans led a wandering life in search of food. Later, some groups began to farm. Native peoples in Mexico began farming crops such as wheat and corn around 7000 B.C. This meant they could live in one place, form villages, and do work other than finding food. Many different civilizations and cultures sprang up in North America and South America.

First people spread
across North America

20,000 B.C.

7000 B.C.

People begin farming
in the Americas

Early American Cultures

The Native peoples in America had many different ways of life. Some groups are known from the big mounds of earth they built that still remain today. As early as 1000 B.C., people built mounds to use as burial grounds, worship places, and sites for leaders' homes. Three main **mound builder** cultures were the Adena, the Hopewell, and the Mississippian.

The Adenas lived in what is now Ohio from 1000 B.C. until A.D. 200. They built mounds in striking shapes, such as the Great Serpent mound near Hillsboro, Ohio. Shaped like a snake, it is ¼ mile (.4 km) long. The Adenas lived in small villages. They lived mostly by hunting, fishing, and gathering.

The Great Serpent mound built by the Adenas is now part of a state park in Ohio.

The Hopewells were farmers of crops such as corn and squash. They lived in what is now Ohio, Indiana, Michigan, Illinois, Wisconsin, Iowa, and Missouri from about 100 B.C. until about A.D. 500. Both the Adenas and the Hopewells put objects in the tombs they built. They felt that a person's spirit would use pipes, jewelry, pottery, and weapons in the next world.

The Mississippian culture built a city around A.D. 600 in what is now Illinois. They named it Cahokia, and at one point, 40,000 people lived there. That means Cahokia was as large as the modern cities of Palm Springs, California; Hoboken, New Jersey; and Muskogee, Oklahoma. Cahokia's largest mound covers about 16 acres (6 hectares). Goods found in

Olmec culture flourishes		Mogollon culture develops	
1200 B.C.	**1000 B.C.**	**500 B.C.**	**100 B.C.**
	Mound-building Adenas appear		Hopewell culture develops

The Anasazis left their cliff dwellings in the 1300s. They may have moved southwest to escape a long drought or warring neighbors.

the mounds show that the Mississippians traded with many of their neighbors.

In what is now the southwestern United States, people known as **cliff dwellers** built shelters in canyon walls and under over-hanging rock formations. The Anasazis lived between A.D. 1000 and 1300 in what is now Arizona, New Mexico, Utah, and Colorado. They were hunters and farmers who lived in two-story or three-story houses built in cliff walls or on ledges. They used ladders to reach entrances on upper levels. The ladders were lowered for residents and raised if enemies approached.

Another Southwest culture was the Mogollon people. They built dams and terraces that helped with their farming. Mogollons lived in Arizona and New Mexico from about 500 B.C. to A.D. 1200. They produced the finest pottery made in North America north of Mexico. They often painted geometric designs in red and brown or black and white on their pottery.

Anasazi ruins often contain decorative art carvings or written pictographs that tell a story. The pictographs tell us much about how these people lived.

Mayas begin to flourish

Anasazis build cliff dwellings; Vikings reach North America

Incan empire dominates western coast of South America

A.D. 300   A.D. 600   A.D. 1000   1300   1400

Mississippians establish Cahokia

Aztecs establish city of Tenochtitlán

Native Americans Before 1492

After Europeans brought horses to America, many Native Americans changed their way of life. For instance, few groups relied on buffalo before 1492 because they were difficult to hunt. With horses, the Plains nation was able to use buffalo as its main source of food, shelter, and clothing.

Millions of people lived in North America in the late 1400s. They lived in hundreds of nations throughout the land. They had many different ways of life. Many nations lived near one another and shared the same culture. They lived in regions called **culture areas** by scientists and historians.

The homes that Native Americans lived in depended on climate and resources in the environment. For example, some people on the Plains lived in tepees made of animal skins, and some people in the Northwest lived in wooden multifamily houses. In the East, the Iroquois made buildings called longhouses, in which several families lived. Other cultures built lodges covered with mud.

These peoples lived in groups with their extended families: grandparents, aunts, uncles, and cousins. Often, families joined together in a **band,** a group of 20 to 300 people. Several bands formed a **nation,** which is a large group of people in a particular area with the same way of life and customs.

The daily life of Native Americans was based on working for food, clothing, and shelter. Men usually hunted for food, and women usually gathered plants and farmed.

The men usually hunted whatever game they could in their area: fish, wild birds, deer, and rabbit. Many groups also gathered berries, nuts, and roots. Some of them farmed, raising mostly beans, squash, and corn.

Native Americans enjoyed playing games. They had foot races and played forms of hockey and basketball. They invented a game of racquetball, which grew into the game of lacrosse. They also developed unique arts and crafts.

Most cultures had ceremonies that reflected their religious beliefs. The Plains nation celebrated a sun dance to offer thanks. They also held a buffalo dance to bring good fortune in hunting. Farming nations held rain dances. Nations in the East held a corn dance in honor of each summer's corn crop.

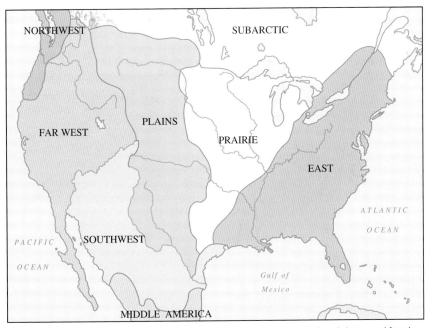

NORTH AMERICAN CULTURE AREAS. The different nations within a culture area shared the same lifestyle, but they often had different customs, religious beliefs, and languages. Some nations would trade with each other, some would fight with each other, and some would do both.

In Search of the East

Henry the Navigator of Portugal watches as one of the expeditions he sponsored returns to port.

Trade with the Middle East

When Europeans began to travel to the Middle East, they were introduced to silk, spices, new jewels, and china. In 1095, Christian crusaders from Europe began a war against the Muslims in the Middle East. The crusaders wanted to control religious sites in the Middle East. They learned about the riches of African and Asian nations from Middle Eastern traders. They eagerly traded for the gold, spices, silk, and other goods from Asia and Africa.

Europeans became interested in Africa and in the Far East, which they called the **Indies.** In 1271, a young Italian named Marco Polo went to China. He wrote a book about his travels that increased European interest in the Asian countries.

Vasco da Gama prepares to set sail from Portugal in 1497 to find a water route to India.

By the 1400s, many Europeans wanted to trade directly with the Asians and avoid the cost of dealing with the Middle Eastern traders. However, the main trade routes were overland and were controlled by the Middle Easterners. This made the products from the Indies very expensive.

Chinese invent movable type

Marco Polo travels to China

1050   **1095**   **1271**

The Crusades begin

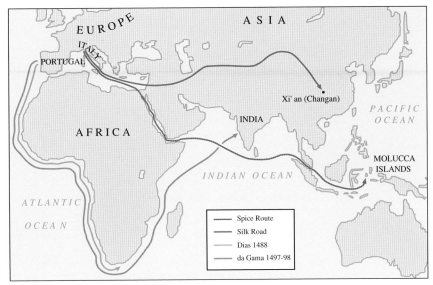

EUROPEAN TRAVEL TO THE FAR EAST, 15TH CENTURY

European explorers, especially those in Portugal and Spain, wanted to find a direct sea route to the Indies. The first Portuguese explorers tried to get to the east by sailing around the coast of Africa. Prince Henry, a son of the king of Portugal, sponsored many trips of exploration. He became known as Henry the Navigator.

A Portuguese explorer, Bartolomeu Dias, sailed around the southern tip of Africa in 1488. Vasco da Gama finally sailed around Africa and reached India in 1498.

These European explorers had new navigational tools to help them sail where they had not gone before. By checking the position of the sun and using an **astrolabe** and a **cross-staff,** they could determine their latitude. They also used a **compass,** an instrument invented in China.

16th century astrolabe

African slaves brought to Portugal

Bartolomeu Dias sails around the southern tip of Africa

| 1416 | 1440 | 1453 | 1488 |

Henry the Navigator sponsors trips along African coast

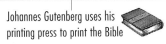
Johannes Gutenberg uses his printing press to print the Bible

Christopher Columbus

Christopher Columbus

A sailor named Christopher Columbus had a new idea of how to reach the Indies by water. Columbus believed Japan was 3,000 nautical miles (5,600 kilometers) west of Lisbon, Portugal. (It is actually 11,000 nautical miles—20,400 kilometers.) He thought he could sail west and reach the Indies.

In the 1480s, Columbus asked King John II of Portugal to sponsor an expedition west. The king refused. Later Columbus persuaded King Ferdinand and Queen Isabella of Spain to support his journey.

On August 3, 1492, Columbus left Palos, Spain, with three ships, the *Niña,* the *Pinta,* and the *Santa María.* They sailed to the Canary Islands and then headed west. On October 12, Columbus landed on San Salvador. He thought he had reached the Indies, and he called the people there Indians. Columbus left 40 sailors on the island of Haiti and returned to Spain with several Indians.

Columbus was welcomed as a hero. Ferdinand and Isabella wanted him to return to the islands to explore further. On his second trip, part of Columbus's crew colonized the island of Hispaniola. On Columbus's third trip, his ships landed on the coast of South America, and he was sure he had discovered a new continent. Columbus made his

Columbus and his crew are welcomed by natives as they arrive in the New World.

Treaty of Tordesillas divides newly discovered lands between Spain and Portugal

Vasco da Gama reaches India by sea

| 1492 | 1494 | 1497 | 1498 | 1500 |

Christopher Columbus reaches the Americas

John Cabot lands at Newfoundland

Pedro Alvares Cabral of Portugal claims Brazil

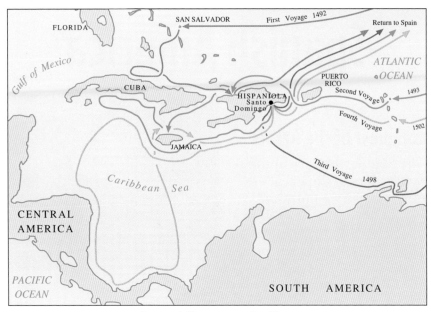

COLUMBUS'S VOYAGES TO THE NEW WORLD

fourth and final voyage in 1502, exploring the islands of the Caribbean and the coast of Central America.

Another explorer, Amerigo Vespucci, made three voyages to the Americas between 1499 and 1502. He claimed that new continents had been found. A mapmaker suggested that the new continents be named America in Vespucci's honor.

Columbian Exchange

With the arrival of Columbus in the Americas, a massive exchange of plants, animals, and diseases began between the Americas and Europe. This chart identifies some of the exchanges made.

From the Americas		To the Americas	
corn	potatoes	horses	cattle
tomatoes	chocolate	sheep	chickens
pumpkins	squashes	wheat	bananas
peppers	peanuts	sugar	grapes
pineapples	cashews	measles	smallpox

Spanish America

This modern painting shows Cortés and his party among the natives.

Conquest of the Aztecs

The Spaniards were among the leaders of the great age of European exploration. A Spaniard named Hernando Cortés sailed to Hispaniola in 1504. In 1511, he helped Diego Velázquez conquer Cuba. Then they heard about the empire of the Aztecs in what is now Mexico.

The Aztecs had formed an advanced civilization. They were a religious people, and the capital city of Tenochtitlán had many temples. The Aztecs fought many wars in the name of religion, and they sacrificed many of their prisoners to their gods. They were very wealthy, partly because they forced the nations they conquered to surrender silver and gold.

In 1519, Cortés sailed to Mexico from Cuba and then down the coast. He and his army traveled inland to Tenochtitlán. On the way, the Spaniards were joined by many Indians

Montezuma's arrest. The Spanish soldiers in the Americas were known as conquistadores.

Spanish bring African slaves to Santo Domingo

Hernando Cortés captures Montezuma; Ferdinand Magellan begins voyage around the world

1501	1513	1519	1521

Juan Ponce de León explores Florida; Vasco Núñez de Balboa sees the Pacific Ocean

Cortés conquers the Aztecs

The Aztecs drive out Cortés and his soldiers. The Spanish returned soon and took permanent control of the empire.

who had been mistreated by the Aztecs. The Spaniards brought guns and horses, which the Indians had never seen before. In Tenochtitlán, the Spaniards captured Montezuma, the Aztec king. They forced him to pay tribute to the Spanish king.

Cortés had too few soldiers to conquer the Aztec capital, but he held Montezuma hostage to ensure the Spaniards' safety. In June 1520, the Aztecs rebelled and killed hundreds of Spaniards. However, Cortés survived. He reorganized his army and gained the support of Spanish and Indian troops. They attacked and destroyed Tenochtitlán in the spring of 1521 and built Mexico City on the ruins of the Aztec capital.

Aztec Civilization

Religion was based on hundreds of gods including a sun god, a corn god, a fire god, and a rain god. The Aztecs practiced human sacrifice.

Classes of society were nobles, commoners, serfs, and slaves. Most people were commoners who farmed or had a trade. Serfs worked the nobles' land. Slaves were criminals or people captured in war.

Aztec calendar stone

Foods were tortillas, chili peppers, corn, avocados, squash, and tomatoes.

Shelters included simple adobe homes for commoners and stone houses with patios for nobles.

Francisco Pizarro conquers the Incas

Juan Rodriguez Cabrillo explores California coast

1533   1535   1542   1565

First viceroy of New Spain is appointed

Spanish found St. Augustine, Florida

Conquest of the Incas

Like Cortés, Francisco Pizarro left Spain to explore the Americas. After living in Hispaniola, he took part in the exploration of Panama with Vasco de Balboa. Living in Panama City, Pizarro heard tales of the wealthy empire of the Incas in South America. He led several explorations down the west coast of South America to find it.

Francisco Pizarro

The Incan empire included parts of present-day Colombia, Ecuador, Peru, Bolivia, Chile, and Argentina. The Incas conquered many peoples through force and then ruled them with a complex political system. They had excellent roads and bridges. They constructed large, strong buildings of stone and made fine artwork of gold and silver. They also developed irrigation and terracing systems to improve their farming.

In 1533, Pizarro and an army of 167 troops captured the Incan leader, Atahualpa. He paid a huge ransom of gold and silver, but the Spaniards executed him anyway. The Spaniards then took over the Incan empire.

A Spanish priest teaches the Incan leader Atahualpa about Christianity. The Spanish worked to convert natives as part of their conquest of the Americas.

Spanish bring African slaves to St. Augustine

 Spanish establish the mission and presidio of San Antonio

1581   **1609**   **1718**

Spanish found the city of Santa Fe

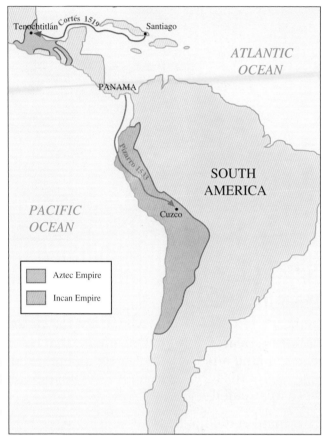

THE SPANISH
CONQUISTADORES VOYAGES
TO THE AMERICAS,
16TH CENTURY

Incan Civilization

Religion was based on many gods, such as the creator god, the sun god, and goddesses of the earth and the sea. The Incas sacrificed crops, animals, and sometimes humans.

Classes of society were based on a family's rank. Groups called ayllus were based on family relationships and land ownership.

Foods included corn and potatoes. They also grew cotton.

Shelters included stone mansions for nobles and adobe or stone houses with thatched roofs for commoners.

Hernando de Soto and his party reach the shore of the Mississippi River.

Spanish America

In the early 1500s, Spain created the *encomienda* system in their American colonies. This meant that colonists received tracts of land and control over the people who lived there. The Spaniards forced the natives to be their slaves, and many were mistreated.

The Spanish did not begin exploring what is now the United States until April 1513, when Juan Ponce de León landed in Florida. Ponce de León had heard stories of a "fountain of youth," and he looked for it in present-day Florida.

The area was explored again by Hernando de Soto in 1539. (He journeyed farther into the mainland and was the first European to reach the Mississippi River.) Yet the area was first colonized by the French. A group of French Huguenots (a Protestant sect) settled near present-day Jacksonville in 1564. The Spanish king sent an army that founded the settlement of St. Augustine and massacred the French. St. Augustine was the first permanent European settlement in what is now the United States.

The Spanish wanted to convert the native peoples to Roman Catholicism. Many priests created missions to help educate them. Some also worked for better treatment of the peoples.

Between 1540 and 1542, Francisco Vasquez de Coronado went in search of the legendary seven cities of great wealth. He ended up in what is now New Mexico and Arizona. Other Spanish explorers traveled through the region and finally colonized it in 1598.

The Spanish Influence in America

Did you know that you can visit a building constructed by the Spanish in America in 1609? The Spanish built the Palace of the Governors in Santa Fe, New Mexico, in 1609 as a fortress. The Spanish builders used adobe, a kind of sun-dried brick.

The Palace of the Governors today.

Although the builders used American materials, the architectural style is mainly Spanish, with a covered porch and European-style doors and windows.

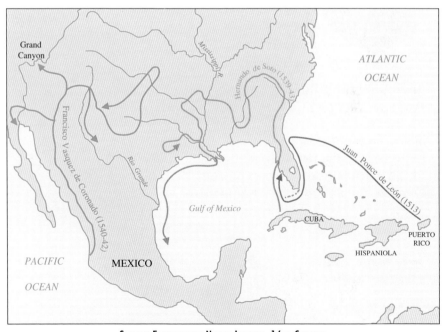

SPANISH EXPLORERS IN NORTH AMERICA, 16TH CENTURY

French and English Exploration

Giovanni da Verrazano

In Search of the Northwest Passage

After Columbus's voyages, the French and English continued to look for a shorter route to the Far East. In looking for a Northwest Passage through North America, explorers from these two countries searched much of the coast of North America. In 1524, Giovanni da Verrazano commanded a French voyage to look for the Northwest Passage. Verrazano explored the Atlantic coast and reported on its beauty to the king of France.

Jacques Cartier

Searching for gold and for a Northwest Passage, Jacques Cartier of France sailed up the St. Lawrence River in 1534 to the site of present-day Montreal. English explorer Henry Hudson, sailing on behalf of the Netherlands, also explored Canada. He sailed into what is now

---

Giovanni da Verrazano explores
the eastern coast of North America

 English bring African
slaves to Hispaniola

English defeat the
Spanish Armada

| 1524 | 1534 | 1565 | 1587 | 1588 |

 Jacques Cartier sails into
the Gulf of St. Lawrence

 English set up their first North American
settlement on Roanoke Island

Henry Hudson did not find a northern route to the Indies, but he did leave a mark on North America. Hudson Bay, Hudson Strait, and the Hudson River all bear his name.

known as Hudson Bay, believing he had found the Pacific Ocean. After a harsh winter, his crew left Hudson and returned to England. Hudson's fate is unknown, but his explorations led to later claims and settlement by the Dutch.

In 1584, Sir Walter Raleigh of England sent explorers to the North American coast to find a good place for a colony. They chose Roanoke Island in North Carolina and started a settlement there in 1587. John White, the settlement's governor, returned to England. When he came back to Roanoke in 1590, the colony had mysteriously disappeared. Search parties found only the word *Croatoan* carved in a tree. The Croatoans were Native Americans who had been friendly with the settlers. Some people thought that the settlers had moved north to the Chesapeake Bay area and fought with nations there. Others thought that the settlers scattered and ended up living with several different nations. No one knows for sure what happened to the settlers, so the group is known as the **Lost Colony.**

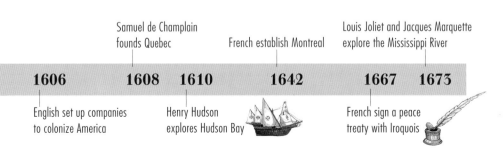

Samuel de Champlain founds Quebec

French establish Montreal

Louis Joliet and Jacques Marquette explore the Mississippi River

1606   **1608**   **1610**   **1642**   **1667**   **1673**

English set up companies to colonize America

Henry Hudson explores Hudson Bay

French sign a peace treaty with Iroquois

Fur traders were some of the first Europeans to successfully settle in North America.

The French in Canada

After Jacques Cartier explored the land around the St. Lawrence River, French fishing crews and traders began to settle in the area. The traders exchanged European goods such as tools and knives with the native peoples for furs from beavers, foxes, minks, and otters. Europeans used the furs to make hats and other clothing; hats made from beaver fur became especially popular. By the late 1500s, the fur trade had become an important industry.

In 1608, the French explorer Samuel de Champlain founded the town of Quebec on the St. Lawrence River. Quebec

Samuel de Champlain selects the site of Quebec.

became an important fur trading center and the center of culture in the growing colony of New France. New France included Canada, Acadia, and Louisiana. In 1660, the colony consisted of only a few thousand fur traders and missionaries. In 1663, King Louis XIV of France sent 2,500 new settlers. By 1720, New France's population was 25,000.

The fur trade remained the most important industry in New France. However, farming also developed. Many young fur traders became farmers when they married. They rented sections of land called *seigneuries.* The king of France gave these parcels of farmland to colonists who had been wealthy nobles or military officers in France.

The colony of New France thrived for 150 years. The Catholic church ran schools and hospitals. The wealthy leaders of the colony lived in large, luxurious houses and enjoyed social events such as formal balls. Merchants lived in smaller stone houses, and farmers lived in small log cabins.

The French colony of Quebec as it looked in 1775.

English Colonies

Natives welcome the English settlers as they land on the shores of Virginia.

Jamestown

On May 6, 1607, a group of 105 English adventurers landed on a peninsula on the James River in what is now Virginia. The colonists had been sent to start a settlement by a business called the Virginia Company of London. They called their settlement Jamestown in honor of their king, James I.

The settlers chose a swampy, unhealthy site for their home. They had poor diets, and two thirds of them died of malnutrition or of diseases such as malaria and pneumonia. In 1608, Captain John Smith took control of the colony. Smith made the settlers plant food crops. He also bought corn from Native Americans. After Smith returned to England in 1609, Lord De La Warr brought new settlers and supplies in 1610.

The Jamestown settlers worried about problems with the natives. Pocahontas, the daughter of the leader of the Virginia nations, helped keep peace for a time. She married settler

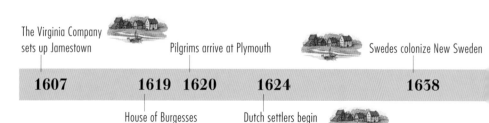

The Virginia Company sets up Jamestown

Pilgrims arrive at Plymouth

Swedes colonize New Sweden

| 1607 | 1619 | 1620 | 1624 | 1638 |

House of Burgesses is formed

Dutch settlers begin New Netherland colony

Pocahontas, daughter of the powerful chief Powhatan, asks that John Smith's life be spared to keep peace during a dispute between her people and the Jamestown colonists.

The first Jamestown settlers work to build their colony.

John Rolfe, who introduced a new tobacco plant that became a valuable cash crop. Soon, the colony raised hogs as well and grew plenty of corn.

In 1619, the Virginia Company sent young women to Jamestown. They married colonists and began families. The native peoples, fearing loss of their homes, attacked the settlement in 1622 and 1644. Fires destroyed the town in 1676 and 1698. Still, Jamestown paved the way for more English colonies.

The House of Burgesses

In 1619, the governor of Virginia called a meeting to be attended by two citizens from each of the divisions of Virginia. At that time, only adult males were considered citizens. These citizen representatives were called burgesses. The **House of Burgesses** first met on July 30, 1619, in Jamestown. The House of Burgesses followed English law, acted on all tax laws, and made other laws. After 1625, the house began managing all of the colony's affairs. The House of Burgesses was an important step in American democracy.

English establish the Carolinas

New Englanders win Prince Philip's War against the Indians

| 1651 | 1663 | 1664 | 1676 | 1732 |

English Parliament passes the first Navigation Act

English take over New Netherland and New Sweden

James Oglethorpe founds Georgia

The first colonists from the *Mayflower* arrive at Plymouth.

Plymouth

The people who later became known as the **Pilgrims** of Plymouth Colony left England because they wanted religious freedom. The official English church was the Church of England. People who did not belong to this religion were often persecuted. The Pilgrims had separated from the Church of England and began practicing religion in their own way. Some fled to the Netherlands, but they were unhappy that their children were not living as English citizens.

Because they wished to worship in their own way in an English environment, the Pilgrims decided to leave for America. Here they believed that they could practice their religion and live under English ways of life. The Pilgrims sailed on the *Mayflower* for more than two months and landed on Cape Cod on November 20, 1620. Although they meant to land farther south near Virginia, the settlers arrived in New England because of navigational errors and bad weather.

The signing of the Mayflower Compact.

While still aboard the *Mayflower,* 41 settlers signed the **Mayflower Compact.** Because they were settling outside the area granted to them, the Pilgrims did not have a set of rules by which to live. The Mayflower Compact set up a few basic rules that all Plymouth settlers had to follow. It was the first guide to self-government created in the American colonies. The Mayflower Compact set up a General Court, which was in charge of electing leaders, imposing taxes, and making laws.

Harvest Festival

After founding the Plymouth Colony in 1620, the Pilgrims suffered through a long, harsh winter. They did not know how to produce the food they needed until their native friend Squanto showed them American crops and farming methods. When they harvested a bountiful crop in the autumn of 1621, they invited the local peoples to join them in a three-day harvest celebration. They enjoyed American foods such as corn bread, duck, goose, turkey, venison (deer meat), and shellfish.

The Narragansets grant land to Roger Williams, who had always encouraged peaceful, humane relations with the nation.

Massachusetts, Rhode Island, Connecticut, and Maryland

In 1630, a group called the **Puritans** came to the Massachusetts Bay area in search of religious freedom. By 1640, the Massachusetts Bay Colony had 10,000 people. The Puritans favored political freedom that gave people certain basic rights. However, only people who practiced the Puritan religion were allowed to live in the colony.

Many settlers left Massachusetts because of the strict religious rules. Some, like Roger Williams, were driven out. In 1636, he bought land from the Narragansets and established the town of Providence, Rhode Island. He set up a government based on religious and political freedom. Other settlers from Massachusetts set up the towns of Portsmouth, Newport, and Warwick.

The Maryland colonists established friendly ties with the peoples in the region.

Colonists from Massachusetts also settled Connecticut. Thomas Hooker, a minister, came searching for religious and political freedom. Others came in search of good farmland. The colonists founded several settlements, and in 1636, they were united as the Connecticut Colony.

In 1634, a group of English colonists settled in Maryland. The owner of the colony's charter in England was Lord Baltimore. Lord Baltimore was a Roman Catholic. He felt that religious freedom would encourage the growth of the Maryland colony. Maryland soon allowed the practice of all Christian religions.

Lord Baltimore

The Road to Democracy

Many of the first English settlers in America insisted on religious freedom. Their search for religious freedom often led them to establish political self-government. In Connecticut, Thomas Hooker's call for a government by the people led to the **Fundamental Orders.** The Orders provided for government elections by citizens. The Puritans of Massachusetts created a similar document, the **Body of Liberties,** in 1641. Massachusetts set up a system that allowed citizens—males who owned property—to enforce their own laws. In Maryland, Lord Baltimore's insistence on religious freedom for all Christians led to the **Toleration Act of 1649.**

Thomas Hooker and his settlers arrive at Hartford, Connecticut.

New Netherland and New Sweden

This painting depicts Dutch settler Peter Minuit negotiating for the island of Manhattan. He paid with a variety of goods worth about 60 guilders, or 24 dollars.

Merchants in the Netherlands wanted to compete with the French and Spanish in the American fur trade. In 1621, they formed the Dutch West India Company. In 1624, the company sent colonists to settle near the mouth of the Hudson River on an island that the native people called Man-a-hat-ta. The Dutch colonists called their settlement New Amsterdam. In 1626, the governor of the settlement, Peter Minuit, bought the island of Manhattan from the natives.

The Dutch claimed land including parts of present-day Connecticut, Delaware, New Jersey, and New York. In order to colonize their land quickly, they set up the **patroon system.** Huge pieces of land were given to patroons (landowners), who were to find 50 adults to settle on the land and farm it. However, the strict patroons gave their workers few rights, so the population grew slowly.

Dutch governor Peter Stuyvesant recaptured Fort Casimir from the Swedish on September 26, 1655. This victory ended a 15-year struggle between Dutch and Swedish colonists by driving the Swedes out of North America.

In 1638, Swedish settlers founded a colony in present-day New Jersey. The Dutch, who lived directly north of New Sweden, believed that the Swedes were on Dutch land. The Swedish colony numbered fewer than 200 people. The Dutch governor, Peter Stuyvesant, took over the Swedish colony in 1655.

Many English colonists from Massachusetts and Connecticut settled eastern Long Island off the coast of New Amsterdam. The Dutch settled on the western part. The Dutch and the English lived in peace for several years, but then they began to fight. The king of England gave his brother, the Duke of York, a charter for the territory. In 1664, English warships sailed into the New Amsterdam harbor. The Dutch colonists would not support Stuyvesant, and they surrendered the colony. The English renamed the area New York after the Duke of York.

Peter Stuyvesant surrendered New Amsterdam to Colonel Richard Nicolls on September 20, 1664, almost nine years to the day after ousting the Swedish colonists.

William Penn establishes a treaty with neighboring peoples. Fair treatment of natives was an important part of Penn's plan for his colony.

Pennsylvania, Carolinas, and Georgia

In 1663, the king of England granted present-day North Carolina and South Carolina to **proprietors,** or owners. They named the land Carolina after their king, Charles II. Beginning in 1670, the proprietors sent colonists to the land and accepted others who came as well. By 1700, the colony contained many wealthy plantations worked by slaves, who made up about half the population.

Meanwhile, North Carolina drew many people from Virginia and England. The proprietors allowed the colonists to govern themselves. Most lived on small farms and had fewer slaves than their neighbors to the south.

In 1681, the king of England granted the Pennsylvania region to William Penn. Penn was a **Quaker,** a believer in a new faith based on peace and goodwill. He planned to establish

King Charles II presents the charter for Pennsylvania to William Penn as payment of a debt owed to Penn's father.

James Oglethorpe

a colony with political and religious freedom. Penn laid out the plan for the capital city of Philadelphia in 1682. Both the city and the colony prospered.

James Oglethorpe wanted to help the jailed debtors of England start a new life, so he and some wealthy friends sent them to settle Georgia in 1732. At first, the colonists were granted only small parcels of land and were not allowed slaves. Georgia later developed a plantation economy.

Penn's Dream

William Penn was a Quaker. The Quakers believed that religious authority came from the Christian spirit in each person, not from the Bible or priests. They thought that killing was wrong, even in war. William Penn wanted to create a colony where Quakers could worship freely. He soon decided to make his colony a refuge for any people who wanted religious or political liberty.

William Penn

On the colonial plantations in the South, life was very different for the slaves *(left)* than it was for the landowners *(below)*.

Colonial Economies

Settlers soon learned how to live off of America's rich resources. Farming became the most important way of life. Most farmers planted the same crop for several years. When the soil ran out of nutrients, the farmers cleared more land. Since the East Coast had plenty of rich soil, farmers produced plenty of food. In addition to growing corn and wheat, they raised livestock. Farmers in Virginia and Maryland grew tobacco. Those in Georgia and South Carolina produced rice and indigo. Another valuable product was timber. Lumber and other tree products were important for the shipbuilding industry.

In the South, African slaves did most of the hard work on tobacco, rice, and indigo **plantations.** By 1750, more than 235,000 African slaves lived in the colonies.

Shipbuilding, whaling, and fishing were all important industries in the colonies.

The farming in New England was more difficult than in the other colonies. The climate was harsher, the land was rockier, and the soil was thinner. Many people turned to fishing and whaling. The nearness of the sea also encouraged the ship-building industry in New England.

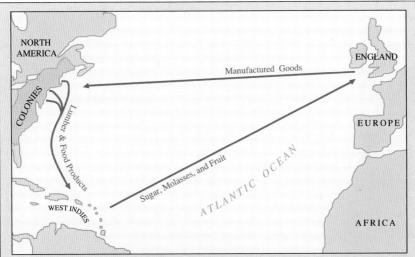

TRIANGULAR TRADE ROUTE, 18TH CENTURY

Trade with the English

When Americans began to produce enough goods for export to other places, England made laws called the **Navigation Acts.** The acts forced the colonies to trade only with England and regulated what could be exported. One of the acts, the Molasses Act, prohibited the colonies from buying molasses from the French colonies in the West Indies. However, the colonists smuggled in French molasses. To get around other navigation laws, the colonies developed **triangular trade routes.** One of these routes involved sending food products and lumber to the West Indies. The West Indies exchanged these products for fruit, molasses, and sugar. These were traded to England for manufactured goods, which were exported to the colonies.

Life in the Colonies

The **New England Colonies** included Massachusetts, Rhode Island, Connecticut, and New Hampshire. New England life centered around towns. Settlers were given a piece of land for a house, a lot on which to plant corn, and part of a common meadow on which their animals could graze. Decisions about the towns were made in town meetings. Salem and Boston, two towns in Massachusetts, were the main trade ports in New England.

THE ENGLISH COLONIES IN AMERICA, 18TH CENTURY

The **Middle Colonies** included Delaware, New Jersey, New York, and Pennsylvania. Many farmers produced so much wheat that the colonies became known as the "bread colonies." The Middle Colonies also manufactured glass and leather goods. The two largest American cities, Philadelphia and New York, were located here.

The **Southern Colonies** included Georgia, Maryland, North Carolina, South Carolina, and Virginia. This is where life on the big tobacco and indigo plantations thrived. Slaves

A typical street in the colony of New York might have looked like this on a given day.

The city of Yorktown, Virginia, as it appeared in 1781.

were the main workers on the plantations, and they made up a large part of the population in the South. Charleston, South Carolina, and Savannah, Georgia, were two of the main port cities where slaves and goods were traded.

The Great Awakening

In colonial times, many people lived far from a church. During the **Great Awakening,** from the mid–1740s until about 1750, several popular ministers traveled throughout the colonies and held huge meetings. These preachers spoke about repenting of sins and turning to God. One result of these revivals was that new Methodist and Baptist congregations sprang up. Also, the preachers helped the colonists think about the equality of all people. Finally, the Great Awakening improved higher education. In order to educate new preachers, church leaders founded the College of New Jersey at Princeton in 1746, King's College (Columbia University) in 1754, the College of Rhode Island (later Brown University) in 1764, and Queen's College (Rutgers University) in 1766.

George Whitfield was an influential traveling preacher.

Jonathan Edwards helped inspire the Great Awakening.

Colonial Strife

DISPUTED BY ENGLAND, RUSSIA, & SPAIN

DISPUTED BY ENGLAND & FRANCE

NEW FRANCE

PACIFIC OCEAN

LOUISIANA

COLONIES

ATLANTIC OCEAN

NEW SPAIN

Gulf of Mexico

HISPANIOLA

CUBA

JAMAICA

Caribbean Sea

England

France

Spain

SOUTH AMERICA

EUROPEAN CLAIMS IN NORTH AMERICA, 1748

The French and Indian War

The French owned land along the St. Lawrence River, the Great Lakes, and the Mississippi River. England claimed the land lying inland from its colonies. The two countries fought over their lands and over control of the fur-trading and fishing industries in America.

The French and Indian War began in 1754. The French had many friends among the native tribes. The English had often cheated and killed their new neighbors. Many Native Americans helped the French fight the English.

The French had several successes in 1755 and 1756. A strong general, Louis-Joseph de Montcalm-Grozon, led the French in

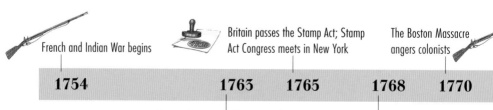

French and Indian War begins

Britain passes the Stamp Act; Stamp Act Congress meets in New York

The Boston Massacre angers colonists

1754 **1763** **1765** **1768** **1770**

Treaty of Paris signed; Britain enforces Navigation Acts in the colonies

The British send soldiers to Boston to keep order

In an early victory, English forces at Lake George stop the French from invading New York.

capturing British strongholds. From 1758 to 1759, the British defeated the French at important forts along the western frontier. Finally, the British captured Quebec in 1759 and Montreal in 1760.

The French and Indian War was part of the Seven Years' War waged by the major European nations. To end the war, the **Treaty of Paris** in 1763 gave Britain almost all the French lands in Canada and east of the Mississippi River. Spain received New Orleans and French lands west of the Mississippi. The war put an end to France's strength in North America.

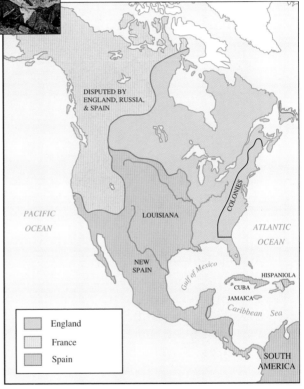

EUROPEAN CLAIMS IN NORTH AMERICA, 1763

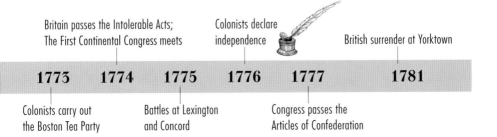

Britain passes the Intolerable Acts; The First Continental Congress meets

Colonists declare independence

British surrender at Yorktown

1773   **1774**   **1775**   **1776**   **1777**   **1781**

Colonists carry out the Boston Tea Party

Battles at Lexington and Concord

Congress passes the Articles of Confederation

After the Boston Massacre, British troops were moved out of the city to ease tensions.
A trial found two of the soldiers involved in the incident guilty of manslaughter.

Stamp Act Congress

After the French and Indian War, Britain had a much greater territory to control in America. Also, the expensive war had greatly increased Britain's national debt. The British Parliament felt that the colonies should help pay for these expenses. To get additional revenue from the colonies, Britain began to exert a tighter rule over the American colonies, which upset many colonists.

The Stamp Act of 1765 required colonists to buy stamps for paper documents, such as newspapers, pamphlets, and legal documents. Many colonists argued that since America was not represented in Parliament, Parliament did not have the right to tax them. Some

Americans throughout the colonies violently protested the Stamp Act.

colonists organized a group called the **Sons of Liberty.** They encouraged colonists not to obey the Stamp Act and not to import British goods.

In October 1765, representatives from nine colonies met in New York to discuss the Stamp Act. This was known as the Stamp Act Congress. The colonists agreed that "taxation without representation is tyranny." Parliament soon repealed the Stamp Act.

In 1767, Parliament passed the **Townshend Acts,** which taxed such British imports as paint, lead, paper, and tea. The British sent troops to New York and Boston to put down protests. The Bostonians especially objected to their presence. On March 5, 1770, an unruly American mob attacked some British soldiers. The soldiers fired on the crowd and killed four Boston citizens. This was known as the **Boston Massacre.**

That same day, Parliament repealed all of the Townshend duties except for the tax on tea. This the British kept to assert their authority over the colonists.

Important Acts and People

Sugar Act was passed to raise revenue. It restricted American exports and put additional taxes on some imports.

Stamp Act of 1765 required American businesses to buy stamps for many kinds of documents.

Townshend Acts of 1767 required Americans to pay taxes on imports of lead, paint, paper, and tea.

John Dickinson published the "Pennsylvania Farmer" letters to convince people to settle the disagreements between Britain and the colonies peacefully.

Patrick Henry led the opposition to the Stamp Act in Virginia.

Samuel Adams helped organize the Sons of Liberty and publicized the unfairness of the Townshend Acts.

Crispus Attucks, an African American and a former slave, became one of the first to give his life in the Revolution when he was killed at the Boston Massacre.

Colonists disguised as Mohawks dump tea from the *Dartmouth* into Boston Harbor.

The Beginning of War

With the new taxes and laws, some Americans feared that the British would soon take away all their freedom. In 1773, Parliament gave the East India Company a monopoly on all tea sent to the colonies. The colonies reacted angrily. In Philadelphia and New York, the tea was returned to England.

In Charleston, the tea was allowed to land but was not sold. In Boston, the Sons of Liberty dumped the tea into the water. This **Boston Tea Party** angered Parliament, and in 1774, England passed several laws to punish the colonies. The Americans called these laws the **Intolerable Acts.**

Patrick Henry

In response to the Intolerable Acts, the colonies planned a congress of all the American colonies. On May 27, 1774, delegates from all the colonies except Georgia met in Philadelphia. This was the **First Continental Congress.** The Congress called for an end to trade with Britain until the Intolerable

Two famous incidents from the beginning of the Revolutionary War: Paul Revere's ride *(left)* and the Battle of Lexington *(below).*

Acts were repealed. It declared that Parliament had no right to pass laws for America except those involving foreign trade. Some of the leaders at the Congress were Richard Henry Lee, Patrick Henry, George Washington, and John Jay.

King George III insisted that the colonies would not become independent without a fight. On April 19, 1775, British troops were sent to seize American ammunition at Concord, outside Boston. Two American patriots, William Dawes and Paul Revere, rode through the countryside to warn the citizens, and the **Minutemen,** armed colonists, were waiting at Lexington for the soldiers. Shots rang out, and the Revolutionary War had begun.

Revolutionary War

	Americans	British
Advantages	•On American land •Leadership of George Washington •Help from France	•Strong government •Trained army •Financial resources
Disadvantages	•Lack of finances •Untrained army •Weak government	•Lack of enthusiasm •Far from home •American sympa- thizers in Britain

The Declaration of Independence

Some members of the Continental Congress signed the Declaration of Independence on July 4, 1776.

Even after Lexington and Concord, the American people disagreed over whether or not they should be independent from Great Britain. In 1775, the Continental Congress sent the **Olive Branch Petition** to King George III. The petition promised loyalty to the king and asked for compromise. King George did not trust the Americans. He declared that the colonies were in a state of rebellion. In January 1776, **Thomas Paine** published a pamphlet called *Common Sense.* It said that Americans must become independent. Paine's words helped change people's minds. In 1776, the Congress passed the Declaration of Independence. Written by **Thomas Jefferson,** the Declaration laid out some basic ideas on which a government should be based. It also gave the reasons why America should become independent.

Loyalists and Patriots

Some people in the colonies remained loyal to England. These **Loyalists** made up about one third of the American population. Many were leaders of the government, church, or military. They feared that they would lose their positions if they opposed England. They also respected the King of England's authority. Many Loyalists left America at the beginning of the war. Others stayed in the colonies. The **Patriots** were Americans who supported war against Britain.

The Revolution

When fighting against the British started, each colony had its own militia. **George Washington,** the general in command of the war, organized the Continental Army, but he had a difficult time recruiting soldiers. One of the colonies' greatest strengths was General George Washington.

The British had a strong army, and they hired German mercenaries (paid soldiers). Britain planned to defeat the colonies in the north first. They

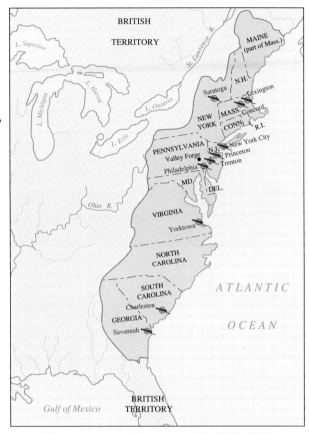

MAJOR BATTLES OF THE REVOLUTIONARY WAR, 1775–1781

hoped that the other colonies would then surrender. The British captured New York City in 1776. Washington countered with a surprise attack on Trenton, New Jersey. The Americans also defeated the British at Princeton, New Jersey.

The British captured Philadelphia on September 26, 1777. Benedict Arnold led battles against British General John Burgoyne near Saratoga, New York. On October 17, 1777, Burgoyne surrendered. This was a turning point of the war, because France then agreed to help the Americans.

Washington's army endured a terrible winter at Valley Forge, Pennsylvania. While they were there, a Prussian soldier named Baron Friedrich von Steuben taught them military methods. By the end of 1778, the British brought forces into

On Christmas day 1776, George Washington led colonial troops across the Delaware River for a successful surprise attack on Trenton, New Jersey.

the Southern Colonies. They captured Savannah, Georgia, and later took Charleston, South Carolina.

Yorktown, Virginia, was the site of the last major battle. French and Americans surrounded British troops led by General Charles Cornwallis. He surrendered on October 19, 1781. The Americans and the British signed the **Treaty of Paris** in 1783.

Some Heroes of the Revolution

Mary Hayes accompanied her husband at the Battle of Monmouth and earned the nickname "Molly Pitcher" for bringing water to soldiers.

John Paul Jones was a naval captain who captured the British ship *Serapis* in 1779. In the midst of battle, Jones said, "I have not yet begun to fight."

Marquis de Lafayette was a French noble who led troops in the Battle of Yorktown.

Francis Marion, known as the "Swamp Fox" for his guerrilla attacks, helped force General Charles Cornwallis to Yorktown.

Casimir Pulaski, a professional soldier from Poland, died in battle at Savannah.

A New Nation

The Articles of Confederation

In 1777, Congress passed the Articles of Confederation. These articles gave the national government the power to declare war and deal with other countries. But the government could not collect taxes. It had no way to pay back the huge debts from the war or to provide for an army. The states limited the power of the national government so that each state would have more control over its own affairs.

UNITED STATES IN 1781

Articles of Confederation

National Congress Could:
•Declare war and peace
•Manage foreign relations
•Establish army and navy
•Issue and borrow money
•Control Indian affairs

Each State Government Could:
•Have one vote in Congress
•Have any powers not specifically given to the Congress

Weaknesses:
•Congress could not raise money through taxes or control trade
•Congress could not enforce its laws on the states
•No federal executive or judiciary branch

The Constitutional Convention

In 1786, farmers in Massachusetts were deep in debt. Their state taxes were very high, and prices for farm products were low. Groups of farmers demanded financial help. The state government refused their demands. Daniel Shays, a Revolutionary War veteran, led a group of 1,200 farmers to take over the Springfield arsenal. They were turned back and arrested. Shays and others were later pardoned. **Shays' Rebellion** helped people realize that the federal government needed more control over finances.

Economic problems in Massachusetts in the 1780s led to violent conflicts between citizens and the government.

In 1787, fifty-five delegates, from all states except Rhode Island, met for the Constitutional Convention and set up an entirely new government. The first plan proposed was the Virginia Plan. Many delegates,

George Washington addresses the Constitutional Convention.

Articles are ratified by all states

Congress passes a Land Ordinance

| 1780 | 1781 | 1783 | 1785 | 1787 |

Pennsylvania becomes the first state to ban slavery

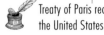

Treaty of Paris recognizes the United States

Congress passes the Northwest Ordinanc
Constitutional Convention assembles

especially those from small states, opposed the plan because it based the number of representatives on a state's population. Some offered the New Jersey Plan. It was much like the Articles of Confederation, but with a stronger Congress. The **Great Compromise** settled the argument. It proposed two houses of Congress with membership in the lower house based on a state's population. In the other house, each state would have the same number of representatives.

The members also disagreed over how to choose an executive, or President. This time, the compromise proposed that an **electoral college** would choose the executive. All 13 states ratified the Constitution by May 1790.

Creators of the Constitution

Benjamin Franklin

The oldest delegate was **Benjamin Franklin,** who was 81 and in poor health.

Alexander Hamilton fought for a strong federal government.

James Madison was called the "Father of the Constitution."

Gouverneur Morris wrote the final revision of the Constitution.

Edmund Randolph proposed the Virginia Plan.

Roger Sherman suggested the Great Compromise.

George Washington was president of the convention.

The Constitution is ratified; the Bill of Rights is proposed

Bill of Rights is ratified

Washington signs Jay's Treaty with England

1788 1789   1791   1793   1795 1796

George Washington elected President

Washington is sworn in for a second term as President

John Adams elected President

The Constitution

The Constitution

The Constitution allows United States citizens to elect the people who will represent them in government. It also sets up a **federal** system. This means that powers are divided between the national and the state governments. In the national government, power is divided among three branches. The **executive branch,** the President, enforces the law. The **legislative branch,** the Congress, makes the law. The **judicial branch,** the Supreme Court, explains the law.

Articles I, II, and III describe the branches of the government. These articles explain how the President, Vice-President, senators, representatives, and Supreme Court justices are chosen. It describes the powers and responsibilities of each office. The federal powers listed include the right to collect taxes, to declare war, and to regulate trade. These are called expressed powers. The Constitution also includes some reserved powers. These are powers, such as marriage and public education, that are not given to the federal government and, therefore, belong to the people or to the states.

Article IV says that all states are equal to one another and that new states may be admitted to the Union. Article V explains how **amendments** may be added to the Constitution. Article VI says that when state laws conflict with national laws, the national laws come first. It also says that a national law must not contradict the Constitution. Article VII explains that the Constitution had to be ratified by at least nine states to become law.

Checks and Balances

The U.S. Constitution provides a system of checks and balances in the government. Each of the three branches of the government has powers that let them influence what the other branches do. This way, all three branches

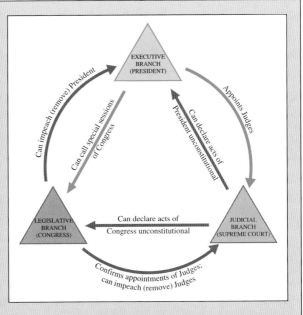

must work together to run the country, and no one branch can become so powerful that it takes control of the country.

A New Nation: The Bill of Rights

The United States Constitution focused on creating a strong government. It did not discuss the basic rights of all citizens. Some states would not ratify the Constitution unless a Bill of Rights was added. The Bill of Rights was ratified on December 15, 1791 and guarantees the following freedoms:

Amendment 1: Freedom of religion, speech, and the press; rights of assembly and petition.

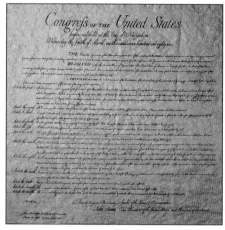

The Bill of Rights

Amendment 2: Right to bear arms.

Amendment 3: No citizen will be required to house soldiers.

Amendment 4: Authorities must have an arrest or search warrant before arresting people or searching their homes.

Amendment 5: Rights in criminal cases.

Amendment 6: Rights to a fair trial.

Amendment 7: Rights in civil cases.

Amendment 8: Bails, fines, and punishments must be fair.

Amendment 9: People have other rights not listed in the Constitution.

Amendment 10: Powers not given to the federal government are reserved for the states or the people.

The founders of the Constitution thought that the Constitution should be flexible. They provided for a way to add amendments, or changes. Two thirds of each house of Congress must pass an amendment. Or Congress may set up a national convention to pass it. Then the legislatures of three fourths of the states must ratify it.

How a Bill Becomes a Law

A bill, or proposed law, can be introduced in either the House of Representatives or the Senate, unless it is a money bill. Only the House of Representatives can propose money bills.

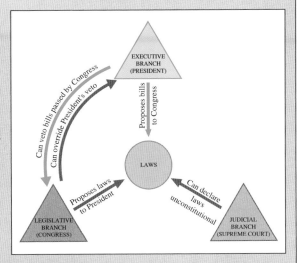

1. A bill is introduced to one of the houses of Congress and assigned a number.

2. A committee collects information about the bill, holds hearings, and suggests changes. Then it is presented to the entire house.

3. The house discusses the bill and then votes on it. If approved by more than half the members, it is sent to the other house.

4. The bill goes through the same process in the other house.

5. The bill goes to a conference committee made up of members of both houses. The conference committee revises it if necessary.

6. Both houses vote on the revised bill. If approved, it is sent to the President.

7. If the President signs it, the bill becomes law.

8. If the President vetoes the bill, the Congress can override the veto. This means that the bill will become law if two thirds of both houses approve it over the President's veto.

George Washington was sworn in as President on April 30, 1789, in New York City.

President Washington

The electoral college unanimously elected George Washington the first President of the United States in 1789. For his **Cabinet,** he appointed **Thomas Jefferson** Secretary of State; **Alexander Hamilton** Secretary of the Treasury; **Henry Knox** Secretary of War; and **Edmund Randolph** Attorney General.

Hamilton wanted to increase tariffs and to tax some products. This money would be used to pay national and state debts. Jefferson did not like the plan, but he agreed to support it in exchange for Hamilton's support of a new capital city on the Potomac River.

One result of Hamilton's tax policies was the **Whiskey Rebellion.** In 1794, liquor producers in Pennsylvania refused to pay the liquor tax. Washington sent in troops to end the rebellion. This showed how national laws could be enforced.

Pennsylvania liquor producers tar and feather a tax collector to protest taxes imposed by the national government.

Hamilton also wanted to create a **National Bank**. Jefferson argued that the Constitution had not mentioned a bank. Hamilton said that Congress could regulate money and trade using any means that weren't forbidden by the Constitution.

Washington agreed with Hamilton, and the bank was chartered. Jefferson's view became known as "strict construction" of the Constitution, while Hamilton's was a "loose construction."

The disagreements between Jefferson and Hamilton led to the formation of political parties. Hamilton's Federalist party supported a strong federal government. Jefferson's Democratic-Republicans wanted to give more power to state governments.

Other Important Events

French War: France went to war against Britain and Spain in 1793. Jefferson wanted to support France, while Hamilton wanted to back Britain. Washington insisted that the United States remain neutral.

Jay's Treaty: Washington sent John Jay to negotiate with England in 1795. The British agreed to remove troops from American territory, but other matters were left unsettled.

Pinckney's Treaty: In 1795, Thomas Pinckney negotiated with Spain to end a dispute over the Florida border and give the United States free use of the Mississippi River.

A Growing United States

Marbury v. Madison

Thomas Jefferson became the third President in 1801. He believed that the country should not need a strong federal government. Jefferson's ideas became known as **Jeffersonian Democracy.**

President John Adams

Soon after Jefferson's inauguration, the Supreme Court, under Chief Justice **John Marshall,** began taking on new power and importance. The first important case was *Marbury v. Madison* in 1803. It concerned an appointment President John Adams had made in 1801 just before Jefferson became the new President. Adams appointed William Marbury a justice of the peace. James Madison, the new Secretary of State, refused to give Marbury his appointment papers. Marbury asked the Supreme Court to make the new administration give him the appointment. The Supreme Court said that Madison had acted improperly, but it struck down the act of Congress that gave Marbury the appointment. This decision

Thomas Jefferson elected President

 U.S. declares war on Great Britain

Missouri Compromise passes Congress

| 1801 | 1803 | 1812 | 1817 | 1820 | 1823 |

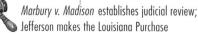 *Marbury v. Madison* establishes judicial review; Jefferson makes the Louisiana Purchase

James Monroe elected President

Monroe issues the Monroe Doctrine

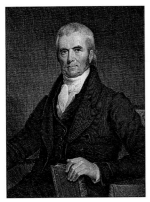

proved that the Supreme Court could declare laws unconstitutional. This power became known as **judicial review.** John Marshall believed that a strong Supreme Court and a strong federal government were necessary.

Chief Justice John Marshall

The Supreme Court and the Constitution

During Chief Justice John Marshall's time, many cases strengthened the federal government.

Fletcher v. Peck (1810)

The court said that a Georgia state law regarding land grants was unconstitutional. This was the first time it had declared a state law unconstitutional.

McCulloch v. Maryland (1819)

Marshall said that Congress had the power to create the National Bank. The ruling said that the Congress had implied powers that were not necessarily stated in the Constitution.

Dartmouth College v. Woodward (1819)

New Hampshire wanted to change the royal charter for Dartmouth College to make it into a state college. The court ruled that the Constitution protects contracts from being changed by the states.

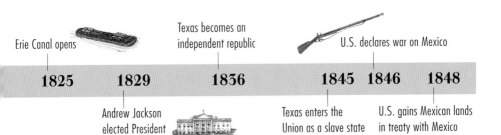

Erie Canal opens

Texas becomes an independent republic

U.S. declares war on Mexico

| 1825 | 1829 | 1836 | 1845 | 1846 | 1848 |

Andrew Jackson elected President

Texas enters the Union as a slave state

U.S. gains Mexican lands in treaty with Mexico

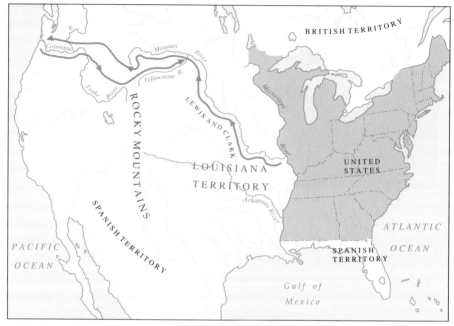

THE LOUISIANA PURCHASE, 1803

The Louisiana Purchase

The huge area between the Mississippi River and the Rocky Mountains had been owned by Spain since 1763. President Jefferson learned that Spain was secretly giving the territory to France. Jefferson wanted to make sure Americans could still use the port of New Orleans. He sent James Monroe to France to negotiate. Unexpectedly, France offered to sell the land for about $15 million in 1803. Congress approved the purchase, adding 827,987 square miles to the United States.

In 1804, Jefferson sent **Meriwether Lewis** and **William Clark** on an expedition through the territory. Jefferson wanted the explorers to find a water route to the Pacific Ocean. He also wanted them to find out more about the territory's plants and animals and to communicate with the area's tribes.

The explorers started in St. Louis in May 1804 and traveled up the Missouri River. With the help of Native Americans, including Sacagawea and her relatives, they reached what is now Oregon in November 1805.

Sacagawea, a 16-year-old Shoshone, helped lead the Lewis and Clark expedition across the Great Plains and over the Rocky Mountains.

Lewis and Clark did not find a water route to the Pacific, but their trip was successful. They claimed the Oregon region. They brought back much information about the geography of the territory, including the Rocky Mountains. They found out about the animals of the region, such as buffalo and grizzly bears. Finally, they had friendly contact with many different Native Americans.

The Great Plains

A Plains buffalo hunt.

Part of the Louisiana Territory east of the Rocky Mountains is a region called the Great Plains. It is a dry grassland area. Few nations had lived in this area before the 1600s, when Spaniards explored the region. The land was hard to farm, and the buffalo were difficult to hunt. After Spanish explorers brought guns and horses to America, Native Americans could hunt buffalo. Nations such as the Blackfeet, Cheyenne, Comanche, Crow, Mandan, Pawnee, and Sioux settled on the Plains.

The War of 1812

In the early 1800s, both Britain and France interfered with American sea trade. British ships often stopped American ones to look for British sailors who had deserted. In doing this, the British attacked the American ship *Chesapeake*, killing four sailors, wounding 18, and damaging the ship. This act angered many Americans.

The USS *Constitution* defeated the *Guerrière* in the Atlantic Ocean on August 19, 1812, boosting American morale.

Americans were also angry about British actions in the Northwest Territory. Britain was encouraging the Native Americans there to fight American settlers. The United States finally declared war on Great Britain in 1812.

Americans defend Fort Niagara against a British attack in 1813.

The Americans' first plan was to defeat Britain in Canada. However, battles at Detroit, Niagara River, and Lake Champlain were unsuccessful. In 1813, Americans captured York (now Toronto) and burned some of its public buildings. Oliver Hazard Perry won an important naval battle on Lake Erie. However, the Americans withdrew from Canada in 1814. The British occupied Washington, D.C., in August 1814. They attacked Fort McHenry. Francis Scott Key, who witnessed the battle, wrote "The Star-Spangled Banner" on this occasion. A peace treaty was signed in December 1814. Fifteen days later at the **Battle of New Orleans,** General Andrew Jackson soundly defeated a final British invasion force.

MAJOR BATTLES OF
THE WAR OF 1812

BRITISH TERRITORY

L. Superior

St. Lawrence River

MAINE

Lake Champlain

L. Michigan

L. Huron

York (Toronto)

N.H. VT.

L. Ontario

MICH. TERR.

NEW YORK

MASS.

CONN. R.I.

Detroit

L. Erie

Lake Erie

PENN.

N.J.

ILLINOIS TERR.

INDIANA TERR.

OHIO

Ft. McHenry (Baltimore)

MD.

DEL.

Washington D.C.

Mississippi River

Ohio River

VA.

KENTUCKY

NORTH CAROLINA

TENNESSEE

SOUTH CAROLINA

MISS. TERR.

ALABAMA

GEORGIA

ATLANTIC OCEAN

LOUISIANA

New Orleans

SPANISH TERR.

Gulf of Mexico

Andrew Jackson and **William Henry Harrison** used their recognition as heroes of the war to start important political careers. In addition, the Federalist party, which had opposed the war, soon lost its power.

The Burning of Washington, D.C.

The First Lady of the United States in 1814 was **Dolley Madison.** When the British began burning the public buildings in Washington, D.C., she escaped, taking with her some papers, some silver, her parrot, and a portrait of George Washington by Gilbert Stuart. The Madisons soon returned to the city, but the White House was not ready to be lived in again until late 1817. Thanks to Dolley Madison, the Stuart portrait of Washington is displayed at the White House to this day.

Dolley Madison

The Monroe Doctrine

James Monroe was President between 1817 and 1825. This time was called "the era of good feeling" because the economy was good and the nation was at peace. With the end of the Federalist party, almost everyone belonged to the Democratic-Republican party. The country was developing industries, and transportation was improving. Pioneers were beginning to settle the West.

President James Monroe

An important event during Monroe's administration was the **Missouri Compromise** of 1820. The Territory of Missouri applied for statehood in 1818. Slavery was legal in the territory. At that time, there were 22 states in the Union—11 free states and 11 slave states. The next year, Maine applied for statehood. The Missouri Compromise said that Maine would be admitted to the Union as a free state and Missouri would be admitted as a slave state. Then the balance between free and slave states would remain. The compromise also banned slavery north of the 36°30' north latitude.

Another one of Monroe's most important acts was the **Monroe Doctrine** issued in 1823. The doctrine said that European nations could not interfere with independent countries of the Western Hemisphere. Many Latin American countries such as Chile and Venezuela had recently become independent from Spain. Americans wanted to make sure that several European nations did not band together against the new Latin American countries. The Monroe Doctrine was important in showing the whole world the high standard of American foreign policy.

Toward Statehood

Article IV of the Constitution allows new states to join the United States. The Constitution does not, however, identify how a territory can become a state. The Northwest Ordinance of 1787 provided a plan for allowing territories to become states with full equality to other states. According to the ordinance, Congress would appoint officials to govern a territory until it had an adult male population of 5,000. Then it could elect a legislature. It could also send a nonvoting representative to Congress. When the territory had a population of 60,000, it could apply for statehood. The ordinance served as a model for allowing states into the Union.

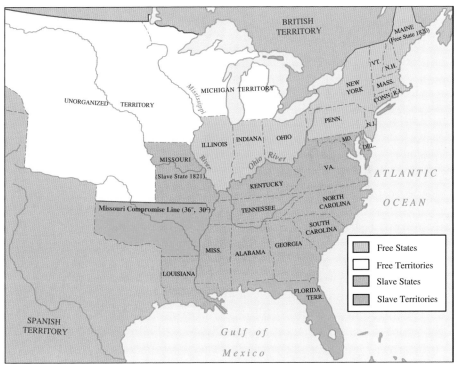

SLAVERY IN THE UNITED STATES AFTER THE MISSOURI COMPROMISE OF 1820

The Jackson Administration

In 1828, presidential nominations were made by state legislatures and public meetings for the first time instead of by Congress. When he was elected President, Andrew Jackson saw himself as a representative of the people. He allowed masses of people to celebrate his inauguration. They crowded into the White House, tracking mud throughout the President's home.

During Jackson's presidency, many Americans were eager to settle new territories. Some wanted lands in the South that native tribes had lived on

President Andrew Jackson enjoyed a wild celebration at the White House after his inauguration in March 1829.

for centuries. Jackson felt that Native Americans (referred to as Indians) and other Americans could not live in peace together. In 1830, he drew up the **Indian Removal Act.** Although many opposed the Indian Removal Act, it became law. During the next ten years, the government forced 70,000 Native Americans to move from their homes in Florida, Louisiana, Alabama, and Georgia to the Oklahoma Territory. They did not have enough food or warm clothing, and many became infected with diseases. Thousands died during the journeys. The Cherokee refer to their relocation as the **Trail of Tears.**

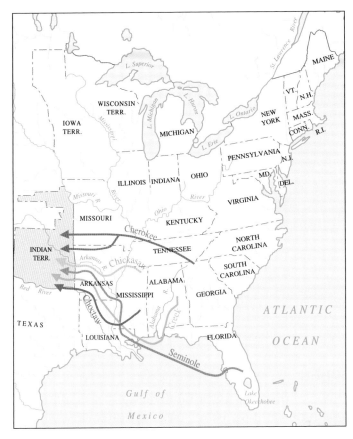

INDIAN RELOCATION
IN THE 1830S

Jackson's War on Banks

Andrew Jackson disliked the National Bank. He thought that the law creating the bank was unconstitutional. He also thought that the bank allowed a small group of Northerners to become rich. Jackson vetoed the bill that would recharter the bank. In 1833, Jackson also had the Secretary of the Treasury remove the government's money from the bank. The money was put into state banks. But the United States suffered a financial panic in 1837, partly because it lacked a strong national bank.

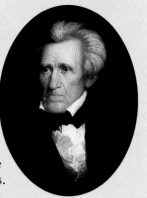

President Andrew Jackson

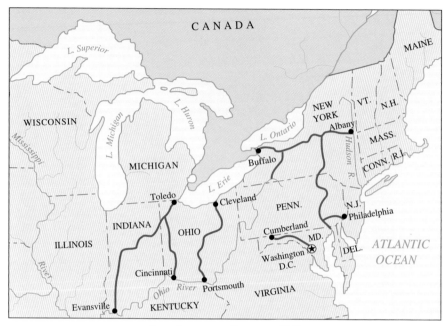

MAJOR CANALS IN THE NORTHEAST, 1860

North and South

In the early 1800s, American manufacturers learned to build and operate machines run on water power. Industries soon sprang up in the North along the eastern coast of the United States, where there were many rivers and waterfalls to power machines. Also, factories began using **mass production** and **standardized parts**. This meant that factories could make products faster and in greater numbers than ever before.

Transportation was changing, too. In 1807, Robert Fulton built the first practical steamboat. Within 20 years, steamboats transported many people and goods by water. New Yorkers built the Erie Canal, a water-

This drawing shows the *Clermont*, Robert Fulton's steamboat, and the internal machinery that made it work.

way connecting Buffalo, on Lake Erie, to Albany, on the Hudson River. The Erie Canal opened in 1825. Soon, other canals were built between the East Coast and the Great Lakes. By the mid–1820s, the North had many industrial centers as well as transportation systems.

In the South, farmers produced tobacco, corn, and other crops throughout the 1700s. In 1793, a new machine made a great change in the southern economy. Eli Whitney's cotton gin separated cotton from its seed quickly and easily. Plantation

The Southern economy was based on crops such as cotton and the slave labor that produced it.

owners soon began to grow large amounts of cotton. They sold it to textile factories in the North and in Europe. Growing cotton required a lot of labor in the fields. More and more slaves were brought to the South to do this job. In 1790, fewer than 70,000 slaves lived in the South. By 1830, there were 2 million.

Slaves and Factory Workers

One of the largest industries in the North was the cloth industry. Francis Lowell's partners built the town of Lowell in 1822 to house textile mills. They brought in young farm women to work in the mills. The women worked up to 70 hours a week. Children also worked long hours in the factories.

A typical textile mill in the North might have looked like this.

Slaves in the South were considered property. Their owners decided what kind of work they would do. Field hands worked from dawn to dusk, especially during harvesting. Slave families were split apart when members were bought or sold. Laws made it illegal to teach slaves to read or write.

Manifest Destiny

Early American pioneers crossed the Appalachian Mountains and settled in the territories of Ohio, Kentucky, Tennessee, and Mississippi. In the 1830s, pioneers went across the Mississippi River to Iowa, Missouri, Arkansas, and eastern Texas. By the 1840s,

In the mid–1800s, settlers traveled west in wagon trains across the Great Plains and over the Rocky Mountains.

people began to make the hard trip to the West Coast. Many Americans came to believe in **Manifest Destiny,** or the idea that the United States should expand across North America. They felt a responsibility to spread the superior form of government and economy they enjoyed.

American settlers in the Oregon Country were in conflict with Great Britain's claim to that area. Britain turned the part of Oregon that was south of the 49th parallel over to the United States in 1846. Searching for a place to freely practice their religion, Mormons led by Brigham Young settled in Utah in 1847. In 1848, James Marshall discovered gold at Sutter's Mill, California. During 1849, people flocked there hoping to find gold. San Francisco grew from a small town to a city of 25,000 people. These gold seekers were called **forty-niners.** Texas became an independent republic after settlers from America defeated the Mexican government there in 1836.

In the first half of the 19th century, fur trappers and traders were among the first European Americans to establish themselves in the lands west of the Mississippi River.

The Texans who died at the Alamo are still remembered for their great courage.

Remember the Alamo

Sam Houston

Settlers in Texas revolted against Mexico in 1835. General Santa Anna led the Mexican army against the American rebels. As Santa Anna approached, a group of 150 Texans retreated behind the walls of the Alamo, an old Spanish mission. The Texans sent a message for help, and they were joined by 37 more fighters. The Mexican forces attacked the Alamo on March 6, 1836, and all the Texans were killed. Under General **Sam Houston,** other Texans rallied with the battle cry "Remember the Alamo." After defeating Santa Anna on April 21, they formed their own country, the Republic of Texas, and elected Houston as President.

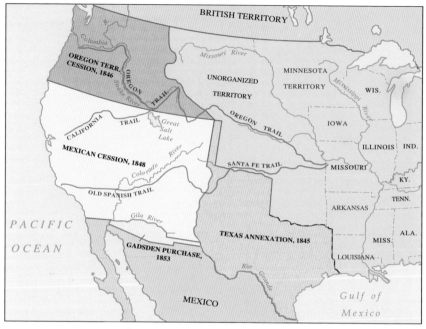

GROWTH OF THE UNITED STATES, 1845–1853

The Mexican War

President James K. Polk

Congress voted to give Texas statehood in 1845. The United States claimed that the Rio Grande was the southern boundary of the United States, but Mexico disagreed. President James K. Polk sent General Zachary Taylor to occupy the land near the Rio Grande. Mexican forces crossed the Rio Grande and attacked Taylor's troops. Congress declared war on Mexico on May 13, 1846.

General Taylor's army soon took the city of Monterrey in Mexico. They defeated the Mexicans at the Battle of Buena Vista in February 1847. The Americans entered Mexico City in September 1847. The **Treaty of Guadalupe Hidalgo** ended the war on February 2, 1848. The treaty gave nearly 2 million square miles of land to the United States. The land included the present states of California, Nevada, and Utah and parts of Arizona, New Mexico, Colorado, and Wyoming. The United States paid Mexico $15 million in return.

With this land came arguments about whether slavery would be allowed in the new territories. In 1850, California applied for statehood as a free state. Proslavery forces objected. **Henry Clay** suggested that California be admitted as a free state and that Utah and New Mexico could allow slavery. He also suggested that the slave trade be abolished from the District of Columbia and that a new law be enacted that would require American citizens to return runaway slaves to their owners. This was **Clay's Compromise** of 1850.

General Zachary Taylor would later be elected President.

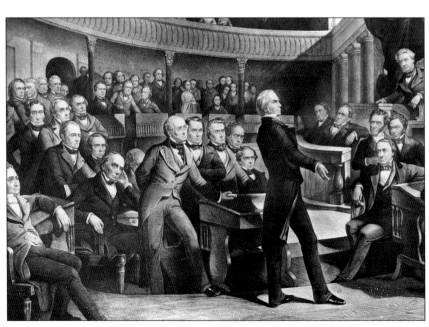

For the second time, Henry Clay temporarily settled the national debate over slavery.

Internal Strife

Slavery and Abolition

In the late 1820s, William Lloyd Garrison, a young newspaper editor in New England, started a movement to end slavery completely. Garrison and his followers believed that slavery was cruel and should not exist in a democracy. He and his followers were known as **abolitionists.**

Frederick Douglass

Many people disagreed with Garrison's movement at first, but more and more people began to support it. In 1841, **Frederick Douglass** spoke at an abolitionist meeting in Nantucket, Massachusetts. He was a former slave who had escaped from Maryland. Douglass told stories about his suffering as a slave. He began to speak at meetings throughout the North. Another great speaker was

Sojourner Truth. She had been freed from slavery in 1827. In 1843, she began speaking of the evils of slavery. Over time, many Northerners became abolitionists.

In 1854, Senator Stephen A. Douglas introduced a bill saying that the two new territories of Kansas and Nebraska could decide whether slavery would be allowed. This contradicted the Missouri Compromise, and antislavery forces were very angry. The bill was passed by Congress.

Sojourner Truth

California becomes a state

Dred Scott Decision finds that slaves are not citizens and the Missouri Compromise is unconstitutional

Oregon becomes a state

1850	1852	1857	1858	1859

Harriet Beecher Stowe publishes *Uncle Tom's Cabin*

Abraham Lincoln debates Stephen Douglas in Illinois

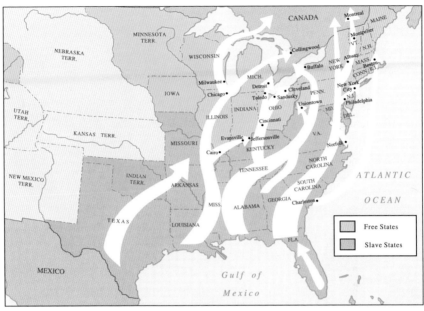

THE UNDERGROUND RAILROAD OF THE 19TH CENTURY

The Underground Railroad

Throughout the years of slavery, many black and white people helped escaped slaves find freedom. The routes escaped slaves took became known as the **Underground Railroad.** People who showed slaves the way to freedom were called conductors.

Harriet Tubman escaped from slavery in Maryland. She returned south many times and helped more than 300 slaves gain their freedom. She was called Moses by the people she helped. She and many members of the Underground Railroad ignored the **Fugitive Slave Law,** which made it illegal to help slaves escape. They continued to help conduct slaves to freedom.

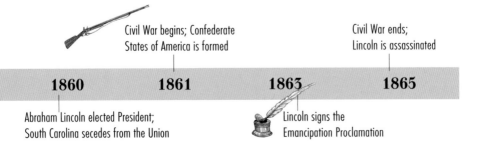

Civil War begins; Confederate States of America is formed

Civil War ends; Lincoln is assassinated

1860   **1861**   **1863**   **1865**

Abraham Lincoln elected President; South Carolina secedes from the Union

Lincoln signs the Emancipation Proclamation

Lincoln and Douglas

In 1854, the slavery issue led to the formation of a new political party—the Republicans. The new party attracted members of the two major political parties of the time—the Democrats and the Whigs—who were against slavery. In 1858, **Abraham Lincoln** was the new party's candidate to run against **Stephen Douglas** for senator from Illinois.

Abraham Lincoln

Stephen Douglas

Lincoln and Douglas agreed to debate before the election. The question of slavery in new territories became the central issue. Large crowds attended the debates, and newspapers eagerly reported them.

Lincoln argued against slavery, but he did not say it should be completely abolished because he knew that could break the country apart. Douglas did not say that slavery was wrong. He said that even in a slave territory, the people could forbid slavery by refusing to pass laws that protected it. He voiced opinions that might win votes both from people who were for slavery and those who were against it. Douglas won the election, but Lincoln became widely known and respected.

People across the country paid close attention to the debates.

Secession

In a very close contest that centered on slavery, Abraham Lincoln was elected President on November 6, 1860. Some Southern states believed that Lincoln's election meant that the North could control the Union without support from the South. Their economies depended on slavery, and they were afraid that Northern abolitionists would pass laws ending slavery. Many states also felt that states had the right to decide whether to

Jefferson Davis

stay in the Union or not. South Carolina was one of these states, and it seceded, or withdrew, from the Union after Lincoln's election. In 1861, ten other states left the Union and joined together as the **Confederate States of America.** They elected **Jefferson Davis** as their president. Lincoln promised to use the government's full power to keep the nation together. The Confederates fired on Fort Sumter in South Carolina on April 12, 1861. Federal troops there surrendered. Lincoln called for Union troops to retake the fort. The Confederacy considered this a declaration of war.

State soldiers from South Carolina fired on Fort Sumter at 4:30 A.M. on April 12, 1861. Low on supplies and with no hope of reinforcements, fort commander Major Robert Anderson surrendered the next day.

Dred Scott

The disagreement over slavery was the main cause of the Civil War. The Compromise of 1850 and the Kansas-Nebraska Act increased disagreement about slavery. Also, in 1857, the Supreme Court had made a decision about a slave, **Dred Scott.** Scott said that he should be free because he had lived for a time in a free state. The Supreme Court said that a slave was not a United States citizen and that Congress could not forbid slavery in the United States. The decision angered abolitionists. In 1859, an abolitionist named **John Brown** tried to seize the federal arsenal at Harpers Ferry, Virginia. He was trying to start a slave rebellion. Brown was captured and hanged, but Southerners were angered by his actions.

John Brown

Advantages in the Civil War

South	North
•Great military leaders	•Strong government
•Possible help from European nations	•Strong economy
	•More farmland
•Soldiers fighting to protect their homes	•More factories
	•More railroads
	•Greater population

MAJOR BATTLES OF THE CIVIL WAR, 1861–1865

The Civil War

After Fort Sumter, the North and South clashed at the First Battle of Bull Run. The North soon realized that the war would not be quick and victory over the South would not be easy.

Robert E. Lee had taken command of the Army of Northern Virginia. He and other Southern generals defended the South. They prevented the Union leader General George McClellan from attacking Richmond.

Robert E. Lee

Ulysses S. Grant

General Ulysses S. Grant commanded Union forces in western Kentucky. He forced Confederate troops at Fort Donelson, Tennessee, to surrender. Also, in the Battle of Shiloh in April 1862, Grant forced the Confederate army to retreat.

The Battle of Antietam on September 17, 1862, was the single bloodiest day of the war. Each side suffered more than 10,000 dead or wounded soldiers.

A turning point of the war occurred at the Battle of Antietam in Maryland in 1862. General Lee's unsuccessful invasion ended Southern hopes of help from Europe. European countries did not want to support a failed Southern rebellion. Another turning point was in Gettysburg, Pennsylvania, in 1863. General Lee tried a daring plan to take Northern territory. However, Lee's army was driven out of the North.

William T. Sherman

Meanwhile, Grant succeeded in capturing Vicksburg on the Mississippi River. The Union now controlled the Mississippi River, which split the Confederacy in half. In 1864, Grant directed his army against Lee in northern Virginia. General William T. Sherman led the North in capturing Atlanta.

After a three-week siege of Island No.10 in Missouri, Union gunboats defeated a small Confederate force controlling the Mississippi River.

Sherman's army captured Savannah and moved into South Carolina. The Union soldiers burned and destroyed everything in sight. Sherman used this "total war" to destroy the South's will to fight.

The Emancipation Proclamation

President Lincoln issued the Emancipation Proclamation on September 22, 1862. The proclamation said that the slaves of the Confederate states would be freed if the states did not return to the Union by January 1, 1863. The South did not give in, so the proclamation took effect on

Abraham Lincoln signs the Emancipation Proclamation, granting freedom to slaves in states that had seceded.

January 1. The proclamation affected the outcome of the war. Many former slaves fought in the Union army. Many also helped the war effort in other ways. The proclamation made the Union effort a war against slavery. European nations did not want to support slavery or slave-holding states. Lincoln himself said the proclamation was "the one thing that will make people remember I ever lived."

Robert E. Lee surrenders to Ulysses S. Grant, officially ending the war. Lee was widely respected for his dignity and great military skill. After the war, he encouraged Southerners to rebuild the nation.

The South's Surrender

General Grant captured Richmond in April 1865. Lee took his army west, hoping to join more Confederate troops in North Carolina. When Union soldiers stopped Lee's army, Lee decided that further fighting was useless. He surrendered to Grant at a small village, **Appomattox Court House**, Virginia, on April 9, 1865.

Union soldiers camp outside Petersburg, Virginia, in one of the last engagements of the war.

The Civil War had been hugely destructive. It was the first modern war. Soldiers used weapons that could kill more easily, such as guns that could fire several shots without reloading. More than 620,000 soldiers died, and half of the deaths were caused by disease. The North and South had waged a "total war," often destroying homes, farms, and towns as a part of their campaigns. Finally, both the North and South had spent huge amounts of money in the war. The country had a long road ahead in repairing the damages from the conflict.

Lincoln was preparing to bring the country back together. Five days after Lee's surrender, Lincoln attended the theater. An actor, John Wilkes Booth, shot Lincoln as he watched the play. Lincoln died the next day on April 15, 1865. Thousands of Americans mourned their lost President.

The Assassination of Lincoln

John Wilkes Booth sided with the South and blamed Lincoln for the war. Booth plotted with several others to murder Lincoln, Vice-President Andrew Johnson, General Ulysses S. Grant, and Secretary of State William H. Seward. After shooting Lincoln in his box in the theater, Booth leaped to the stage. Some people believe he shouted the Virginia state motto "Sic Semper Tyrannis," which means "thus always to tyrants." Booth broke his leg in the jump, but he escaped. Federal troops found him, and when he did not surrender, shot him to death. Several of his friends were convicted of plotting the assassination. Four of them were hanged.

John Wilkes Booth

Abraham Lincoln was the first U.S. President ever assassinated.

African-Americans worked to gain a new place in society during Reconstruction. This drawing shows several of the first African-Americans to be elected to the national Congress.

Reconstruction

After Lincoln's death, Andrew Johnson became President. His Reconstruction plan made it easy for Southerners to rejoin the Union, but it did not help the freed slaves very much. The Southern states began passing laws, called **Black Codes,** which limited the rights of African-Americans.

Congress thought the President's plan was wrong. The members wanted the South punished and the former slaves helped. Congress passed the **Fourteenth Amendment,** which gave African-Americans the right to vote. Then it passed its own Reconstruction Acts that set up new governments in the South. Congress also tried to limit the President's power, but the President tried to avoid these laws. In 1868, the House of Representatives voted to impeach President Johnson. They held a trial to remove him from office. The final Senate vote did not support removal. In 1869, Congress proposed the

President
Andrew Johnson

Laws protecting the rights of African-American citizens were passed during Reconstruction, but they were not always effective.

Fifteenth Amendment. This made it illegal to deny citizens the right to vote because of their race.

During Reconstruction, new groups gained power in the South. Many Northerners, called **carpetbaggers,** moved there to help rebuild and to get wealthy. Southerners who had become Republicans were called **scalawags.** African-Americans also gained some power. Most white Southerners refused to support the Reconstruction governments. They found ways to keep African-Americans from voting. For example, "grandfather clauses" in some areas of the South required a voter to have an ancestor who had voted before 1867. This left out former slaves. Southern Democrats regained control of the South in the 1870s. Many of the gains made by African-Americans during Reconstruction were lost at this time.

Impeachment

Only the House of Representatives can impeach the President or Vice-President. If a majority of the House votes for impeachment, the Senate serves as a court to hear the trial. The Senate must have a two-thirds majority to convict the official. The Constitution says that officials can be removed from office by impeachment and conviction only for very serious crimes such as treason or bribery.

Industrial America

Transportation

The United States grew quickly in the 1800s. New industries were built, especially in the Northeast, and many people were moving west. But travel was hard and slow. People needed better ways to travel and to transport goods.

On May 10, 1869, the Union Pacific and Central Pacific lines met at Promontory Point, Utah.

The first big improvement in transportation was the steamboat, which Robert Fulton perfected in 1807. Later, railroads became the century's most important form of transportation. In 1830, a train powered by horses ran on tracks between Baltimore and a nearby mill town. The first steam locomotive, named the *Best Friend of Charleston*, also ran in 1830. Rail travel grew quickly. By 1835, the United States had more than 1,000 miles of railroad tracks. During the Civil War, both North and South used railroads to carry troops and supplies. The North's better railroad system gave the Union an advantage.

In 1862, President Lincoln signed the Pacific Railroad Act. Two companies were to build the first transcontinental railroad. The Central Pacific Railroad Company moved eastward, and the Union Pacific Railroad Company moved westward. On May 10, 1869, the track was completed. Four more transcontinental railroad lines would soon be built.

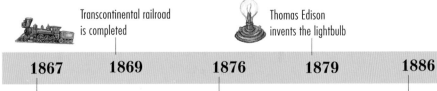

Transcontinental railroad is completed

Thomas Edison invents the lightbulb

| 1867 | 1869 | 1876 | 1879 | 1886 |

United States purchases Alaska

Alexander Graham Bell invents the telephone

American Federation of Labor (AFL) is formed

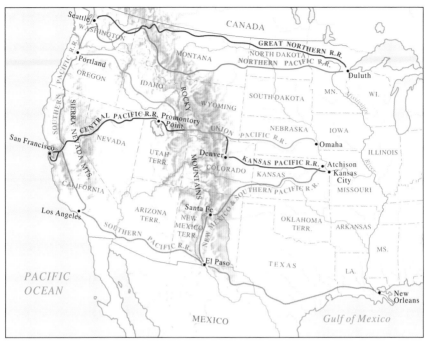

RAILROADS IN THE WEST, 1869–1893

Who Built the Railroads?

The railroad companies needed many workers. The Union Pacific brought in 10,000 workers to build its tracks. Many of them were Irish immigrants. Others had been soldiers in the Civil War. The Central Pacific hired more than 10,000 immigrants from China. The workers for the Central Pacific had to build tracks across the Sierra Nevada Mountains. Building tracks up and down mountains, across gorges, and sometimes through tunnels was a difficult job. All the railroad workers were faced with intense heat in the summer and cold, snow, and avalanches in the winter. Other dangers included landslides, explosions, falls, and fights with Native Americans. Many died.

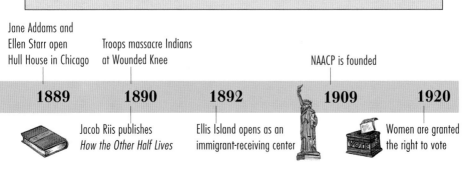

Jane Addams and Ellen Starr open Hull House in Chicago

Troops massacre Indians at Wounded Knee

NAACP is founded

1889   **1890**   **1892**   **1909**   **1920**

Jacob Riis publishes *How the Other Half Lives*

Ellis Island opens as an immigrant-receiving center

Women are granted the right to vote

The Indian Wars

During the 1800s, European settlers spread from east to west across North America. They often took the lands of Native American nations, forcing the peoples to live on reservations, or lands especially set aside for them. Some nations tried to change their way of life so they could live alongside the growing United States. Others fought against the settlers and the U.S.

Sioux chief Sitting Bull

Army. In the end, none of the nations were able to win against the modern technology and tactics of the United States.

The Sioux had kept settlers out of South Dakota until 1874, when gold was found in the Black Hills. Miners and Sioux fought over the land, and the government ordered the Sioux onto reservations. Led by Sitting Bull and Crazy Horse, several groups joined to protect their lands. They defeated the forces of Lieutenant Colonel George Custer near the Little Bighorn River on June 25, 1876. Eventually, the Sioux and their allies were defeated and brought to reservations.

Farther south, the Plains nation in Kansas, Colorado, New Mexico, and Texas also refused to be moved to reservations.

U.S. soldiers attacked a peaceful camp of Arapaho and Cheyenne peoples in the Sand Creek Massacre of 1864. In the Red River War of 1874, Lieutenant General Philip Sheridan defeated Comanche and Kiowa warriors, who were fighting to stop the destruction of their main food source—the buffalo—by American hunters.

This late-19th-century photo shows an Native American encampment along South Dakota's Brule River.

MAJOR BATTLES OF THE INDIAN WARS, 1862–1890

In the Northwest, the Nez Percé leader Chief Joseph tried to take his people to Canada to avoid reservation life. Army soldiers pursued them, and the badly outnumbered Nez Percé were able to fight them off for five days. They were finally captured only a half day's march from the border.

In Arizona, New Mexico, and Texas, the Army fought with Apache raiders such as Cochise and Geronimo. Although some Apache groups continued fighting until 1900, Geronimo surrendered in 1886.

The final event of the Indian Wars was in 1890 at Wounded Knee Creek in South Dakota, where several hundred Sioux were killed by soldiers the day after they had surrendered. Acts of Congress took away the separate way of life that the Native nations had known. The Dawes Act of 1887 broke up land held by native nations. Lawmakers gradually did away with tribal law. Native Americans had to obey the laws of the United States. In 1901, all Native Americans became U.S. citizens.

Alexander Graham Bell *(seated)* invented the first phone, making instant communication possible.

Industrial Revolution

Building new railroads required millions of tons of steel. Also, settlers in the West needed axes, tractors, and other products. In the East, factory owners built new factories to meet this growing demand. They also bought new machines and hired more workers. **Division of labor** made production faster and cheaper by having different groups of workers each do a different step in making a product. As products became less expensive, more were sold. Many people moved to industrial cities to work in factories.

At the same time, many inventions began to change people's lives. Thomas Edison invented the electric light in 1879. Alexander Graham Bell invented the telephone in 1876. The invention of the typewriter in 1867 made business writing

Other important inventions of the period included the "type-writing machine" *(above)* and the "horseless carriage" *(left)*. The first automobiles were playthings for the wealthy. Henry Ford changed all that when he introduced his affordable Model T in 1908.

The First Oldsmobile — 1897

faster and easier. Transportation changed dramatically with the invention of the gasoline-run automobile in 1885. Henry Ford and Ransom E. Olds used new methods to **mass produce** huge numbers of automobiles.

America's Self-Made Millionaires

Most Americans have heard of Carnegie Hall in New York City. This famous concert hall was named for a businessperson. Andrew Carnegie came to the United States from Scotland in 1847. Carnegie worked hard and began to invest in the iron industry. He built a steel factory near Pittsburgh that became the largest steel mill in the country. In 1901, Carnegie was the richest man in the world. He spent much money to help educate others. Besides financing Carnegie Hall, he gave money to create public libraries, universities, and research centers.

Andrew Carnegie

Other Americans also created amazing wealth in this era. **John D. Rockefeller** entered the oil business in 1862. He reorganized the system of refining and producing oil. By 1882, his company, Standard Oil, controlled almost the entire oil business. Like Carnegie, Rockefeller gave much money to educational organizations.

John D. Rockefeller

Other self-made millionaires included **Philip Armour** and **Gustavus Swift.** They started as butchers and ended up developing the meat processing business. **Cornelius Vanderbilt** made a fortune in the railroad business.

Cornelius Vanderbilt

Cowhands and Farmers

Trail driving was dirty, lonely, and sometimes dangerous work. The men who did it were called cowhands.

In the West, early settlers on the frontier used the huge open spaces for grazing cattle. Cowhands took the cattle herds to grazing lands in the spring and returned them to the ranch in the fall. They also took herds to cattle towns and put them on trains to be sent east and sold.

Later, families settled down on small farms. Farmers plowed over the grass that the cattle liked and planted crops, usually wheat. A conflict soon arose between the farmers and the ranchers. The farmers used barbed wire to fence off their land. The ranchers did not like to have their watering places or trails blocked. Fights, called the **range wars** or **barbed wire wars,** broke out. In 1886 and 1887, terrible winter blizzards killed millions of cattle on the open range. Ranchers began raising cattle on fenced-in fields.

The Oklahoma Run

In the late 1880s, people demanded that Indian Territory in Oklahoma be opened to settlement. Although this land belonged to the nations, the government agreed. At noon on April 22, 1889, thousands of homesteaders raced to claim millions of acres of land for settlement in

This painting shows the rush to Native American lands.

the first Oklahoma land rush. The last land rush was held in September 1893. The Native Americans had once again lost land that was promised to them.

The skyscraper became America's most important contribution to world architecture.

Cities

In the East, cities grew rapidly to accommodate new factories and workers. Land was expensive, so builders built upward. The first "skyscraper" was built in Chicago in 1884–1885. Electric lights replaced gas lamps on streets and in buildings, and huge steel bridges were built for the first time.

The growing, crowded cities created poor living conditions. Many people lived in tenement buildings with small rooms and few windows. Families had to share water and toilet facilities. These conditions spread diseases such as tuberculosis and smallpox. Crime also became a problem. City areas with many tenements were known as **slums.**

Many people from rural areas of the United States moved to the cities to find jobs. Other city residents were **immigrants** from other countries. Between 1890 and 1914, 16 million European immigrants came to America to escape persecution or find opportunity. Many immigrants landed at **Ellis Island** in New York harbor. About a third of these people stayed in New York City. Many others moved to nearby cities in the Northeast.

A marvel of 19th-century engineering, New York's Brooklyn Bridge opened in 1883.

"The Pen" at New York's Ellis Island as it appeared in 1907.

Before the first unions, many workers toiled under miserable conditions.

This 1908 photo shows a young girl working at a cotton-spinning mill in South Carolina instead of attending school.

Unions

The growth of industry in the late 1800s brought many people into cities to work. People made products in factories, mills, and workrooms called **sweatshops.** Pay was very low. Men, women, and even children worked ten to twelve hours a day, six or seven days a week.

The country was becoming very wealthy, yet many families had low-paying jobs that left them in poverty. Many Americans became angry about child labor, low pay, and poor working conditions. They began to organize unions to help American workers. In 1869, reformers organized the Knights of Labor with both skilled and unskilled workers as members. In 1886, skilled workers formed the American Federation of Labor (AFL). Union members tried to make changes by threatening to **strike,** or stop work, if their demands were not met.

Sometimes union activities and strikes resulted in violence. In 1886, a bomb blew up in a meeting of workers in Haymarket Square in Chicago. A riot followed in which eight police officers and others were killed. In 1892, the manager of a steel factory had troops sent to fight striking workers. Sixteen people were

Railroad workers set up a blockade during Chicago's famous Pullman Strike of 1894.

killed and many wounded. In 1894, workers for the Pullman Company, which made railroad cars, went on strike. To support these Chicago workers, the American Railway Union refused to haul railroad cars made by the Pullman Company. This action interfered with mail delivery, and the government sent troops to Chicago. Violence broke out, but the government ended the strike.

Some Leaders of the Union Movement

| Eugene V. Debs | "Big Bill" Haywood | Mother Jones |

Eugene V. Debs, leader of the American Railway Union, was arrested in Chicago during the Pullman Strike for refusing to call off the strike.

Samuel Gompers, a cigar maker, founded the American Federation of Labor (AFL) in 1886.

"Big Bill" Haywood, a miner, organized workers from many different fields into the Industrial Workers of the World, nicknamed the Wobblies.

Mother Jones organized unions and strikes for coal miners.

By 1917, women's suffrage groups across the country were organizing street marches, such as this one in New York City, to demand the right to vote.

Progressive Era

In the late 1800s, many Americans worked together to improve living conditions. They formed groups to improve education and to help women and poor people. This period became known as the Progressive Era.

After the Civil War, many women began working to gain the right to vote (also called suffrage). Susan B. Anthony and Elizabeth Cady Stanton founded the National Woman Suffrage Association in 1869. In 1920, the Nineteenth Amendment granted women the right to vote.

After 1890, religious leaders and social workers called for improvement in the lives of poor people in the cities. States passed laws to improve housing conditions. Reformers like Jane Addams and Ellen Starr built **settlement houses.**

Bandit's Roost in New York, photographed in 1888, was typical of urban slums of the day.

These were centers where neighborhood residents and leaders worked together to help the poor. Other reformers supported the temperance movement to reduce people's drinking of alcoholic beverages.

Some people objected to government corruption and the growing power of big businesses. They wanted to get rid of dishonest city officials. In July 1892, a group of reformers formed a new political party called the People's, or Populist, party. The Populist party called for a graduated income tax. This meant that people who earned more money would pay a higher percentage of their income in taxes.

Local and state governments passed many laws that helped give people more power. **Initiative and referendum laws** allowed voters to recommend and approve laws. **Direct primary laws** allowed voters to nominate candidates. The Seventeenth Amendment to the Constitution, adopted in 1913, allowed voters to elect senators.

Reformers

Jane Addams founded Hull House in Chicago. Her center included child care and college courses.

Susan B. Anthony was an important early leader in the campaign for women's rights.

Jane Addams

Susan B. Anthony

Robert M. La Follette, governor of Wisconsin, led the state to adopt the first direct primary law in 1904.

Jacob Riis was a journalist whose writings and photographs influenced the public to improve life for the poor.

Lincoln Steffens exposed corruption in several city governments.

Ida Tarbell wrote a book about corruption in the oil business that led to laws against unfair business practices.

The U.S. and the World

Spanish-American War

By the 1890s, some Americans felt that the United States should become a world power. These **expansionists** wanted America to gain overseas territories.

U.S ships destroyed Spain's underequipped Cuban navy in a four-hour battle on July 3, 1898.

Spain had long owned colonies, including Cuba, Puerto Rico, and the Philippines. When Cubans revolted against Spain, many Americans wanted to help the Cubans. American newspapers boosted their circulation by printing inaccurate or exaggerated stories that encouraged people to support the war; this type of reporting was called **yellow journalism.** On February 15, 1898, a U.S. battleship called the *Maine* blew up in Havana harbor. Many people blamed Spain for the explosion, even though its cause was never known. They used the slogan "Remember the *Maine*" to gain support for a war. On April 25, 1898, Congress declared war on Spain.

The Spanish-American War was over quickly. On May 1, the United States Navy defeated the Spanish fleet in the

Spanish-American War

Theodore Roosevelt becomes President

The first movie with a story, *The Great Train Robbery*, is produced

| 1898 | 1901 | 1903 | 1907 |

The United States annexes Hawaii

Wilbur and Orville Wright build the first successful airplane

Building of the Panama Canal begins

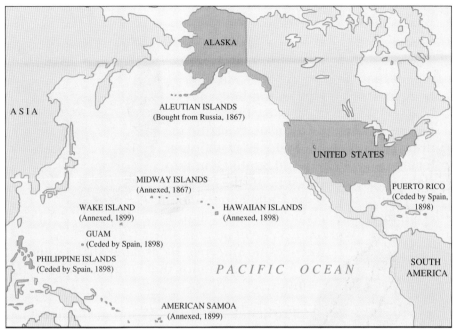

GROWTH OF THE UNITED STATES, 1867–1899

Philippines. By July, the army had defeated Spanish forces in Cuba. The Treaty of Paris, signed December 10, 1898, made Cuba an independent nation. The United States gained Guam, Puerto Rico, and the Philippines, even though many Americans opposed the United States owning other countries as colonies.

The United States also gained Hawaii in 1898. Hawaii had been ruled by kings and queens throughout the 1800s. But in 1893, the queen was removed from power and Hawaii became a republic. American business leaders controlled the government. On August 12, 1898, the United States annexed Hawaii. It became a U.S. territory in 1900. All Hawaiians became American citizens.

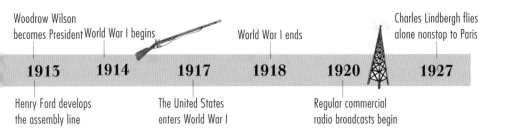

Woodrow Wilson becomes President | World War I begins | World War I ends | Charles Lindbergh flies alone nonstop to Paris

1913   **1914**   **1917**   **1918**   **1920**   **1927**

Henry Ford develops the assembly line | The United States enters World War I | Regular commercial radio broadcasts begin

Roosevelt and Wilson

"Speak softly and carry a big stick." These words of Theodore Roosevelt meant that the United States should back up its relations with other countries with a strong military force. Roosevelt used the Monroe Doctrine to prevent European countries from interfering in Venezuela and Santo Domingo. He used the Navy to support the country of Panama so that the United States could build the Panama Canal. Roosevelt also worked to reform business practices in America. He created stricter government regulations that companies had to follow.

President Theodore Roosevelt

President Woodrow Wilson got Congress to pass his Federal Reserve Act, which created a new government banking system. He also brought about other laws that regulated trade in America and with other countries. In 1914, Wilson said that the United States must remain neutral during World War I. He tried to maintain peace, but he finally asked Congress to declare war after Germany repeatedly provoked America.

President Woodrow Wilson

On April 6, 1917, the United States entered the war.

President Woodrow Wilson meets with his cabinet members in 1914, his second year in office. He accomplished most of his economic changes in those first two years.

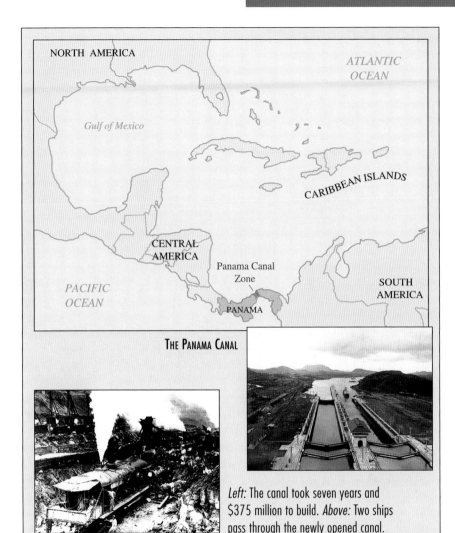

THE PANAMA CANAL

Left: The canal took seven years and $375 million to build. *Above:* Two ships pass through the newly opened canal.

The Panama Canal

To shorten the sea route from the eastern United States to the western United States, President Theodore Roosevelt planned to build a canal across the Isthmus of Panama. One of the biggest problems in building the canal was getting rid of the malaria, yellow fever, and bubonic plague on the Isthmus of Panama. Colonel William C. Gorgas, an American doctor, led the fight against the mosquitoes and rats that caused these diseases. The first two years of the Panama Canal project were spent clearing out brush and grass where these pests lived. The Canal opened on August 15, 1914.

ALLIED COUNTRIES

CENTRAL POWERS

NEUTRAL COUNTRIES

EUROPE DURING WORLD WAR I

World War I

World War I began in 1914 with the assassination of Archduke Francis Ferdinand of Austria-Hungary. This caused a war between Serbia and Austria-Hungary. Many European nations had treaties of alliance, and they joined the war to honor their treaties. Russia supported Serbia, and France joined the war as Russia's ally. Great Britain entered the war on France's side. France, Great Britain, and Russia were known as the **Allies.** Austria-Hungary and its ally Germany were known as the **Central Powers.**

President Woodrow Wilson tried to keep the United States out of the war. After many hostile acts by Germany, including attacks on passenger ships, the United States declared war on Germany in April 1917. By the spring of 1918, ships carried 100,000 American soldiers per month to fight in Europe. American assistance was extremely important in finally ending the war on November 11, 1918.

Nearly 10 million soldiers died in World War I. About 116,000 of these were Americans. Many new weapons appeared,

The Battle of Verdun was one of the major engagements of the war. It lasted from February to December in 1916 and caused 700,000 casualties.

including airplane bombers, tanks, poison gas, submarines, and machine guns.

President Wilson went to Paris in 1919 to help draw up a peace treaty. He had prepared a list called the **Fourteen Points** to settle the disputes among the nations. The list also created the League of Nations. The **Treaty of Versailles** made Germany disband its armed forces, accept full blame for starting the war, and give back large amounts of land and money.

Wilson and the League of Nations

President Woodrow Wilson proposed a League of Nations to help resolve disagreements without war. The League of Nations would be an international group of nations that would try to keep peace among the nations of the world. Wilson convinced other

A League of Nations meeting in 1920.

countries to join the league, but the United States Senate would not approve it. The league did not succeed in ending conflicts because all major nations were not members. It was disbanded in 1946 and replaced by the United Nations.

Prosperity

After World War I, the United States enjoyed a time of peace and prosperity. It is sometimes called the Roaring Twenties.

Automobiles became more common. In 1913, Henry Ford had improved assembly line methods so that cars could be made quickly and cheaply. In 1910, there were 500,000 automobiles in use in America, while in 1920, there were more than 8 million. The country also improved its highways.

By the 1920s, autos were a common convenience.

Another new form of transportation was the airplane. In 1927, Charles Lindbergh thrilled the country by flying a small plane across the Atlantic Ocean alone in 33½ hours.

An audience watches comedian Buster Keaton perform in *Sherlock, Jr.* in 1924.

New forms of entertainment appeared, too. People could listen to recorded music on phonographs. Almost every town and city had motion-picture theaters. In 1927, the first "talkie," *The Jazz Singer,* appeared. By 1929, as many as 100 million people went to movie theaters each week. Another form of mass entertainment was the radio. Millions of people listened to news, music, sporting events, and comedy on radios in their homes.

Families across the country frequently gathered around their radios for news and entertainment.

With the growth of movies and radio, Americans shared the same culture more than ever. People admired the same sports heroes and movie stars. Clothing styles spread more rapidly. And with the invention of labor-saving devices such as washing machines and refrigerators, people had more time to enjoy these forms of entertainment.

Women and the Roaring Twenties

The Roaring Twenties brought new clothing styles to young women. Many of them began wearing comfortable short dresses. They cut their hair into short bobs. Even more important was women's new position in society. During World War I, many women had taken on business responsibilities. After the war, women made new places for themselves in business and education. Women also got the legal right to vote in 1920.

In the 1920s, American women became much more independent and influential. They found many ways to increase the role that they played in America's social world, business world, and political world.

Facing Challenges

Pride and Prejudice

Throughout the early 1900s, black Americans continued the struggle to find their place in American society. They still suffered from discrimination. Many lived in the South, where the economy was suffering. During World War I, 360,000 black Americans left their homes to serve in the armed forces.

Troops clash with black protesters during a 1919 protest march in Washington, D.C.

Hundreds of thousands of others moved from their homes in the South to cities in the North. Between 1910 and 1930, about a million black Americans made this move. They soon

found that many of their problems followed them north. They often could not find jobs because they did not have the necessary skills or education. Many ended up living in crowded tenements in run-down neighborhoods.

Carrying American flags, members of the Ku Klux Klan parade past the Capitol in 1926.

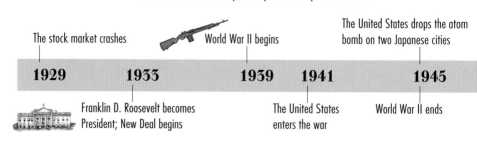

The stock market crashes

World War II begins

The United States drops the atom bomb on two Japanese cities

| 1929 | 1933 | 1939 | 1941 | 1945 |

Franklin D. Roosevelt becomes President; New Deal begins

The United States enters the war

World War II ends

Formed in 1905, the Niagara Movement called for equality for black Americans. The group merged with white activists in 1909 to form the NAACP.

Relations between the races grew more and more strained. The **Ku Klux Klan,** a racist organization that had grown up in the South after the Civil War, made a comeback, especially in the North. The Ku Klux Klan attacked black Americans and used many methods to deny them their rights. In 1918 and 1919, several race riots took place around the country. At least 100 people were killed and many others injured. Many people joined organizations such as the **National Association for the Advancement of Colored People (NAACP),** which worked for racial equality.

Some Writers of the Harlem Renaissance

During this time, Americans of all races enjoyed the artistic talents of the Harlem Renaissance. This was a group of black writers, artists, and musicians who lived and worked in Harlem, part of New York City, in the 1920s.

Countee Cullen wrote poems about black life in a traditional style.

Langston Hughes, the best known of the Harlem movement, wrote many volumes of poetry.

Claude McKay wrote *Home to Harlem,* a best-selling novel.

Jean Toomer wrote *Cane,* a book that combined fiction, poetry, and prose in describing black life.

Supreme Court makes the *Brown v. Board of Education* decision

Civil Rights Act passed

| 1950 | 1954 | 1963 | 1964 | 1965 |

Korean War begins

President John F. Kennedy is assassinated

Troops build up in Vietnam War

The Great Depression

By the end of the 1920s, American industries were no longer showing profits. Other economic problems arose in the New York stock market. In 1929, stock market prices started to go down. On October 24, 1929, the market crashed. People tried to sell their stock, but there were few buyers. Many investors lost their entire fortunes in the crash.

Thousands of unemployed New Yorkers line up to apply for federal "relief jobs" during the Depression.

The poor economy and the stock market crash led to the Great Depression, which lasted for more than 10 years. Banks stopped making loans to businesses. Businesses then had to reduce production. People lost their jobs. By 1933, 13 million Americans were out of work.

Farming suffered the same hardships as the rest of the economy. To make matters worse, the Southwest became a barren Dust Bowl. When the normal amount of rain did not

A mountainous dust cloud rolled through Clayton, New Mexico, in May 1937.

Martin Luther King, Jr., and Bobby Kennedy are assassinated

Richard Nixon resigns the presidency; Gerald R. Ford becomes President

1968   **1969**   **1974**   **1989**

Astronauts land on the moon

The Berlin Wall is knocked down

fall in 1932, wheat crops were ruined and the land was bare. Winds began blowing the dry soil. Huge dust storms blinded travelers and covered the insides of homes. The dust traveled hundreds of miles, some of it settling in New York City. With no crops for eight years, many farmers lost everything. Normal rainfall returned in 1940, and farmers had to learn better conservation methods to protect the soil.

Effects of the Great Depression

Shacks built by jobless and homeless people dot an area once filled with shipyards in Seattle, Washington. Before the Depression, hundreds of vessels had been built here.

During the Great Depression, millions of Americans were poverty stricken. Many people depended on charity or the government for food. Many people made neighborhoods of shacks built of cardboard and crates. People called the neighborhoods **Hoovervilles** after President Herbert Hoover. They blamed the President because he could not end the Depression. Many farmers in the Dust Bowl moved to California. They often had to work as migrant farm workers, picking fruits and vegetables for low wages.

The Soviet Union no longer exists

Terrorists attack the United States

1991

2001

2003

The United States and allies fight in the Persian Gulf War

U.S. troops embark on Operation Enduring Freedom

U.S. and British forces begin Operation Iraqi Freedom

The New Deal

The Great Depression continued, and frustrated Americans elected **Franklin D. Roosevelt** President in 1932. Roosevelt and Congress immediately passed laws for a program called the New Deal. It aimed to help the poor, to create new jobs and build up businesses, and to prevent another severe depression. The program created many new government agencies. The **Federal Emergency Relief Administration (FERA)** gave money to states for the

President Franklin D. Roosevelt

poor. The **Works Progress Administration (WPA)** gave people jobs building public projects such as parks, highways, and bridges. The **Social Security** system still provides money to people coping with retirement, disability, unemployment, or death.

Roosevelt's programs helped restore a strong economy. Their success made him very popular. He was the only President elected to four terms. Since the New Deal, the government has taken a greater role in regulating the nation's economy.

World events also demanded Roosevelt's attention. Japan seized an area of China in 1931. In 1939, Germany invaded Poland. Roosevelt wanted to help countries fighting Germany, Italy, and Japan. But American **isolationists** did not want to

get involved. The isolationists believed that the United States should take little or no part in the affairs of other nations.

WPA workers in Washington, D.C., chop firewood for the coming winter. From 1935 to 1943, the WPA put 8.5 million jobless Americans to work.

World War II

On December 7, 1941, Japanese aircraft bombed U.S. Navy ships at Pearl Harbor in Hawaii. The next day, the United States declared war on Japan. As Japan's allies under the **Axis** treaty, Germany and Italy also declared war on

Winston Churchill, President Franklin Roosevelt, and Joseph Stalin met in 1945 to plan the final assault on Germany.

the United States. The United States joined the **Allies**—Great Britain, China, and the Soviet Union—to fight the Axis powers. Britain and France had declared war on Germany after the Germans invaded Poland. At first, the Soviet Union had a treaty with Germany. Germany invaded the Soviet Union, though, and the Soviets joined the Allies.

Leaders such as Adolf Hitler in Germany and Benito Mussolini in Italy had taken advantage of unsettled conditions in Europe. Hitler and his Nazi party built up armies and conquered other countries. In 1939 and 1940, Germany conquered Poland, Denmark, Norway, Belgium, the Netherlands, and France. Germany attacked Great Britain. Britain's Royal Air Force (RAF) fought the German Luftwaffe in the Battle of Britain, the first battle over control of the air.

The United States lent materials and weapons to the Allies. When the United States entered the war in December 1941, Roosevelt joined with British Prime Minister Winston Churchill and Soviet leader Joseph Stalin to plan the Allied strategy. These leaders became known as the **Big Three.** American bombers soon began helping the RAF bomb Germany.

U.S. sailors cross the English Channel on D-Day as part of the largest invasion force ever assembled.

On **D-Day** (June 6, 1944), General Dwight D. Eisenhower led the Allied forces in a huge attack on the German army in France. American Lieutenant General George S. Patton led his army to Paris and freed the city on August 25. The Allies finally defeated Germany on May 7, 1945.

Japan was still fighting in Southeast Asia and the Pacific Ocean. On August 6, 1945, America dropped the first atomic bomb ever used in war on the city of Hiroshima, Japan. The United States later dropped another bomb on Nagasaki. Japan surrendered on September 1, 1945.

With the defeat of Germany, the Allies investigated the horrible crimes of the Nazis. Millions of Jews and others had been murdered or imprisoned in concentration camps. In all, 11 million civilians were killed; about 6 million of them were Jews. The mass murder became known as the **Holocaust.**

The countries where the war was fought suffered great damage. Many cities were destroyed, and more than 40 million soldiers and civilians died. The Soviet Union lost 7½ million people in battle; Germany, 3½ million; Japan, 2½ million; China, 2 million; and the United States, 400,000. World War II was the most destructive war the world has ever known.

The Women's Army Corps lands in North Africa. Women were important in the military during WWII.

The Home Front

In America, many women went to work in factories during the war. Factory production was amazing. For example, Americans built 86,000 planes in 1942. People bought and collected 10- or 25-cent stamps, which they could then use to buy a Defense Savings Bond. They planted "victory gardens," growing vegetables for their families.

With so many men drafted into military service, all-female factory crews became a common sight.

Some products needed by the armed services were rationed. Americans received coupons for items such as sugar, coffee, butter, and gasoline. Other items such as automobile tires were difficult to get.

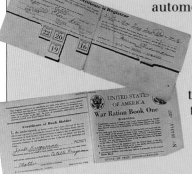

After the Japanese attack on Pearl Harbor, 110,000 Japanese-Americans living on the West Coast were sent to internment camps until the end of the war. The government thought that some of these people might be traitors. Men, women, and children had to leave their homes, jobs, and schools to go to the camps.

Above: War Ration Books allowed Americans to get limited amounts of hard-to-find items such as coffee.
Right: First arrivals at the Japanese internment camp at Manzanar, California, await processing.

The Cold War

The Soviet Union and the United States fought alongside each other in World War II. After the war, the two powerful countries began to distrust one another. The Soviet Union was a **communist** country. In a communist country, the state owns all means of

Soviet Premier Nikita Khrushchev *(right)* meets with American President John F. Kennedy.

production and tries to distribute the wealth of the country equally to its citizens. Communist states often limit the personal freedom and rights of citizens, also. The Soviet Union and China tried to spread communism to other nations. The United States opposed this. This conflict became known as the Cold War. It was called a "cold" war because it did not lead to direct fighting between the countries involved.

The Soviet Union began cutting off contact between Western nations and the Eastern communist countries. In March 1946,

Winston Churchill said that "an iron curtain has descended across the continent" of Europe. People used the phrase **Iron Curtain** to describe the separation of the communist nations from the rest of the world.

The spread of communism worried many Americans. In 1950, Senator Joseph

Senator Joseph McCarthy displays the *Daily Worker,* a Communist party newspaper, at a 1954 hearing.

An aerial photo from 1962 shows three Soviet ships and various nuclear missile parts near Havana, Cuba.

McCarthy of Wisconsin held hearings that accused many liberal Americans of being communist spies. McCarthy never proved that anyone was a spy, but some people lost their jobs and other rights after being accused. Eventually, people saw that McCarthy's charges were irresponsible. The term **McCarthyism** is used to describe careless accusations about citizens.

The Cold War reached a dangerous point in October 1962 with the **Cuban Missile Crisis.** The United States discovered that the Soviets were putting nuclear missiles in communist Cuba, only 100 miles from Florida. The President told the Soviet leader that Americans would stop any Russian ship carrying weapons. Russia finally removed the missiles from Cuba.

President Kennedy and the Peace Corps

When John F. Kennedy ran for President in 1960, he proposed a Peace Corps, an army of people who would work overseas to help people in developing countries. Kennedy created the Peace Corps on March 1, 1961. After training, the Peace Corps volunteers went to foreign countries and helped the people improve living conditions. More than 178,000 people have served in the Peace Corps.

Peace Corps worker in Nepal.

Civil Rights

In the 1950s, black Americans still did not have the same rights as white citizens. In the South, especially, they were segregated from whites. In 1950, the father of a black girl, Linda Brown, went to court in Kansas. He wanted his daughter to attend a nearby all-white public

Rosa Parks was arrested twice for her role in protesting Alabama's segregation laws.

school. The federal court ruled in favor of segregation, so the case went to the Supreme Court. It ruled in **Brown versus Board of Education** that segregation violated the Constitution. The case was tested when nine black students went to an all-white high school in Little Rock, Arkansas, in 1957. U.S. Army troops were sent to guard the students' rights.

Another important civil rights case involved **Rosa Parks** in Montgomery, Alabama. Parks refused to give up her seat and move to the back of the bus, as blacks were required to do

People all across the country organized peaceful marches and protests in support of civil rights for all black citizens in the 1960s.

under Alabama law. She was arrested. Once again, the case went to the Supreme Court. The Court ruled that a city could not segregate people on its buses.

On August 28, 1963, 250,000 people held a peaceful demonstration in Washington, D.C. They wanted Congress to enact a new civil rights bill. President John F. Kennedy proposed a bill. Congress passed the **Civil Rights Act of 1964.** It outlawed discrimination against blacks and other minorities. Many groups, including women, Hispanics, and Native Americans, staged peaceful protests to demand their civil rights.

Martin Luther King, Jr.

In 1956, Martin Luther King, Jr., was a young minister in Montgomery, Alabama. In the next few years, he led many marches and rallies, including the 1963 March on Washington. His goal was to end unjust discrimination. But he always insisted that this had to be done without violence. King was a great speaker who inspired millions of Americans. He received the Nobel Peace Prize in 1964. He was assassinated in Memphis, Tennessee, in April 1968.

Thousands gathered to hear King and others speak at the Lincoln Memorial after the 1963 March on Washington.

King's ideas and words continue to inspire the ongoing civil rights movement in America. Since his death, his widow Coretta and many other people have carried on his efforts to achieve peace and equality for all people.

Into Space

During the 1950s and 1960s, the United States and the Soviet Union were in a space race. The Soviets launched *Sputnik*, the first satellite to orbit Earth, in October 1957. In April 1961, they sent the first person, cosmonaut Yuri Gagarin, into space. About one month later, an American

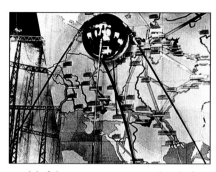

Model of the Soviet Union's *Sputnik I*, the first successful artificial satellite.

astronaut, Alan Shepard, went on a 15-minute flight into space.

After Shepard's flight in 1961, John Glenn orbited Earth in a space capsule. And on July 20, 1969, the *Apollo 11* lunar module landed on the moon. Neil Armstrong became the first person to walk on the moon.

The space shuttle represented a new era of space travel. The first space shuttle was launched April 12, 1981. Two American space tragedies have occurred: January 28, 1986, the space shuttle *Challenger* exploded on take-off, killing seven people; February 1, 2003, the *Columbia*, with a crew of seven aboard, disintegrated upon reentry into Earth's atmosphere. Despite this, exploration of space continues.

The space shuttle was the first spacecraft that could land on a runway and be reused.

The *Apollo 11* mission of 1969 put American astronauts on the surface of the moon.

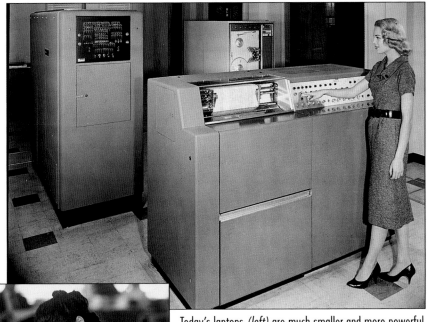

Today's laptops *(left)* are much smaller and more powerful than the first computers of the 1940s and 1950s *(above)*.

The Growth of Technology

Technology has created a revolution that affects Americans' everyday lives. The first television transmission occurred in 1936. Today most Americans have cable, video recorders, and video games. The first electronic digital computer was built in 1946. It took up more than 1,500 square feet (140 square meters) of floor space. Now, Americans use personal computers on their desks or carry them around. PDAs (personal digital assistant) and other handheld computers keep users in touch with just about everything available electronically. In the 1890s, many homes had telephones. Now people have cellular telephones that enable them to make phone calls while they are driving their cars or walking down the street. They can also use them to take pictures, play music, and even record videos! Technology continues to develop at breathtaking speed and to change our lives.

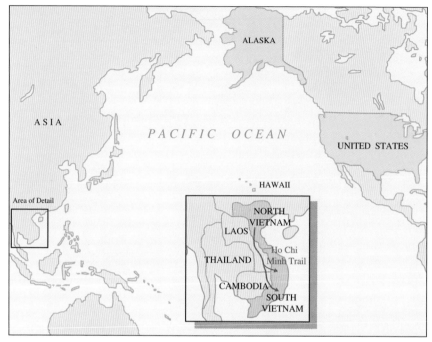

THE VIETNAM WAR, 1964–1973

The Vietnam War

In 1954, a communist government took power in the north
of Vietnam, a small country in Southeast Asia. Communists in
the North encouraged Viet Cong rebels in the South to over-
throw their government. Most Americans approved of aid to
South Vietnam from 1961 to 1963. On August 4, 1964, two U.S.
Navy warships were attacked by North Vietnam. President
Lyndon Johnson sent U.S. troops to South Vietnam.

The American strategy was to bomb North Vietnam. The
rebels used **guerrilla warfare,** or ambushes and hit-and-run
raids, to fight the South Vietnamese and the U.S. armies.
By 1967, thousands of Americans had been killed. Many
Americans began to protest the war. In October 1967,
50,000 protesters marched in Washington, D.C.

In 1969, President Richard Nixon began removing American
troops from Vietnam. The last troops left in early 1973. South
Vietnam surrendered to North Vietnam on April 30, 1975.

By 1968, when this photograph was taken, more than 500,000 American soldiers were stationed in Vietnam.

The war ruined the South Vietnamese economy and made refugees of half its population. It also damaged the country's forests and animal life. In the United States, many people were bitter about losing the war and 58,000 American lives. Americans remain divided over the Vietnam War today.

The Fall of a President

President Richard M. Nixon

June 17, 1972 Five people are arrested for attempting to break into Democratic party headquarters at the Watergate Hotel to plant electronic listening devices.

January 30, 1973 All five are found guilty.

April 30, 1973 President Richard Nixon states he had no part in planning the crime or covering it up.

May 1973 During Senate hearings, a former aide testifies that Nixon knew about the cover-up.

July 23, 1973 Nixon refuses to turn over tape recordings of meetings where he discussed the break-in.

October 20, 1973 Attorney General Elliot Richardson and Deputy Attorney General William Ruckelshaus resign after refusing Nixon's order to fire Watergate special prosecutor Archibold Cox.

November 1973 Nixon agrees to turn over the tape recordings.

March 1974 Nixon's top advisers are charged with covering up the break-in.

August 8, 1974 Nixon resigns.

September 8, 1974 President Gerald Ford pardons Nixon for all crimes he may have committed.

A New World Order

By 1988, the Cold War was coming to an end. The United States and the Soviet Union signed a treaty agreeing to destroy their most dangerous nuclear missiles. They also agreed to reduce the total number of other nuclear weapons. Soviet leader Mikhail Gorbachev encouraged more freedom in the Soviet Union.

President George H. W. Bush and Russian leader Boris Yeltsin signed several historic agreements in June 1992.

Poland, Hungary, East Germany, and Czechoslovakia in Eastern Europe broke free of the Communist party in 1989. In November 1989, East Germany opened its borders to the West. East and West Germany reunited in October 1990.

In June 1990, Gorbachev agreed to give ten Soviet republics self-government. On December 8, 1991, Boris Yeltsin, the new Russian leader, announced that the Soviet Union no longer existed. The Soviet republics became independent nations.

For decades, the United States. had planned its place in world politics around its rival, the Soviet Union. Now that it was no longer a threat, the United States needed to change its role as a world leader.

The United States and several other nations launched Operation Desert Storm in January 1991 to remove Iraqi forces from the oil-rich country of Kuwait.

New challenges came from other governments. In 1990, Iraqi troops invaded the country of Kuwait. President George H. W. Bush helped form a coalition of countries to oppose Iraq. On January 17, 1991, the coalition forces began bombing Iraq. By February 27, Kuwait had been liberated.

On September 11, 2001, middle-eastern terrorists crashed two jetliners into New York's World Trade Center towers. A third crashed into the Pentagon, and a fourth crashed in rural Pennsylvania. Thousands perished in the worst terror attack in American history.

Those claiming responsibility, along with their leader Osama Bin Laden, were being harbored in Afghanistan. President George W. Bush announced Operation Enduring Freedom, and U.S. troops and their allies began war against Afghanistan. After defusing the power of the terrorists, the Afghan people voted in their first free election in 2004.

West German demonstrators place flags atop the Berlin Wall under the watchful eyes of East German soldiers.

The Berlin Wall

After World War II, Berlin was divided. East Berlin became the capital of communist East Germany. West Berlin remained a part of West Germany. In 1961, the communists built the Berlin Wall to prevent people from escaping to West Berlin. More than 170 people died trying to escape over the Wall. The Wall became a symbol of the Cold War. In 1989, the communist government finally allowed East Germans to travel freely. Germans celebrated as the Berlin Wall was knocked down.

The 2000s

On March 19, 2003, American and British forces (plus a few smaller nations) began Operation Iraqi Freedom. President George W. Bush committed thousands of troops and billions of dollars in an attempt to continue the war on terror. The ongoing war in Iraq overshadowed the earlier invasion of Afghanistan.

Americans are also focusing on problems at home. Homelessness, unemployment, equal rights among minority groups, and quality education remain as major issues.

The AIDS Quilt, on display here in Washington, D.C., bears the names of many people afflicted with this tragic disease.

In the last 20 years, dangerous new diseases such as AIDS have struck throughout the world. Scientists are continually working to fight these diseases.

Despite some advances, crime and poverty continue to plague American cities.

Despite the challenges they face, Americans are optimistic. They believe that the democracy created by the Constitution in 1787 will help them meet the challenges of their country and of the world.

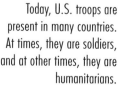
Today, U.S. troops are present in many countries. At times, they are soldiers, and at other times, they are humanitarians.

Index

handy homework helper

Geography

Writers:
Susan Bloom
Maggie Ronzani

Consultant:
Phil Klein, Ph.D.

Publications International, Ltd.

Susan Bloom is a writer and editor with Creative Services Associates, Inc.

Maggie Ronzani is a writer and editor with Creative Services Associates, Inc. She has more than 25 years experience in educational publishing.

Phil Klein, Ph.D., is a Geography Education Specialist. He has written numerous publications including *Geographic Inquiry into Global Issues, Europe and the World in Geography Education,* and the *Journal of Geography.* His teaching experience includes geography education at both the pre-collegiate and college levels. He is a member of the Association of American Geographers and the National Council for Geographic Education.

Cover Illustration: Dave Garbot

Photo credits: Bettmann Archive: 64, 93, 98 (bottom), 101 (bottom); **Corbis:** 29 (top right), 107 (bottom); **FPG International:** 44; Gary Buss: 29 (bottom); Charles Fitch: 102; Kenneth Garrett: 63 (top left); Greg Gilman: 30 (top); Jeri Gleiter: 75; Peter Gridley: 27 (bottom); Richard Harrington: 108; Michael Hart: 34 (bottom); S. Kanno: 31 (bottom); Alan Kearney: 27 (top); Ed Taylor Studio: 72 (bottom left); T. Tracy: 72 (bottom right); Travelpix: 29 (top left), 48 (top); **Globe Photos, Inc.:** 19 (bottom); **International Stock:** Roberto Arakaki: 69 (top); Warren Faidley: 120 (top); Bob Firth: 120 (bottom); Michele & Tom Grimm: 52 (top); Andre Jenny: 35 (top); Buddy Mays: 19 (top); Mark Newman: 115 (top); Stockman: 11 (bottom); Johnny Stockshooter: 58; Vision Impact: contents (bottom right), 86 (top); Brent Winebrenner: 72 (center); **Erich Lessing/Art Resource, NY:** 84; **Musee Dubardo,**

Tunis/Bridgeman Art Library: 6 (top); **Photri, Inc.:** 39 (bottom); **SuperStock:** contents (bottom left & bottom center), 5, 11 (center), 21 (bottom), 26 (top), 28, 30 (bottom), 32, 33 (top), 34 (top), 35 (bottom), 37, 39 (top), 43 (bottom), 51, 52 (bottom), 54 (top), 55 (top), 63 (top right), 69 (bottom), 77, 78, 86 (bottom), 88, 97 (bottom), 98 (top), 105, 106, 109, 111, 113 (bottom), 115 (bottom), 117, 122 (top & bottom right), British Library, London: 6 (bottom); Rosenth: 122 (bottom left); **Tony Stone Images:** Gay Bumgarner: 42; Willard Clay: 26 (bottom); Sue Cunningham: 90 (top); Wayne Eastep: 97 (top); Chad Ehlers: 101 (top); Robert Frerck: 90 (bottom); Yann Layma: 122 (center); Cathlyn Melloan: 63 (right center); John Running: 48 (bottom); Hugh Sittion: 94; Art Wolfe: contents (top left), 47.

Map and Chart Illustrations: Thomas Cranmer; Karen Minot.

Additional Illustrations: Brad Gaber; Mike Garner; Bob Masheris; Anita Nelson; Lorie Robare.

Contents

About This Book

Homework takes time and a lot of hard work. Many students would say it's their least favorite part of the school day. But it's also one of the most important parts of your school career because it does so much to help you learn. Learning gives you knowledge, and knowledge gives you power.

Homework gives you a chance to review the material you've been studying so you understand it better. It lets you work on your own, which can give you confidence and independence. Doing school work at home also gives your parents a way to find out what you're studying in school.

Everyone has trouble with their homework from time to time, and *Handy Homework Helper: Geography* can help you when you run into a problem. This book was prepared with the help of educational specialists. It offers quick, simple explanations of the basic material that you're studying in school. If you get stuck on an idea or have trouble finding some information, *Handy Homework Helper: Geography* can help clear it up for you. It can also help your parents help you by giving them a fast refresher course in the subject.

This book is clearly organized by the topics you'll be studying in Geography. A quick look at the Table of Contents will tell you which chapter covers the area you're working on. You can probably guess which chapter includes what you need and then flip through the chapter until you find it. For even more help finding what you're looking for, look up key words related to what you're study-ing in the Index. You might find material faster that way, and you might also find useful information in a place you wouldn't have thought to look.

Remember that different teachers and different schools take differ-ent approaches to teaching Geography. For that reason, we recom-mend that you talk with your teacher about using this homework guide. You might even let your teacher look through the book so he or she can help you use it in a way that best matches what you're studying at school.

Introduction to Geography

What Is Geography?

When you think about the subject of geography, maybe you think about where a place is and who lives there. The field of geography includes these facts, but it also includes much more.

Geography is the study of the features of the earth and the location of living things on the planet. Geographers study rivers, mountains, plants, and other physical features of the earth. They examine where and how people live. They determine how people change to suit their environments and how people change their environments. For example, geographers studying the city of San Diego might examine its climate, its location near the Pacific Ocean, and its other physical features. They might study how these features have affected the people of the city and their ways of life. They might also examine how people have changed the environment of the area.

Geography can be as simple as studying the path of a stream in your neighborhood and the life in that stream. It can be as complex as using a satellite to study earth's pollution.

Finding Out About the Earth

The word "geography" comes from the Greek word *geographia*, which means "earth description." The ancient Greeks were the first people to study geography in an organized way. They tried to explain the relationship between the physical features of a place and the lives of the people there. Other peoples, such as the Egyptians, Phoenicians, and Arabs, were great travelers and traders. As they traveled, they learned more about the earth. The ancient Romans also added to the knowledge of earth's geography. During the Middle Ages, much knowledge of geography was lost. Later, the 1400s and 1500s were a time of

This Roman mosaic depicts an ocean-going Greek vessel. The Greeks were the first to study geography.

A map from the 1500s shows the level of geographic knowledge at the time.

great discoveries by European explorers. These centuries brought a huge increase in geographic knowledge.

From as early as around 600 B.C., thinkers such as Aristotle and Ptolemy thought the earth was a sphere (a ball) in space. They were right! Earth is one of nine planets in our sun's solar system. It revolves around a star we call the sun. Earth is covered with water, rock, and soil. It is close enough to the sun to receive warmth and light. But it is far enough from the sun so that temperatures are not too hot for living things to survive. Earth is home to human beings and many kinds of plants and animals.

Earth has a **North Pole** at one end and a **South Pole** at the other. The planet is not perfectly round but is slightly flat at the poles. Halfway between the two poles is an imaginary line that circles the earth. This line is called the **equator.**

Location

Our Home, Earth

The earth's surface is composed of about 71 percent water. Almost all the water is in the oceans. An **ocean** is a huge body of salt water. Together, the oceans contain about 97 percent of all the water on the earth.

Some people think of the oceans as one huge body of water. However, we usually divide them into four major bodies of water. The Pacific Ocean is the largest, followed by the Atlantic Ocean, the Indian Ocean, and, finally, the Arctic Ocean.

The oceans include smaller bodies of water, such as seas, gulfs, and bays. A **sea** is any body of salt water that is smaller than an ocean and partly or completely enclosed by land.

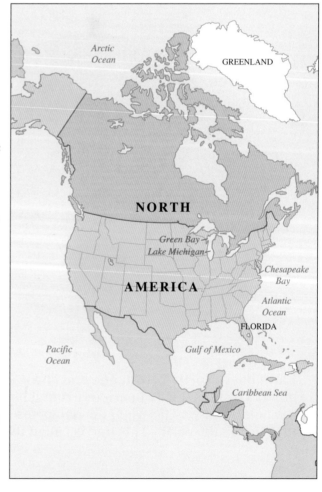

Look on a globe to find the Sea of Japan in the Pacific or the Caribbean Sea in the Atlantic. Sometimes, however, the word "sea" is used to refer to the oceans in general. A **gulf** is a part of an ocean that extends into land. Examples are the Gulf of Mexico and the Persian Gulf. A **bay** is also a body of water that extends into land. It is smaller than a gulf. A bay may be part of an ocean, such as Chesapeake Bay, or part of a lake, such as Green Bay.

Land makes up 29 percent of the earth's surface. The largest landmasses are **continents.** They are surrounded by water. The largest continent is Asia, followed in size by Africa, North America, South America, Antarctica, Europe, and Australia. Smaller bodies of land completely surrounded by water are **islands.** Islands vary greatly in size. Greenland is the largest island on earth. It covers 840,000 square miles (2,175,600 square kilometers). Some islands are smaller than a city block.

Many continents and islands have **peninsulas,** areas of land that extend out from the rest of the land and are mostly surrounded by water. Most peninsulas, like Florida, are narrow strips of land. The largest peninsula is the Arabian Peninsula, part of Asia. It has about 1,160,000 square miles (3,004,000 square kilometers) of land. Check the map on page 8 to locate examples of different bodies of water and landmasses.

Earth's Size

Circumference around poles: 24,860 miles (40,008 kilometers)

Circumference around the equator: 24,902 miles (40,076 kilometers)

Total area: 196,800,000 square miles (509,700,000 square kilometers)

Water area: about 139,500,000 square miles (361,300,000 square kilometers)

Land area: about 57,300,000 square miles (148,400,000 square kilometers)

Maps: Pictures of Earth

A **globe** lets you see the earth's entire surface. Because it is shaped like a sphere, the globe is the only model that gives a correct picture of the earth as a whole. But a globe cannot fit in a book or give details about a specific place. When you need information from a book or specific information about places on earth, you use a map. A **map** is a flat picture of all or part of the earth.

Globes and Maps

People use maps for many different reasons. You may use a map to help you find your way around a city. Airplane pilots and ship navigators use maps to find their way in air or on water. We can learn about the rivers, lakes, mountains, and even the soil in an area by reading a map. A map can give information about a place's climate, population, industry, and much more.

Lines, colors, and symbols on a map stand for features such as bodies of water, elevations, roads, and cities. You can tell what the lines, colors, and symbols mean by using a map's legend. A **map legend** lists what each symbol stands for. For example, a road map may use one kind of line for highways

Globes	Maps
• duplicate the earth's shape	• show the earth or part of it on a flat surface
• show all land and water surfaces in correct position	• can provide a wide variety of information
• show size and shape in correct proportion	• give detailed information about specific places
• show distance and area without distortion	• can be printed in books

The table lists the strengths of both globes and maps. You can see how globes and maps differ. Maps cannot show true shape, proportion, direction, or distances for all the earth at once. Only globes can show all four of these features correctly at the same time.

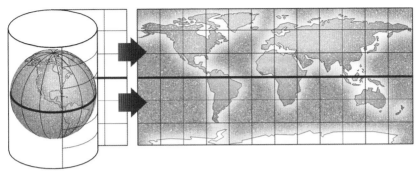

On this map, Alaska looks larger than Mexico. But Mexico is actually larger than Alaska. To show the round earth on a flat map, mapmakers stretch the top and bottom of the map. As a result, places in the far north and south often look larger than places in the middle of the map.

and other kinds of lines to stand for state or county roads. The legend explains what each line means. You need to understand the legend in order to use the map.

Another map feature is called a **compass rose.** It shows the points of the compass. A compass rose shows where to find north, south, east, and west on the map.

A very important map feature is its scale. Maps are just pictures of places on earth. The **map scale** compares the distances shown on maps to the distances in real life. For example, a map may read "1 inch equals about 1,000 miles." This means that one inch on the map

Different types of maps show different types of information. *Top:* A political map shows such data as country borders, capital cities, and major cities. *Bottom:* A terrain map shows mostly mountains, bodies of water, and other land formations.

represents 1,000 miles on earth. A scale may be shown as a ruler that marks off distances along a line.

Words to Know

compass rose: a symbol that indicates direction on a map

map legend: a listing and explanation of symbols and colors on a map

map scale: a line or ratio that shows the relationship of distances on a map to distances on the earth

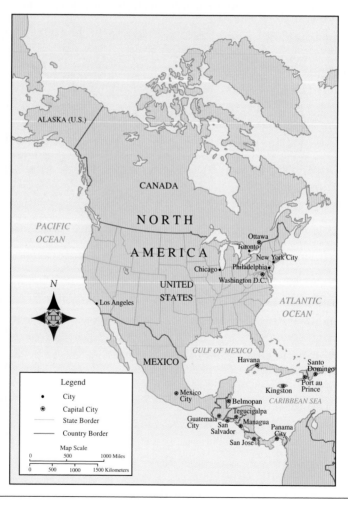

Maps with Grids

Grids are sets of lines that help us locate places on a map. Many maps use an **index grid:** lines that make horizontal rows and vertical columns. The vertical columns are identified by letters that run across the map's top and bottom. The horizontal rows are identified by numbers that run down each side. The map index lists the places on the map and the letters and numbers that identify their location. For example, the index to a map of Mexico might list the city of Guadalajara with the identifying symbol D3. The city is found in the area where the vertical column marked D crosses the horizontal row called 3.

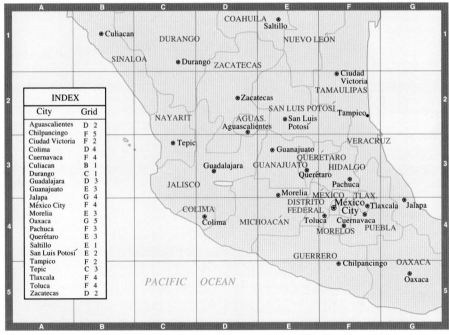

INDEX	
City	Grid
Aguascalientes	D 2
Chilpancingo	F 5
Ciudad Victoria	F 2
Colima	D 4
Cuernavaca	F 4
Culiacan	B 1
Durango	C 1
Guadalajara	D 3
Guanajuato	E 3
Jalapa	G 4
México City	F 4
Morelia	E 3
Oaxaca	G 5
Pachuca	F 3
Querétaro	E 3
Saltillo	E 1
San Luis Potosí	E 2
Tampico	F 2
Tepic	C 3
Tlaxcala	F 4
Toluca	F 4
Zacatecas	D 2

If you were looking for the city of Aguascalientes on this map, you would look at the grid location D2. The city of Oaxaca is at G5.

Latitude and Longitude

By using two grid coordinates, you can locate any point on earth. These two coordinates are latitude and longitude.

Latitude describes the position of any point on earth in relation to the equator. Latitude is measured by parallels. A **parallel** is an east–west line on a globe. Each parallel is the same distance from the parallels on either side of it.

Longitude is measured by meridians. A **meridian** is a line that goes from the North Pole to the South Pole. All meridians meet at the poles.

LINES OF LATITUDE

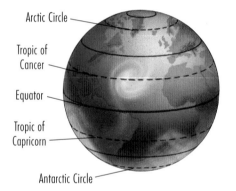

Arctic Circle
Tropic of Cancer
Equator
Tropic of Capricorn
Antarctic Circle

LINES OF LONGITUDE

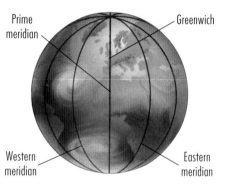

Prime meridian
Greenwich
Western meridian
Eastern meridian

Latitude and longitude are measured in degrees of a circle. Degrees can be divided into smaller units called minutes. The equator has a latitude of 0 degrees. The North Pole has a latitude of 90 degrees north. The South Pole is at 90 degrees south. The latitude of any place between the equator and the poles is between 0 and 90 degrees.

The measurement of longitude begins at the meridian that passes through Greenwich, England. This line is known as the **prime meridian.** It is identified as 0 degrees longitude. The 180-degree meridian lies halfway around the world from the prime meridian. Lines of west longitude lie west of Greenwich. Lines of east longitude lie east of Greenwich.

By identifying the latitude and longitude of a place, we can locate any place on the earth. We use latitude and longitude to find **absolute location,** the exact spot on the earth where a particular place is found. For example, the large city located close to 40 degrees north and 80 degrees west is Pittsburgh, Pennsylvania. You can also identify where Pittsburgh is by giving its **relative location.** The relative location

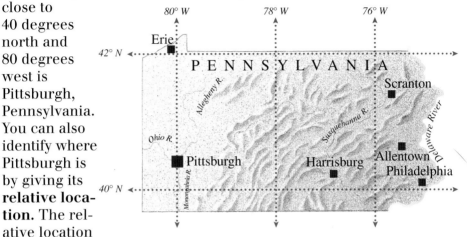

is where something is in relation to other features. For example, you might say that Pittsburgh is in southwestern Pennsylvania where the Allegheny and Monongahela rivers join to form the Ohio River.

Words to Know

absolute location: a place's position on a grid of latitude and longitude lines

latitude: imaginary parallel lines that circle the earth from east to west

longitude: imaginary lines that stretch north and south from the North Pole to the South Pole

meridian: line of longitude running from the North Pole to the South Pole

parallel: line of latitude running east–west around the globe

prime meridian: the 0-degree line of longitude that passes through Greenwich, England

relative location: the position of one place in relation to another place

Hemispheres

The name for any half of the globe is **hemisphere.** The prime meridian divides the Eastern Hemisphere from the Western Hemisphere. It cuts through Europe and Africa. For convenience, geographers say that the Eastern Hemisphere includes all of Europe, Africa, Asia, and Australia. The Western Hemisphere includes North America and South America. Antarctica is in both hemispheres.

The earth can also be divided into the Northern and Southern hemispheres. The equator is the dividing line for these hemispheres. Every place north of the equator is in the Northern Hemisphere, and every place south of the equator is in the Southern Hemisphere.

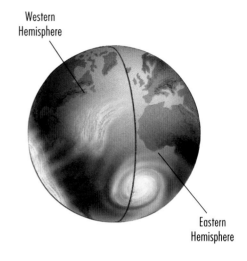

Western Hemisphere

Eastern Hemisphere

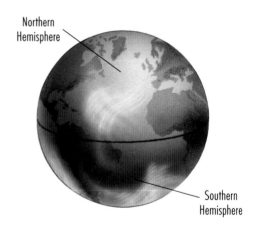

Northern Hemisphere

Southern Hemisphere

If you live in Chicago, Illinois, you live in the Northern and Western hemispheres.

The Physical Environment

Earth's Rotation and Revolution

Earth is one of nine planets that circle the sun. It is the third planet from the sun. A **planet** is a very large body that travels around a star.

Earth is always moving. It spins around on its axis like a top. At the same time, it revolves around the sun.

Imagine a line going through the planet from the North Pole to the South Pole. This imaginary line is called earth's **axis.** The earth spins eastward on its axis, making a complete **rotation** every 23 hours and 56 minutes. The spinning of earth on its axis causes day and night. On the side of earth facing the sun as it rotates, it is daytime. On the side of the earth facing away from the sun, it is night. As the earth turns eastward, people see the sun come up in the eastern sky.

You can demonstrate earth's rotation by shining a flashlight on a globe. Hold the light steady as

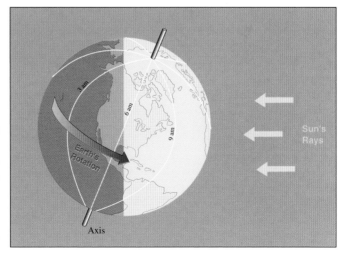

The rotating of the earth on its axis causes day and night. The side of the earth facing the sun is in daytime. It takes 23 hours and 56 minutes to make one complete rotation.

you spin the globe. The area the light is shining on is in daylight. The other side of the globe is in darkness.

While the earth spins, it also slowly **revolves,** or circles, around the sun. If you move a tennis ball (earth) around a basketball (sun), you will get an idea of earth's revolution. The planet completes one revolution in 365 days, 6 hours, and 9 minutes. Earth's path around the sun is called its **orbit.**

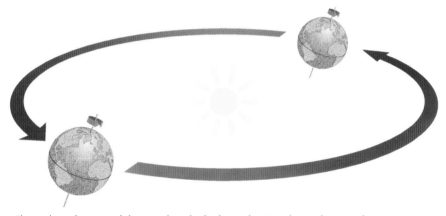

The earth revolves around the sun relatively slowly. It takes 365 days, 6 hours, and 9 minutes to make one complete revolution around the sun.

Our 24-hour day and 365-day year are based on earth's rotation and revolution. But one revolution is actually slightly more than 365 days, and one rotation is slightly less than 24 hours. These differences between actual time and calendar time are made up during leap years, which occur every four years.

Words to Know

axis: imaginary line through the earth from the North Pole to the South Pole; earth turns on its axis

orbit: the path of earth around the sun

planet: large body that travels around a star

revolve: to move in a curve around a point; earth revolves around the sun

rotation: the turning of earth on its axis

Seasons

Do you have a favorite season of the year? Perhaps you like the crispness of autumn or the snows of winter best. Or maybe in the place you live, winter is warm and summer is hot. The **seasons** of the year are spring, summer, autumn (or fall), and winter. With each new season,  the weather and amount of daylight change in most parts of the world. The farther you are from the equator, the more seasonal change you will see.

Seasons are caused by earth's tilt on its axis and its movement around the sun. Seasons change because different areas on earth get different amounts of sunlight during the year. Earth is tilted on its axis about 23½ degrees from an upright position. You can demonstrate how different areas of earth receive different amounts of sun by holding a ball at an angle as you circle a lighted lamp. Always face the same direction as you circle the lamp. Do not turn to face the lamp as you move. Notice how one part of the ball gets more light than another at certain times.

During the fall *(top)* and winter *(above)* in the Northern Hemisphere, the temperatures are cool and there is less direct sunlight.

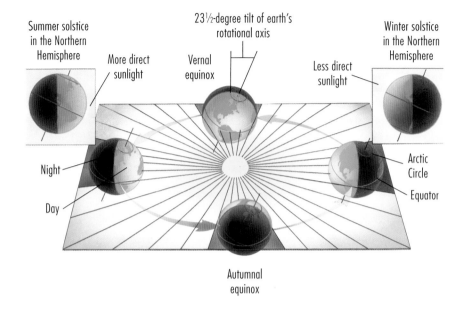

The Northern Hemisphere tilts away from the sun during the winter. It receives less direct sunlight and has cooler temperatures than at any other time of the year. It tilts toward the sun during the summer. During this time, the Northern Hemisphere receives more direct sunlight and has warmer temperatures.

Geographers and other scientists mark the beginning of each new season by earth's position in relation to the sun. The beginning of spring in the Northern Hemisphere is marked by the **vernal equinox** on March 19, 20, or 21. The **autumnal equinox,** the beginning of autumn, occurs on September 22 or 23. During an equinox, the sun appears directly above the equator. On these days, all places on earth have a 12-hour day and a 12-hour night.

In the Northern Hemisphere, summer begins on the summer solstice, June 20 or 21. On this day, the hemisphere gets more hours of daylight than on any other day of the year. The sun's rays at noon shine directly over the line of latitude at 23 degrees 27 minutes north. This parallel is called the Tropic of Cancer. The winter solstice, December 21 or 22, is the first day of winter in the Northern Hemisphere. On this day, the hemisphere gets the fewest hours of daylight than on any other day. During the winter solstice, the noon sun shines directly over the latitude 23 degrees 27 minutes south. This line is called the Tropic of Capricorn. The area between the two Tropics is called the tropical zone. Most areas in the tropical zone are warm all year long.

Tropic of Cancer

Tropic of Capricorn

Did You Know?

When it is summer in the Northern Hemisphere, it is winter in the Southern Hemisphere. If you have a friend in Australia, he or she may be basking in December's hot summer sun as you shiver in December's cold winter wind.

Summer in Australia, which is in the Southern Hemisphere, begins in December.

Weather

Weather is the condition of the atmosphere at a specific time and place. The **atmosphere** is the air that surrounds earth. The weather where you are may be warm or cold, sunny or cloudy, rainy or dry today. Tomorrow, it could be very different. The weather will almost certainly change from season to season.

The weather depends on four factors: temperature, air pressure, wind, and humidity. **Temperature** is based on the sun's heat energy in the atmosphere. Only a tiny amount of the sun's heat energy ever enters earth's atmosphere. Of this heat energy, 34 percent is reflected back into space by clouds and dust; 19 percent is absorbed by the atmosphere, warming the air; and 47 percent reaches earth's surface, warming the surface. (See the illustration below.) The ground and the oceans absorb the heat energy and then eventually release it back into the atmosphere. The atmosphere prevents much heat from escaping back into space.

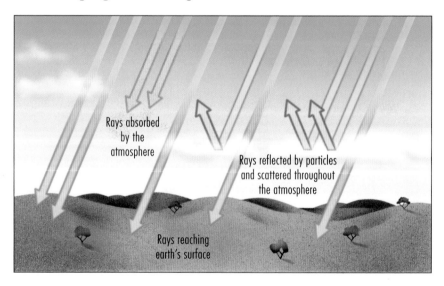

Rays absorbed by the atmosphere

Rays reflected by particles and scattered throughout the atmosphere

Rays reaching earth's surface

The term **air pressure** refers to the atmosphere's force on the earth. Warm air is less dense than cool air. It puts less pressure on the earth. It forms a **low-pressure area.** Cool air puts more pressure on the earth and forms a **high-pressure area.** High-pressure areas tend to push into low-pressure areas.

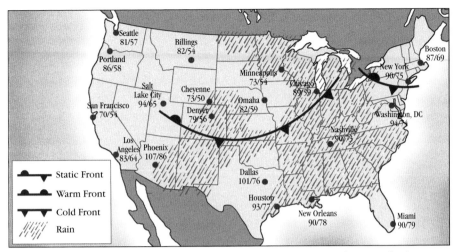

When a high-pressure area (cool air) and a low-pressure area (warm air) move close to each other, a wall called a **front** forms between them. When the cold air mass is advancing, the wall is called a cold front, as shown on this weather map. When the warm air mass is advancing, it is called a warm front.

When air in a high-pressure area moves into a low-pressure area, it creates the air movement you know as **wind.** If two areas have a large difference in air pressure, strong winds will result.

Humidity is the amount of water vapor in the atmosphere. Most water vapor comes from the oceans. If the air contains a lot of water vapor, the humidity is high. Warm air can hold more vapor than cool air. When moist air cools, water vapor may turn into water droplets. The water falls to the earth in the form of rain, snow, sleet, or hail. These types of falling water are called **precipitation.**

Amazing Weather Records

Highest temperature in the United States: 134 degrees Fahrenheit (57 degrees Celsius) in Death Valley, California, July 10, 1913

Lowest temperature in the United States: 80 degrees below zero Fahrenheit (62 degrees below zero Celsius) at Prospect Creek, Alaska, January 23, 1971

Highest wind: 231 miles per hour (372 kilometers per hour) at Mount Washington, New Hampshire, April 12, 1934

Climate

The weather where you live may change from day to day and from season to season. But the climate where you live stays about the same from one year to the next. **Climate** is the average weather conditions in a place over a period of at least 30 years. Many different factors influence the climate of a place.

Latitude is one important factor. It helps determine how warm or cold an area's climate will be. It also influences how much the weather will change from season to season.

Places near the equator, the tropical zones, receive direct overhead heat from the sun throughout the year. These areas have a warm climate. Places near the North and South Poles receive slanted rays from the sun. This indirect light produces less heat than direct rays. The areas close to the poles have colder temperatures. In both polar and tropical areas, the temperatures do not change much in different seasons.

Because of the earth's tilt, places in the middle latitudes have more direct sunlight and longer periods of sunlight in the summer than in the winter. So temperatures vary from season to season. Summer brings warmer temperatures. Winters are colder.

The amount of moisture in the air is another factor in climate. Winds blow moist air from the ocean over nearby land. Over land, it becomes precipitation. Warmer air can hold a lot more water vapor than cool air. So areas near the warm oceans around the equator have the most precipitation. The cold places near the poles have the least precipitation. Also, coastal areas may be cooler in summer and warmer in winter than inland areas. That's because the nearby water changes temperature more slowly than land. It helps keep the air temperature of land that is near water more moderate.

Winds also affect climate. Different places on earth have different wind systems. Winds can carry heat and moisture from one place to another. They can also change directions in different seasons. In some seasons they might bring moist air. In others, they might bring dry air.

Finally, differences in altitude affect climate. Air becomes colder as it rises. It cannot hold as much moisture as warm air. Mountains have cooler temperatures and more precipitation than lower-lying places.

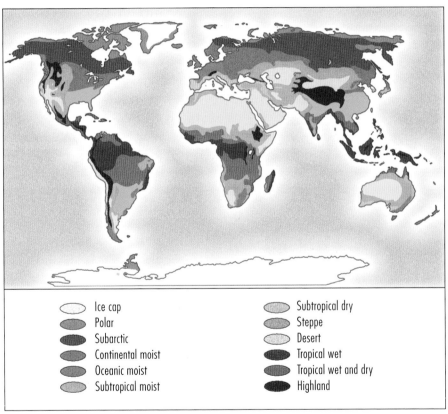

Ice cap
Polar
Subarctic
Continental moist
Oceanic moist
Subtropical moist

Subtropical dry
Steppe
Desert
Tropical wet
Tropical wet and dry
Highland

This map shows the different types of climates that exist in the world. What type of climate do you live in?

Weathering and Soils

When you plant a seed in a garden or a pot, you put the seed in soil. **Soil** is the material that covers much of earth's land surface. Plants depend on nutrients in the soil for life.

Top: The soil on this soybean farm in Iowa is an example of a **mollisol**, or "soft soil." *Bottom:* The dry soil of the deserts of the southwestern United States is **aridisol**, or "dry soil."

Soil is made up of minerals, decaying plants and animals, water, and air. Earth has many different kinds of soil. Geographers put soils in categories according to color, texture, structure, and chemical makeup. For example, most of the Midwestern prairies in the United States have a soil called a **mollisol,** which means "soft soil." This soil is very rich in plant nutrients. It is excellent for growing crops such as corn or wheat. In fact, prairies are known as the "world's breadbaskets" because of this rich soil. On the other hand, the deserts of the southwestern United States are often known as **aridisols,** which means "dry soil." These soils do not contain as much organic material. It takes a lot of work to grow crops in desert soils.

The rocky, dry soil of this California desert was caused by physical weathering.

What makes soil? Rocks break up through the work of water, ice, plants, or changes in temperature. This process is called **weathering.** Soil results from weathering, acting over long periods of time.

One kind of weathering is **physical weathering.** In physical weathering, rocks break into pieces. Sometimes water fills cracks in rocks and then freezes. As it freezes, the water expands and splits the rocks apart. Roots of trees and other plants may also break rock as they grow in cracks. Physical weathering is common in places where temperatures change greatly over 24 hours. In the dry western United States, days are hot and the nights are cool. Much of the soil there has been formed by physical weathering.

Chemical weathering is caused by water. Water in rivers, oceans, and rainfall dissolves certain minerals from rocks and causes the rocks to break apart. Chemical weathering occurs most often in moist climates. It creates a thick, rich soil. Chemical weathering is common in the eastern part of the United States.

Chemical weathering caused the rich soil on this West Virginia farm.

Erosion and Deposition

The face of the earth is constantly changing. Water and other natural forces break down rock and create soil through weathering. At the same time, water, ice, and wind wear down mountains, create new valleys, and wash away fertile soil. This process is called **erosion.**

Water causes much erosion. The weathering process is one form of erosion. Water also moves rocks and soil from one place to another. As rainwater fills streams and rivers, the moving water flows downhill and cuts into the land.

Have you ever visited the Grand Canyon? This spectacular site is one example of land eroded by water. The Colorado River carved out the canyon over millions of years.

The ocean also causes erosion, changing the land along the seashore. The eroding action of waves and tides creates beaches and cliffs in coastal areas. Glaciers have also carved the landscape through erosion.

The Colorado River began breaking down rock in the Grand Canyon 5 million years ago.

Wind erosion occurs when strong winds blow dust, sand, and soil. The wind changes the landscape by moving these materials from one place to another. In addition, strong winds carry

Top left: Wind erosion formed these sand dunes in Death Valley, California. *Above:* A mudslide is another form of erosion, which often results in the destruction of property. *Bottom left:* A **delta** is the area of land built up at the mouth of a river. This is called **deposition.**

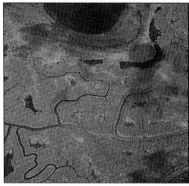

particles of sand. When the winds blow, the particles rub against rocks and wear them down.

Landslides and mudslides are dramatic forms of erosion. They change the shape of mountains and valleys.

Sometimes erosion in one place causes a buildup of land in another. For example, a **delta** is a fan-shaped area near the mouth of a river. Mud and other materials are deposited by the river in the delta. Or, the wind may blow sand from one part of a coastal area to another, forming sand dunes. This process of land buildup is called **deposition.**

The Earth's Highs and Lows

Highest land: Mount Everest, 29,028 feet (8,848 meters) above sea level

Lowest land: shore of the Dead Sea, about 1,312 feet (400 meters) below sea level

Deepest part of ocean: Mariana Trench, Pacific Ocean, southwest of Guam, which descends to a depth of 35,797 feet (10,911 meters) below the surface

Landforms

If you visit Death Valley in California, you would be at one of the lowest land areas in the world. If you climbed to the peak of Mount Everest in Nepal, you would be at the highest land area in the world. Mountains and valleys are **landforms,** or natural features of the land's surface. Landforms are the shape of earth's surface, including natural features such as mountains, plains, valleys, and hills.

The word **elevation** describes the distance above or below sea level of a landform. Mount Everest has the highest elevation in the world: 29,028 feet (8,848 meters) above sea level. A place in Death Valley has the

Left: Mount McKinley, Alaska, the highest peak in North America, is 20,320 feet (6,194 meters) above sea level. *Below:* Death Valley was named by pioneers on their way to California because of its barren terrain. It includes the lowest point in the Western Hemisphere.

A **relief map** shows land features such as mountains, plateaus, and valleys.

lowest elevation in the Western Hemisphere: 282 feet (86 meters) below sea level.

Relief refers to the high and low levels of land. Relief is the vertical distance between the highest and lowest points in a specific landscape.

Some maps show land features such as high mountains and low valleys. These are called **relief maps.** Relief maps show elevation as well as relief. Some relief maps use lines and colors to show elevations. Others are three-dimensional, using bumps and grooves to illustrate mountains and valleys. A three-dimensional map is called a **raised relief map.**

The shore of the Dead Sea is the lowest land area in the world.

Mountains, Plateaus, Hills

Have you ever wondered about the difference between a mountain and a hill? In general, a **mountain** is defined as an area that is much higher than its surroundings. Geographers define a mountain as a landform that includes two or more different zones of climate and plant life at different altitudes. In most

Mount Athabasca in Alberta, Canada, towers above its surroundings.

parts of the world, this means that a mountain must be at least around 2,000 feet (600 meters) above its surrounding area. A mountain has steep slopes and peaks that are sharp or slightly round.

The tundralike area near La Cumbre, Bolivia, is called the Altiplano.

The environment on the highest mountains includes a cold, snowy climate near their peaks where very few plants and animals can live. The next level down is **tundra,** a barren, rocky area. A tundra has some shrubs and mosses. A few animals such as mountain goats and sheep may live here. A timber line divides this area from land on which trees grow. Below this line there may be vibrant forests where plants and animals thrive.

A **hill** is also an elevated landform. It has a distinct summit, or top, but it generally has a relief of less than 1,000 feet (305 meters) Hills and mountains are formed differently and are made of different types of rocks and soil.

This lush green hill with its rich soil is in New Zealand.

Another kind of elevated landform is a plateau. A **plateau** usually has a relief of between 300 feet (91 meters) and 3,000 feet (910 meters). It does not have a sharp peak but covers a wide area. A high plateau is located in North America between the Rockies and the Sierra Nevada ranges.

The Roan Plateau near Douglas Pass in Colorado covers a large area near the Rocky Mountains.

Mountains

Tundra

Hills

Plateau

Island

Valleys and Plains

A **valley** is a place that has a lower elevation than the ground around it. Valleys are often found between hills or mountains. Many have rivers that drain inland areas to the ocean. Valleys

are often formed by the course of rivers and streams and the erosion of the land around them. The flat bottom of a valley is called a **floor.** Valley floors are usually very fertile. People often farm valley floors. A valley floor along the banks of a river is called a **floodplain.** When the river overflows its bed, it floods the surrounding land. The sides of a valley are called **walls** or **slopes.**

A **canyon,** such as the Grand Canyon in Arizona, is an especially deep valley with steep walls. A valley that is located on a coastline and flooded by the ocean is called a **drowned valley.** Chesapeake Bay is a drowned valley.

An especially deep valley with steep walls is called a **canyon.** The Black Canyon is located in Colorado.

A valley may also be located between plains. A **plain** is a wide stretch of land with a level elevation and little relief. A **coastal plain** is a broad, flat stretch of land along an ocean. A coastal plain slopes gradually toward the ocean. Plant life on an inland plain depends on its climate. An inland plain in a humid area may have lush forests. The plains in a dry climate are usually covered with grasslands. The Great Plains in the United States are a dry, grassy plain.

The Great Plains of the United States are home to wheat farms and grasslands.

Above: Dairy cattle graze in Switzerland, where grass and clover grow in the narrow, steep valleys.
Right: Cattle also graze in the Shenandoah Valley in Virginia, which is located on a flat floodplain.

Switzerland is a country with huge mountains that rise as high as 15,000 feet (4,572 meters) above sea level. Farmers there have a hard time tilling the soil of extremely narrow, steep valleys. Grass and clover grow well, however, so many Swiss farmers are dairy farmers.

Dairy cows are raised in the Shenandoah Valley in Virginia, also. This land is located on the floodplain of the Shenandoah River. It is much flatter than the land in Switzerland. Floods are not always bad news to the farmers here. The water helps spread nutrients throughout the soil. However, every few years the rainfall may be much higher than average. Then, a flood may damage crops, buildings, and animals.

Coasts

You have seen how wind and water erosion change earth's surface. Because a coastline is the area where the land and the water come together, it is a place that is constantly changing.

The land area next to the ocean may be high, rocky cliffs or wide, sandy **beaches**. Beaches may contain black sand from volcanic materials, white sand from the shells of marine animals, or rocks ranging from gravel to boulders.

Winds create waves that change beaches and wear away cliffs. **Tides** also change the coastline steadily day after day. Tides are the rise and fall of the water in the ocean. They are caused by the moon's gravity pulling up the water directly beneath it. When the moon's gravity pulls the water up, a high tide results. At the same time, a high tide occurs on the opposite side of the planet because the moon pulls the earth away from the water there. The action of tides causes the water in the oceans to rise gradually for six hours, until it reaches high tide. The water then slowly goes back down. It reaches its lowest point, low tide, in another six hours. Then the cycle begins all over again. Most coastal areas have two high tides and two low tides each day.

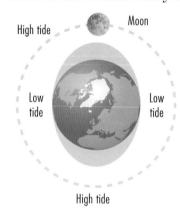

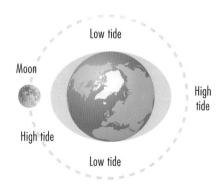

One interesting kind of coastal area is the **tidal marsh**. A tidal marsh is found inland from a beach. The place must be low and flooded by high tides some of the time. The first area of a tidal marsh is

The pull of the moon's gravitational force (gravity) causes high and low tides in earth's oceans and seas.

the tide flats. Tide flats are next to the sea floor and are exposed only at very low tides. The low marsh areas farther inland are exposed during low tide and flooded during high tide. The high marsh areas are flooded only at very high tides. These areas have been considered to be wasted land in the past. They have been developed for use as garbage dumps, airports, and even sports stadiums. However, tidal marshes

Tidal marshes *(top)* and **coral reefs** *(bottom)* are coastal areas.

have a unique ability to hold water. They help refill ground water supplies. They also have a rich nutrient supply that allows many plants and animals to flourish.

Another type of environment that forms between land and water is a **coral reef.** Coral is made up of the hard outer skeletons of small ocean organisms. New organisms live on top of the shells of dead organisms. Over time, they build up a large structure. Reefs form in warm, tropical seas. When a reef breaks the water's surface, a thin soil can form on top. The reef then becomes home to tropical vegetation. A coral reef can shelter a diverse community of tropical fishes and other organisms.

Glaciers and Glaciation

Many of the world's hills, mountains, and valleys were shaped by **glaciation,** the action of glaciers.

Glaciers are made of snow that has partially melted and refrozen. As new snow is added to the old snow, the air is squeezed out, eventually turning the snow to glacial ice. In Alaska, glacial ice forms quickly, over about 30 to 50 years. Alaska receives a great deal of new snow every winter. The snow does not melt completely over the summer, and the layers build up from year to year. In Antarctica, temperatures stay extremely cold but very little snow falls. Also, the snow rarely melts, even partially. Antarctic glacier ice may take 3,500 years to form. Many places in North America receive several feet of snow every winter, but they do not have glacial ice. That is because the snow melts completely every summer.

Once glacial ice is formed into a body, the body of ice may begin to move. At this point the ice is called a glacier. A glacier may move as slowly as 1 to 2 inches (3.5 to 5 centimeters) a day. Sometimes, a glacier will **surge,** suddenly moving faster than 100 feet (30.5 meters) per day.

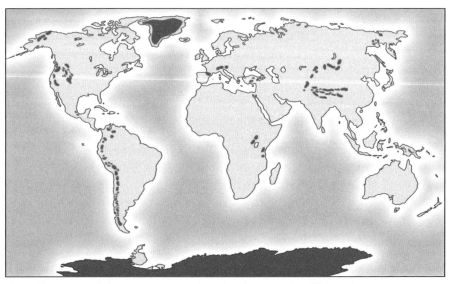

The world's continental glaciers (ice caps) are located in the areas colored blue on this map.

A **valley glacier**, such as Hailugou Glacier in Sichuan Province in China, looks like a river of ice.

The two main kinds of glaciers are valley glaciers and continental glaciers. A **valley glacier** is like a river of ice, following a channel down a mountain. Most valley glaciers are less than 2 miles (3.2 kilometers) long. The Hubbard Glacier in Alaska, however, is more than 200 miles (320 kilometers) long. Valley glaciers are also known as **alpine glaciers.**

Continental glaciers are large, thick ice sheets. These are the largest glaciers. They are also called **ice caps.** Continental glaciers bury both valleys and mountains. Greenland and Antarctica have large ice caps. Greenland is covered by one continental glacier. Antarctica is covered by two. The Greenland glacier is more than a mile (1.6 kilometers) deep in some places.

Greenland is covered by one huge **continental glacier**, or **ice cap.**

Glaciers change the earth's surface through erosion and deposition. Moving ice picks up rocks that grind the solid rock beneath it. It also pushes rocks and soil ahead of it and gouges out low areas. The moving ice may deposit the rock material in ridges or hills as it melts.

The Water Cycle

On earth, there is more water than any other substance.
The oceans are massive bodies of salt water, and glaciers are
huge bodies of frozen water. Water fills lakes, ponds, rivers,
and streams. Even the air we breathe contains water. Earth's
water moves in a continual cycle from the surface to the air
and back to earth. This circular movement of water is called
the **water cycle** or the **hydrologic cycle.**

1. The heat from the sun warms the earth's surface and air
above it.

2. This heat causes water to **evaporate,** or form invisible
water vapor. Water evaporates from the oceans, lakes, and
rivers. Water also evaporates from the land and living things,
such as plants.

3. The water vapor cools and **condenses,** or forms small
droplets of liquid water on dust and dirt in the atmosphere.
These droplets come together as clouds.

4. As the clouds become cooler, the water droplets become
heavier. They fall to the ground as rain, snow, sleet, or hail.
Rain, snow, sleet, and hail are called **precipitation.**

5. Most precipitation falls into the oceans. Some falls into
lakes and rivers that flow into the oceans. Precipitation that
falls on the land may **run off** into rivers and streams. Or it
may soak into the ground where plant roots can absorb it.
Some of the water that soaks into the ground becomes part of
the **groundwater.** Groundwater takes up the spaces between
underground gravel or rock layers. The groundwater moves
very slowly into lakes and rivers and eventually drains into
the oceans.

Step 1. Heat from the sun warms the earth's surface and air above it.

Step 3. Warm, moist air rises and cools as it moves upward. Water vapor condenses into clouds.

Step 4. Precipitation forms and falls.

Step 2B. Water from living things transpires (is released as water vapor) into the air.

Step 2A. Water from oceans, lakes, rivers, and the ground evaporates (becomes water vapor) into the air.

Step 5. Runoff precipitation flows into rivers, lakes, and underground reservoirs (aquifers) and back to oceans.

Freshwater Ecosystems

Freshwater is water that is not salty. Much of the earth's freshwater is in lakes, ponds, streams, and rivers. A **lake** is a body of water that is surrounded by land. A **pond** is a small lake that has shallow water. A **river** is a body of water that flows over land in a long channel. **Streams** are small, often fast-moving, channels of water that combine to form a river.

Teeming with life, ponds feature a variety of plants and animals, such as frogs.

Most of earth's freshwater is in the form of ice caps, glaciers, and groundwater. Only a very small percentage is found in ponds, lakes, rivers, and streams. See the chart on the opposite page to compare the amount of earth's freshwater to salt water, and to understand where that freshwater is located. Like the oceans, bodies of freshwater are filled with life.

Lake Facts

Largest lake in the world: Caspian Sea, 143,550 square miles (371,800 square kilometers)
Largest Great Lake: Lake Superior, 31,700 square miles (82,100 square kilometers)
Largest lake entirely in the United States: Lake Michigan, 22,300 square miles (57,760 square kilometers)
Deepest lake: Lake Baikal in Russia, 5,371 feet (1,637 meters)

River Facts

Longest river on earth: Nile, 4,160 miles (6,695 kilometers)

Longest river in the United States: Missouri, 2,540 miles (4,090 kilometers)

Second longest river in the United States: Mississippi, 2,340 miles (3,766 kilometers)

River carrying the most water: Amazon in South America

Ponds, in particular, have a vast variety of plants and animals. The shallow waters of ponds allow sunlight to reach the bed, or bottom, of the pond. Plants with roots can grow there. As a result, ponds attract many animals that feed on the plants, and these animals, in turn, attract animals that feed on them. In or near a pond, you might find frogs, toads, mosquitoes, ducks, minnows, and many other species.

Rivers are also home to an amazing variety of life. In the Mississippi River, the huge paddlefish can grow up to six feet in length and weigh 200 pounds. Other types of fish located in various rivers include trout and salmon. The fish eat insects or other fish. In turn, they might be eaten by bears or other predators, or even caught by human anglers.

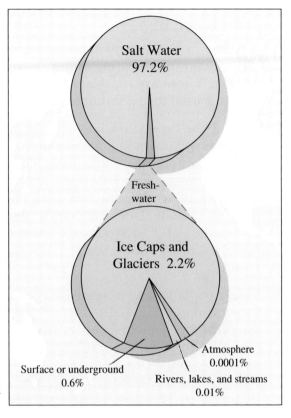

Salt Water 97.2%

Fresh-water

Ice Caps and Glaciers 2.2%

Atmosphere 0.0001%

Surface or underground 0.6%

Rivers, lakes, and streams 0.01%

Coho salmon swim upstream in an Alaskan river.

Words to Know

lake: body of water surrounded by land

pond: small lake with shallow water

river: body of water that flows over land in a long channel

stream: small, fast-moving channel of water

World Biomes

A **biome** is a plant and animal community that thrives in a large geographical area. Many geographers identify six major biomes. These are tropical forest, desert, grassland, temperate forest, boreal forest or taiga, and tundra.

A biome has specific kinds of plant and animal life. It is also defined by its climate. For example, the temperate forest biome is found in the eastern half of the United States. This biome is moist, with cold winters and warm summers. Trees such as elm, maple, and oak grow well in this environment's soil and climate. Deer, raccoons, squirrels, and other animals are native to the area. Europe has a climate similar to the eastern United States. It also has a large temperate forest biome.

The way plants and animals relate to one another is an important element of the biome. Each plant and animal occupies a **niche**. A niche is an organism's role in its environment. It includes where the organism lives and what it feeds on. For example, cattle graze on grasses in the grasslands biome of North America. Kangaroos graze in the grasslands of Australia. The two animals are **ecological equivalents**: they occupy the same niche in different places.

Tropical Forests

If you have seen movies that take place in a tropical rain forest, you may picture this biome as a sweltering jungle overgrown with lush vegetation. The facts about tropical forests may surprise you.

The tropical forest climate has the least change in moisture and temperature from season to season. The

Most of the Amazon tropical rain forest is located in Brazil, but large portions also exist in neighboring Peru, Colombia, and Ecuador.

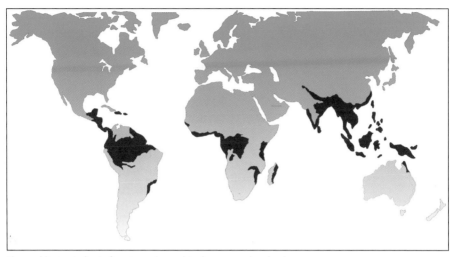

The world's tropical rain forests are located in the areas colored red.

tropical forest biome is found between the Tropic of Cancer and the Tropic of Capricorn. Because the sun's light is evenly distributed all year in the areas around the equator, the forests stay quite warm. But they almost never get as hot as places such as Dallas, Texas, or Atlanta, Georgia, in summer.

Many tropical forests are **rain forests.** The average temperature in a rain forest is at least 75° Fahrenheit (24° Celsius). A rain forest receives from 80 to 288 inches (203 to 732 centimeters) of rain per year. Five out of every seven days rain falls for part of the day.

Tropical rain forest biomes have different layers of plant growth. The top layer, the **emergent layer,** consists of trees that rise above the rest of the forest. In the rain forest, these trees range from 130 to 250 feet (40 to 76 meters) in height.

The next level down is the **canopy.** The tops of the trees in the canopy are very close. They form a kind of green roof over the forest. The canopy absorbs much of the sunlight received by the forest. It cools the forest floor during the day and keeps warmth in at night. Because of the light-absorbing canopy, little vegetation grows on the ground. That's why the lush jungles you may have seen on television do not exist on the rain forest floor. They are only found near rivers or in areas that have been cleared.

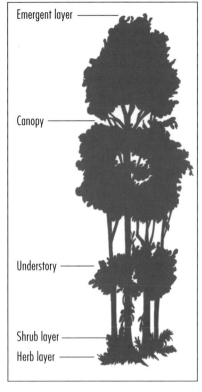

Emergent layer

Canopy

Understory

Shrub layer

Herb layer

The next layer down is called the **understory.** It is made up of the tops of young trees, the trunks of tall trees, and smaller trees. The next layer, the **shrub layer,** is about 20 to 30 feet (6 to 9 meters) off the ground and includes the few shrubs that can find enough light filtering down through the canopy. On the ground is the **herb layer,** made up of small plants that could not survive the elements without the canopy's protection.

Because it is never cold or dry in the tropical rain forest, a huge variety of plant species grow there. Many different animals feed on the plants. In fact, more than half the world's plant and animal species live in the rain forest.

Other tropical forests that are not rain forests exist in places such as southern Asia. These areas are dry for three or four months of the year and then experience extremely heavy rains for several months. Because of these heavy rains, the forest vegetation is similar to that of tropical rain forests. Other tropical forests exist on the middle slopes of some mountains in tropical areas. These forests have trees like those in rain forests. But winds and cooler temperatures prevent the great diversity of plant and animal life found in the rain forest.

The Amazon Tropical Rain Forest

The largest tropical rain forest, the Amazon, covers about a third of South America. In one square mile (2.6 square kilometers) of Amazon forest, scientists have found more than 3,000 species of plants. This area is home to exotic plants such as water lilies more than 6 feet (1.8 meters) across. Animals have adapted to the rain forest environment. The

The Parson's chameleon can change its skin color.

emerald tree boa is a snake that lives in tree branches. Because of its bright green color, it can hide among the leaves and surprise its prey and squeeze it to death. The sloth hangs upside down from branches with the help of large hooked claws. Chameleons, such as the Parson's chameleon, can lighten or darken their skin to blend into their surroundings. Other rain forest inhabitants include the poison arrow frog, the toucan bird, and the golden lion tamarin. A huge array of insects also live in the Amazon rain forest. The morpho butterfly is bright blue and has a wingspan of 8 inches (20 centimeters).

You may have heard a lot lately about working to save the rain forest. This is because people are destroying it at an alarming rate. They want to farm or to produce wood for paper and other products. Many people in the Amazon rain forest make a living by cutting down trees. The trees are used to produce paper, mostly for people in countries such as the United States and Japan. People of many nations are working together to find ways to live off the rain forest without destroying it. These include getting rubber from trees, gathering nuts and fruits, and raising fish and turtles in rain forest streams.

The poison in the tiny poison arrow frog is one of the world's strongest natural poisons. The frog is brightly colored to warn predators that its skin is deadly poisonous.

Deserts

Deserts seem like harsh, difficult places to live. But some plants and animals have adapted to the hot, dry conditions of the desert biome. A desert is an area that receives an average

of less than 10 inches (25 centimeters) of rain per year. The rains in a desert are usually not evenly spaced throughout the year. Instead, long dry spells are followed by pouring rain. Many deserts are very hot. It is not unusual for the temperature to reach 110° Fahrenheit (43° Celsius), and it may go as high as 125° Fahrenheit (52° Celsius). The desert floor may get as hot

The Sonoran Desert in southwestern United States is famous for its tall saguaro cactuses.

as 175° Fahrenheit (79° Celsius) because it is not shaded by much vegetation. Nights in the desert are cooler. The temperature falls as much as 80° Fahrenheit (26° Celsius) at night. This happens because there is little moisture or clouds to hold in the daytime warmth.

You may be familiar with the desert in the western United States. The North American desert is one of the smaller deserts in the world. The largest, the Sahara, is in Africa. The Sahara has an area of more than 3½ million square miles (9 million square kilometers). About half the continent of Australia is covered by desert.

The desert landscape has many unusual features. Sand covers about 10 to 20 percent of most deserts. The wind blows the sand into large hills called **dunes.** Dunes are constantly changing shape and loca-

The Gila monster of the American Southwest has adapted to the harsh desert climate.

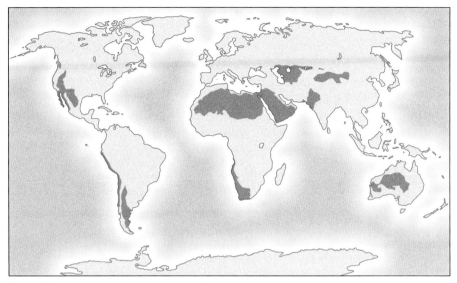

The world's deserts are located in the areas colored orange.

tion. Because the desert is so dry and supports little vegetation, its landscape is easily eroded. One formation, an **arroyo,** is a channel with vertical walls and flat floors. It is caused by flooding that has worn away the soil and rocks. Wind erosion causes desert rocks to take many strange, sculptured shapes. **Mesas** are large, flat hills with steep slopes. They are formed when soft materials wear away and leave behind hard rock. In the middle of the desert's dryness, there are some streams and underground springs. The land around these often forms an **oasis.** This is a green, fertile area.

Desert plants have unusual ways of living in their dry environment. The mesquite tree grows roots 40 feet (12 meters) beneath the ground. These roots draw on water that is hidden far below the surface. Other plants, such as cacti, store water in their roots, leaves, or stems. Animals, too, must adapt to the desert's harsh environment. One of the best-known desert animals, the camel, may drink as much as 30 gallons (113 liters) of water at one time and then go without water for a week. Other animals survive by avoiding the hot desert floor. They burrow underground during the day or fly high above the heat. Many desert animals only come out at night, when temperatures are cooler.

Grasslands

Natural grassland is any area where only nonwoody plants grow naturally and in plenty. Woody plants are bushes and trees. Nonwoody plants include many kinds of grasses and flowering plants. Most grasslands are in temperate climates that receive between 10 and 30 inches (25 to 75 centimeters) of rainfall per year. That's more rain than deserts and less than forests.

Many areas that are grasslands today are not natural grasslands. They have been formed as people cleared wooded areas to provide land for crops and grazing. Grains such as wheat, rice, and corn are actually types of grasses. That's why grasslands are also important grain-growing regions.

Several different kinds of grasslands are located in different parts of the world. Some are called **prairies** and others are called **steppes.** The prairies of North America are located on continental plains. These are lowland regions with fairly small amounts of rainfall and a long dry season. Some of the American grasslands are described as desert grasslands. They are so dry that only a few species of grass manage to survive.

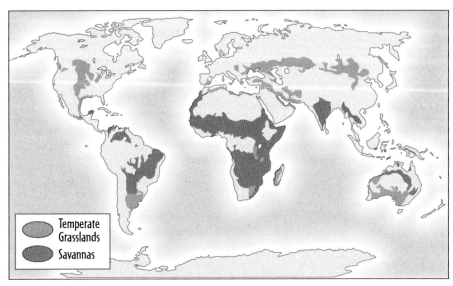

The world's temperate grasslands are located in the areas colored light green. Tropical savannas are located in those colored orange.

Top: The Masai steppe in Kenya, Africa, is an example of a grassland. *Right:* Lions roam the African savanna, another type of grassland.

The steppes of Russia are not quite as dry as the desert grasslands. They cover the largest continental plains in the world, stretching 2,500 miles (4,023 kilometers) from Ukraine to the heart of Asia. These naturally formed grasslands have been developed as farmland only beginning in the twentieth century. They are the natural home of a species of grass that can grow as tall as a human and of bright flowers including wild tulips, irises, and peonies. These grasslands, like the desert, can be a hostile environment. The summer sun scorches the treeless plains, and the winter winds force small animals into burrows.

The dry-grass plains in the tropics are often classed as **savanna**. The African savanna is located south of the Sahara. It changes from desert-grass savanna to tropical savanna with trees and lush grasses. The acacia is a tree commonly found in the African savanna. Several species of this tall, flat-topped tree grow throughout Africa. In the dry savanna areas, the acacias have developed leaves and roots that help them survive drought. They can also survive fires. Because the savanna has more moisture than other grasslands, it supports a wide variety of plant and animal life.

Fire is important to the grassland biome. Fire prevents dead grasses from building up and releases nutrients from the dead grasses back into the soil. It also helps keep out species from other areas that invade grasslands. Native grasses and plants have adapted so that they can survive fires.

Temperate Forests

The temperate forest biome contains both coniferous and deciduous trees. **Conifers** are evergreen trees, such as pines,

firs, spruces, and cedars. Conifers are constantly losing and replacing their leaves, so they appear to be constantly green. **Deciduous** trees, such as oaks, maples, and beeches, lose their leaves every autumn. This helps them avoid losing moisture during the winter months when they cannot get water from the frozen

Temperate forests, such as Glacier Bay Forest, feature coniferous trees or a mixture of coniferous and deciduous trees.

ground. Because deciduous trees have large leaves, they are able to produce more food in the spring and summer.

Temperate forests are located mainly in the Northern Hemisphere, in areas with wide seasonal changes. The forests farthest north contain coniferous trees or a mixture of coniferous and deciduous trees. Farther south, many natural forests contain mostly deciduous trees.

A temperate forest goes through dramatic changes with each season. In the autumn, the trees prepare to shut down growth for the winter. The leaves' colors change to bright orange, yellow, and red before they fall.

A gray wolf speaks its mind.

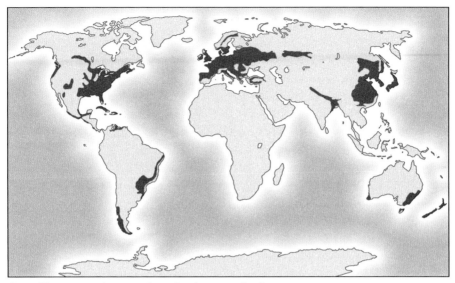

The world's temperate forests are located in the areas colored green.

In the winter, the trees enter a state similar to the hibernation of forest animals. Insects of the forest also die during the winter. But spring brings new insect birth as well as the rebirth of the trees and other plants. In summer, the forest is lush and green.

Temperate forests are home to large animals such as bears, deer, and wolves. Smaller animals such as squirrels, rabbits, raccoons, and opossums also live there. Some of these animals hibernate during the winter. Many birds live in the forests in spring and summer and go south for the winter.

People have a huge effect on the growth of temperate forests. For example, before the Civil War, many of the natural deciduous forests in the South had been cleared for farms. After the Civil War, many plantations were no longer used. The land was planted with pine trees. Now most of the southern forests are coniferous. Today, humans are still a threat to forests. Some forests are cleared for farms, factories, and cities. Pollution from industry endangers forest life. And in some forests, trees are often cut for lumber.

Boreal Forests

North of the temperate forests is a belt of coniferous forests that spreads across the northern continents. This is the boreal forest biome, also called **taiga.** Mountain environments have a timberline, which marks the place above which no trees grow. In the same way, the northern continents have a tree line. No forests are found

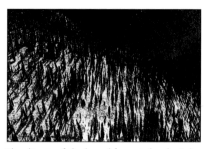

The climate of the boreal forest is harsh. Only a few types of trees are able to survive.

north of this line. Between the tree line and the temperate forests are the coniferous forests of the taiga.

The trees of the boreal forests live in an environment that offers many challenges. The climate brings bitter cold, winds, drought, and snow. The ground has poor, thin soil. The winter lasts eight or nine months, and the growing season is only three to four months long. Because of these harsh conditions, few species of coniferous trees can survive. Many kinds of small mammals live in the boreal forest. These include beavers, porcupines, and rabbits. Ducks, owls, woodpeckers, and other birds also make their home there. Many of these birds travel south for the winter. Large animals in this biome include bears, caribou, and moose.

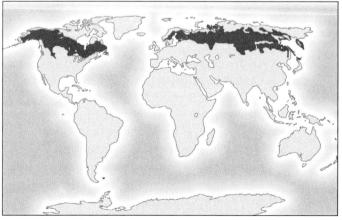

The world's boreal forests are located in those areas colored dark green.

People who live in boreal forests often work in the logging industry. But, the harsh climate and poor transportation in the northernmost boreal forests make logging difficult.

Tundra

North of the tree line in the Northern Hemisphere lies the **tundra,** a barren region. From September through April or May, snow covers the ground. In the summer, temperatures range from 37° to 54° Fahrenheit (3° to 12° Celsius). Even in the summer, the ground from 1 to 5 feet (30 to 150 centimeters) beneath the surface stays frozen. This frozen ground is called **permafrost.** True tundras cover regions in Greenland, Canada, Europe, Asia, and Alaska. Tundralike areas are found above the timberline on temperate mountains such as the Rockies and the Himalayas. Although no trees grow in tundra, there is a wide variety of plant life in the summer: mosses, lichens, grasses, flowers, and shrubs. Arctic foxes, bears, and reindeer live in the tundra.

A polar bear surveys the tundra.

On the tundra of far northern Canada, the Inuit people have made their home for thousands of years. The Inuits first made their living in this harsh environment by hunting, fishing, and gathering. Now, many of them work in modern industries that mine the tundra's rich mineral deposits.

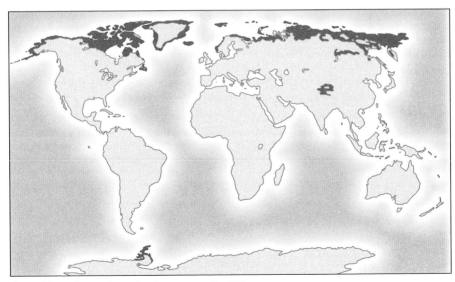

The world's tundras are located in those areas colored blue.

Human Geography

Where People Live and Why

The world population in 2004 was about 6½ billion people. Studying the world's physical features gives you an idea of the size of our planet and its wide variety of physical features and climates. How do these features affect the places people live?

The world's people are not spread out evenly across the planet. If they were, about 100 people would live on every square mile (2.6 square kilometers) on earth. **Population density** means the average number of people per square mile (or square kilometer) living in an area. People must live in a place where they can produce food or earn money to buy food and other necessities.

Valleys and plains are well populated because they often have fertile land that can be easily farmed. Mountains have fewer people because the soil is thin and easily eroded. Most cities develop near large bodies of water, where major water transportation routes have been established. Cities offer many jobs in trade, industry, business, and transportation. They are more densely populated.

Fertile land and fresh water are **natural resources.** Other natural resources include iron ore, oil, and natural gas. Regions with plentiful natural resources can support large populations. In the past, people could not live very far from natural resources. Now, transportation and communication are much better. Food and fresh water can be carried great distances. Today, populations are still more dense near natural resources, but people can live in places that could not have supported them in the past. For example, many parts of the state of Arizona are dry desert. In the past, these areas could not support a large human population. But today, large cities such as Tucson and Phoenix thrive in the desert.

Climate also plays an important role in population density. For example, no people live in Antarctica year round. Many deserts have few or no people. Europe and southern and eastern Asia have the most densely populated regions in the world. They have temperate or subtropical climates.

The continents of Africa, Australia, and South America have coastal areas with dense populations. The interior areas have sparser populations. North America has densely populated coastal areas and also densely populated central regions.

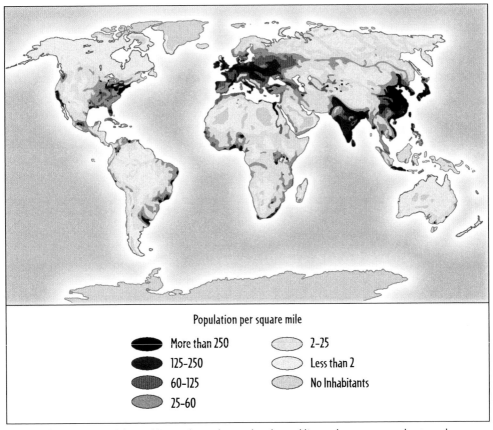

Population per square mile

- More than 250
- 125–250
- 60–125
- 25–60
- 2–25
- Less than 2
- No Inhabitants

It is clear from this map of the world's population density that the world's people are not spread out evenly across the planet.

Patterns of Settlement

Have you ever thought about whether you prefer the country, city, or suburbs? Geographers think about this issue also. When they talk about **patterns of settlement,** they mean where people live and how these settlements are distributed. A pattern of settlement may be described as mainly urban, suburban, or rural. The United States has an urban pattern of settlement that is becoming more and more suburban.

An **urban** area, or a **city,** is a densely populated settlement. Cities usually have more than 1,000 people per square mile (2.6 square kilometers). City residents make a living in ways other than producing food. Since World War I, more and more people in America have moved from rural areas to cities. A city is the center of economic, religious, and social life. A **town** is a similar center that is smaller than a city.

With a population of 8,008,278 (2000 census), New York City is one of the most densely populated places in the world. It is also an American economic and cultural center.

Suburbs are the towns surrounding a large city. There have been suburbs since ancient times when cities had smaller settlements outside their walls. Because they did not have the protection of the walled city, these suburbs were often home to people of less wealth and lower social class. During the Renaissance, wealthy citizens began the trend of building summer homes outside the city. They wanted to enjoy fresh air and beautiful scenery. During the Industrial Revolution, cities became even more crowded. (See pages 72–73 for more information on the Industrial Revolution.) Transportation also improved. Now people could

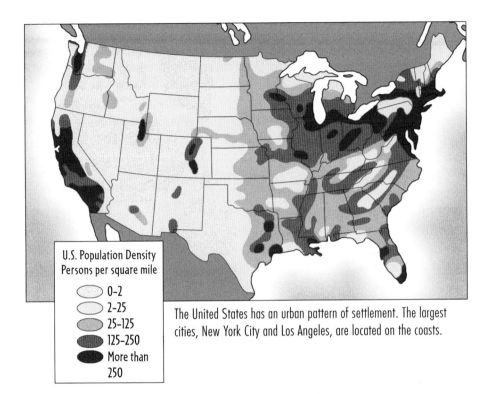

U.S. Population Density
Persons per square mile

- 0-2
- 2-25
- 25-125
- 125-250
- More than 250

The United States has an urban pattern of settlement. The largest cities, New York City and Los Angeles, are located on the coasts.

live outside the city and travel to and from work on streetcars or railroads. The growth of suburbs in many developed countries continues today.

Rural areas have a less dense population than cities and suburbs. They have large open spaces of land that are often used for farming.

If you live in or near a city, you have probably heard the term **metropolitan area.** A metropolitan area is a city and the suburbs that surround it. The city and suburbs in a metropolitan area are closely connected. People from the suburbs might work in the city. People from both the city and suburbs might shop in the suburbs. "Metropolitan area" is a useful term to describe the community of people who live in and around a city. Some cities have very large metropolitan areas.

Migration

Have you ever been to a Chinatown or a Little Italy? Many American cities have neighborhoods like these, named for the people who live there. **Migration** is the movement of people from one place to a permanent settlement in another place. Migration may be internal, such as when people move from a rural area to an urban one in the same country. External migration is when people move from one country to another one.

When people move away from their country, they **emigrate.** When they move into a new country, they **immigrate.** People leave their home countries for many different reasons. They may leave because it is hard to get food or housing in their home country. Or maybe they cannot find work. They may leave because they are persecuted for their religious or political beliefs. For example, in the 1600s the Pilgrims left England because they were not allowed to worship as they wanted. They settled in Massachusetts, where they could worship and govern themselves as they chose. Today, people in all parts of the world migrate for many of the same reasons as they did in the past.

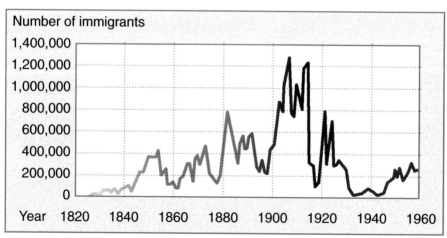

This chart indicates the number of legal immigrants admitted to the U.S. annually, according to the U.S. Immigration and Naturalization Service.

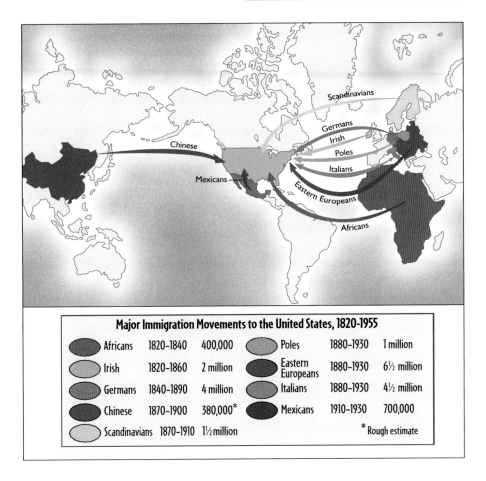

Major Immigration Movements to the United States, 1820-1955

Africans	1820–1840	400,000	
Irish	1820–1860	2 million	
Germans	1840–1890	4 million	
Chinese	1870–1900	380,000*	
Scandinavians	1870–1910	1½ million	
Poles	1880–1930	1 million	
Eastern Europeans	1880–1930	6½ million	
Italians	1880–1930	4½ million	
Mexicans	1910–1930	700,000	

* Rough estimate

Between 1820 and 1955, the United States received more immigrants than any other country. Around 40 million people, mostly from Europe, settled in the United States. In the mid–1800s, more than 2 million people immigrated from Ireland alone. In Ireland, many people depended on potatoes for food. When the potato crop failed, 750,000 died of starvation or disease. Many others emigrated. Because many who migrated to the United States had little money, they settled near where they landed, on the East Coast. Because of the famine and emigration, the population of Ireland today is only about half of what it was in 1845.

Natural Increase

Every ten years, the United States government collects information about the country's population. This collection is called a **census**. A census also gathers other important information, such as how old people are and where they live. The study of population and information about people in a population is called **demography.**

The population of a place can become larger or smaller. Birth rate, death rate, and migration cause a population to increase or decrease. **Birth rate** is the number of births per year per 1,000 people. **Death rate** is the number of deaths per year per 1,000 people. To find out how fast a population is growing, demographers subtract a place's death rate from its birth rate. The number they get is called the rate of **natural increase.** It is expressed as a percentage. For example, in 2004, the birth rate in the United States was 14 per 1,000. Its death rate was 8 per 1,000. So its rate of natural increase was 0.6 percent.

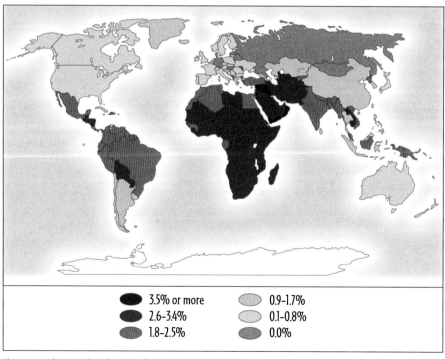

● 3.5% or more	◯ 0.9–1.7%
● 2.6–3.4%	◯ 0.1–0.8%
● 1.8–2.5%	● 0.0%

This map indicates what the rate of natural increase was by country during 1995.

Demographers look at both natural increase and migration when they calculate how fast a population is growing. To calculate how fast the earth's population is growing, you only need to know the natural increase. No people are emigrating from earth or immigrating to earth!

Mexico City *(top left)*, Sao Paolo, Brazil *(top right)*, and old Delhi, India *(above)*, are among the most crowded cities in the world.

In 1999, the world's population passed 6 billion people. It is increasing at a rate of about 1½ percent per year. If this rate of population growth continues, the world's population will double every 45 years. Because of improvements in living conditions, the death rate has dropped for the last 200 years. If the rapid population growth continues, some economists think that the world will not be able to feed all the people well. It would not be possible for everyone to have good food or enough shelter. This situation is called **overpopulation.** To fight overpopulation, many governments have urged that people have smaller families. These governments want the birth rate to be the same as the death rate. Some economists do not feel overpopulation will become a problem. They believe that better technology and new inventions will make it possible for the earth to feed its growing population.

World Countries

A **country** is a recognized territory with definite boundaries. Its government legally rules over the people living within the boundaries.

A map that shows the boundaries of counties, states, or countries is called a **political map.** Many different things cause changes in the political map of the world. In the sixteenth through nineteenth centuries, the exploration and settlement

of the New World made many changes in country boundaries. Wars can also make changes in countries and their boundaries. For example, as a result of World War I, many new nations were created in Europe. Austria and Hungary were two of these. In 1991, the Communist government of the Soviet Union fell. This huge country broke into 15 smaller ones, including Russia.

Russia is troubled by many economic problems, which have not been lessened by the fall of Communism. Here peddlers display illegally obtained goods at an open market.

The most common form of government in the countries of the world is **democracy.** In a democracy, the citizens elect representatives to make and enforce laws. Countries with democratic governments include the United States, Great Britain, Canada, Australia, Japan, and most western European countries. Some countries have **authoritarian** governments. This means that only a few people make government decisions. For example, the Communist Party rules the government of Cuba. Rulers called **dictators** govern some countries in Asia and Africa with the help of their armies.

The Soviet Union broke into 15 separate countries after the Communist government fell in 1991.

Many organizations help countries work together. Nearly every country of the world belongs to the United Nations. The United Nations helps settle disagreements among countries. It helps improve health and education in countries around the world. Other organizations, such as the European Union, help countries do business with each other.

The largest nation in area in the world is Russia. Canada is the second largest. The country with the largest population is China. The two smallest countries are Monaco and Vatican City. Each of these countries has an area of less than 1 square mile (2.6 square kilometers).

States and Provinces

You probably know that some countries are divided into states or provinces. The United States consists of 50 states. A **state** is a unit of regional government within a country. Some other countries that have states are Brazil and India.

The United States has a **federal** system of government. This means that the national government has some powers and the state governments have others. For example, the national government coins money, negotiates with other governments, and controls immigration and emigration. The state governments have authority over public schools, and they make civil and criminal laws. In some situations, the national and state governments both have power. For example, both can collect taxes and build highways.

Some countries, such as Canada and China, are divided into **provinces.** Canada has ten provinces and three **territories.** The territories are areas in far northern Canada with severe

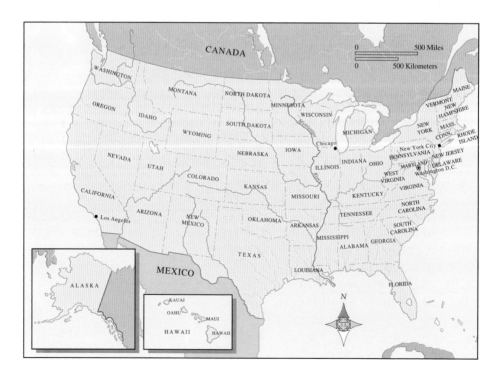

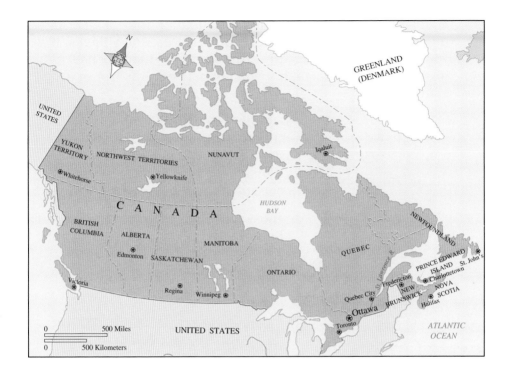

climates and small populations. Canada's provinces are similar to the U.S. states—they have many governmental powers. Those in China, however, have little power.

States and provinces, as well as countries, have a **capital**. A capital is a city where the government has its headquarters. For example, Ottawa, in the province of Ontario, is Canada's capital. The capital of the province of Ontario is Toronto.

Have you ever heard people use the word "state" when they were not talking about one of the 50 United States? The word "state" has more than one meaning. Sometimes, it is used as a synonym for "country." Other times, people use it to mean "government." In a sentence such as, "The state has power over its people," the speaker is talking about a government. This may sound confusing, but it's not. If you pay attention to the rest of the sentence, you will understand what the speaker is talking about when he or she says "state."

Local Political Divisions

States and provinces contain many smaller units of government. These include counties, cities, towns, and villages. If you live in the United States, you might not live in a city, a town, or even a village, but you almost certainly live in a county.

Almost all the states in the United States are divided into **counties.** Louisiana is divided into parishes, and Alaska has boroughs or census divisions. These units are very similar to counties.

In most states, the county is the largest unit of local government. Each state has authority over its county governments. Cities and towns lie within a county or sometimes cover parts of two or more counties. Important local government tasks are usually divided between

A county is a smaller unit of government within a state. This map shows the counties of Idaho.

the county government and the city or town government. For example, the county may run the courts while the city is in charge of the fire department and the police department.

Louisiana is divided into parishes instead of counties. The plantation called Oak Alley is located in the St. James Parish.

Other countries have different kinds of local divisions. For example, Italy is divided into 20 regions. The regions are divided into provinces, and the provinces are divided into communes.

Alaska is divided into boroughs or census divisions instead of counties.

Economic Activity

You practice economics every day. If you want to buy lunch or a game, you must decide whether you have enough money to pay for it. If you earn some money, you decide how you will spend it. The governments of nations must make these same kinds of decisions.

Long ago, people often got what they needed by direct trade, or bartering. For example, if you had a pig and you wanted a goat, you might make a trade with someone. But this was not always practical. What if the person did not want a pig? The use of money allowed people to buy what they needed. To earn money, you make a product or provide a service. You spend your money on other people's products and services. The study of how goods and services are produced and distributed is called **economics**.

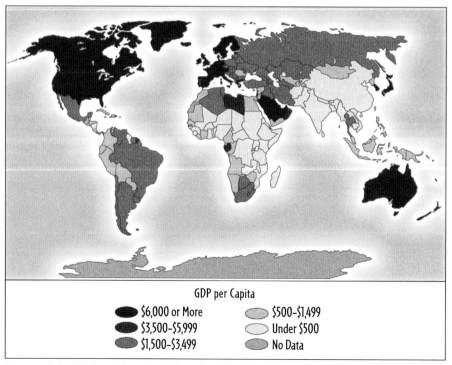

GDP per Capita

- $6,000 or More
- $3,500–$5,999
- $1,500–$3,499
- $500–$1,499
- Under $500
- No Data

This map of the GDP (gross domestic product) shows the total value of the goods and services produced by country in 1991.

A country's government has much to do with the country's economy. The government collects taxes, issues money, and provides services. A country's economy can be put into one of three categories based on how much control the government has over the country's businesses. In a **capitalist** economy, private citizens own and run most of the businesses. They decide how much to charge for goods and services. The United States, Canada, and Japan have capitalist economies. In a **socialist** economy, the government owns some of the important industries, such as steel mills and railroads. Private citizens own other businesses. Cuba has a socialist economy. In a **communist** economy the government owns and regulates almost all of the businesses. China has a communist economy.

The total value of the goods and services produced in a country in one year is called its **gross domestic product,** or **GDP.** This number is stated in dollars. For example, in 2004 the GDP of the United States was $10.99 trillion. France's GDP for that year was $1.661 trillion. To compare GDP by countries, a number called the **per capita GDP** is used. "Per capita" means "per person." The per capita GDP is the average value of goods and services produced by each person in a country. This number is found by dividing the GDP of a country by its population. The per capita GDP of the United States in 2004 was $37,800. That means the average American citizen produced $37,800 worth of goods or services.

The countries of the world can be divided into two groups: **developed countries** and **developing countries.** Developed countries have many industries and usually have a higher per capita GDP than developing countries. The United States, Japan, and most of the countries in Europe are developed countries. Developing countries have an economy based more on farming than on industry. They generally have a lower per capita GDP. Most of the world's developing nations are in Asia, Africa, and Latin America. People in developing countries often receive fewer years of education and less advanced health care. It can be hard to get information because there are fewer newspapers, phones, and televisions. Developing countries also usually have higher population growth rates than developed countries.

Economic Diversification

Up until about 10,000 years ago, people spent almost their whole lives searching for food. They wandered over the land, hunting wild animals and gathering wild plants. Then people gradually learned how to grow plants for food. They also began to domesticate wild animals such as sheep, goats, and cattle. That means they tamed the animals and herded them. People settled down to live in one place. As agriculture developed, people produced bigger food supplies. Not everyone had to spend all their time on food production. People were now able to **diversify**: develop other means of making a living. People started to work in crafts and trades. This great change has been called the Agricultural Revolution.

Economic activities are often grouped in four **sectors**. The primary sector is agriculture, mining, forestry, and fishing. The secondary sector is industrial manufacturing. The ter-

tiary (third) sector is services, such as retail stores and banking. The quaternary (fourth) sector is information, including computers and telecommunications.

From the Agricultural Revolution until the 1700s, most people worked in the primary sector. Then came the Industrial

Top: Agriculture, such as rice farming, is part of the primary sector. *Above left:* This woman selling coffee participates in the tertiary sector. *Above right:* The quaternary sector includes computer information services.

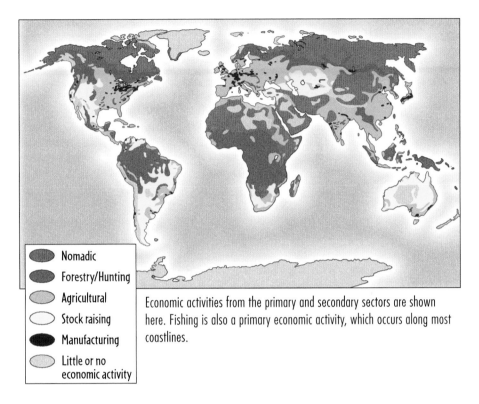

Legend:
- Nomadic
- Forestry/Hunting
- Agricultural
- Stock raising
- Manufacturing
- Little or no economic activity

Economic activities from the primary and secondary sectors are shown here. Fishing is also a primary economic activity, which occurs along most coastlines.

Revolution. In the 1700s, many people went to work in factories instead of on farms. They were working in the secondary sector. To find jobs in factories, people moved from rural areas to cities. As the Industrial Revolution spread, many countries began turning away from an economy based only on agriculture. The United States, Belgium, France, and Germany were among these countries.

Economic diversification continues today. Developing countries have had economies based on agriculture and selling their natural resources, such as lumber. They are turning more to technology and industry, and improving transportation and communications.

Keep in mind that developed countries with jobs in the quaternary sector still have agriculture and manufacturing. Diversification means that a country has industries from all the sectors. This leads to a country that offers a large variety of goods and services. It includes a population that is well educated and can expect to live a longer life.

Agriculture

The development of farming around 10,000 years ago greatly changed people's lives. The industrial age may have given people new ways to earn a living, but farming is still the world's most important industry. More people the world over work in agriculture than in any other industry. About half the workers in the world work in farming.

There are many different kinds of farms in the world. They give us an amazing range of products. If you traveled around the world you might visit a rubber tree farm in Indonesia, a silkworm farm in China, a banana plantation in Brazil, and a sheep ranch in Australia.

The two main kinds of farms are **specialized farms** and **mixed farms.** A specialized farm grows only one **cash crop:** a crop that is grown to sell. Cash crops can be wheat, rice, bananas, sugar cane, or many others. A specialized livestock farm raises cattle, poultry, or sheep. Specialized farms can be risky because disease, insects, or bad weather could wipe out an entire season's production. A mixed farm produces a variety of crops and animals.

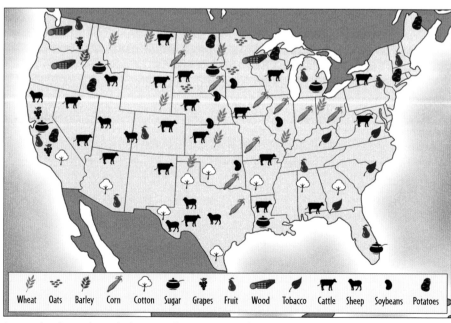

An agricultural map shows the locations of important agriculture activities.

More and more, farms in the United States are owned and operated by big businesses. Today there are more than 2 million farms in our country. The average size of a farm is about 470 acres. Many farmers sell their produce through contract farming. In **contract farming,** the farmer promises to sell a certain amount of the farm's produce at a specified price. The farmer often sells to companies that sell grain or that make food products.

Farmers decide what to grow based on their environment. They must begin with fairly level land and soil that can be tilled. Some soils are richer in nutrients. Plants grow more easily in these soils. Some soils are better for some crops than for others. Climate is an important factor in deciding which crops to grow. Some crops, such as cocoa beans and sugar cane, grow well in a tropical climate. Others, like potatoes, grow well in a cooler climate. Different crops also need different amounts of sunshine and rain.

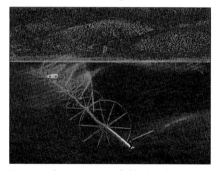

Some of the earliest farm inventions were irrigation and the plow (pulled by oxen). **Irrigation** is bringing water to fields that do not get enough water from rain.

Irrigation brings water to fields that do not get enough water from rain.

In the last few centuries, many inventions have helped farmers do their work. The cotton gin, reaper, combine, and steel plow were invented in the 1700s and 1800s. These allowed farmers to produce larger quantities of crops more successfully. The mid–1900s brought electricity to farm equipment. At the same time, scientists improved the breeding of plants and animals. Other scientists developed new fertilizers, insecticides, and herbicides (weed killers).

One of the greatest challenges facing agriculture today is how to increase food production in developing countries. Most developing countries have rapidly increasing populations, and they cannot feed the increasing numbers of people. Many farming improvements have been made, but the problem has not been solved yet. One promising approach is to adapt traditional farming methods to produce more food.

Manufacturing

Manufacturing industries produce goods. Manufactured products may satisfy our basic needs for clothing, food, and shelter. Or they may make our lives easier or healthier. Some manufactured goods are steel, paper, automobiles, shoes, and refrigerators.

Manufacturing industries take raw materials and make a finished product from them. **Raw materials** are things found in nature that are made into manufactured products. Wood is a raw material. The word **output** describes the manufactured products. The word **input** describes the machinery and raw materials used for the product. Five basic inputs are needed for production. The first input is **natural resources,** such as land, water, and minerals. The second is **capital:** the thing used to make a product, such as buildings, machines, and trucks. Capital can also refer to the money used to start or expand a business. The third is **labor,** or human input: work done by employees. The fourth input is **technology:** knowledge of machines, tools, and how to use them. **Management,** the fifth type, describes the employees who supervise the other employees. Management makes decisions such as how much to produce and what prices to charge.

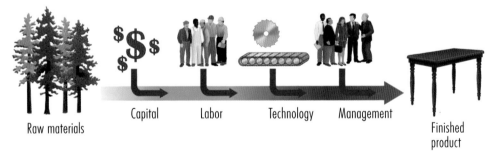

Raw materials   Capital   Labor   Technology   Management   Finished product

Developed countries produce many more manufactured goods than developing ones do. Developing countries often lack the capital, trained labor, and management needed for production. Many of the industries in developing countries

Among those goods manufactured in the United States are cars. This photo of an auto assembly plant shows two of the inputs needed for the production of goods—**labor** and **technology**. Over the years, improvements in technology in some industries have resulted in the replacement of human labor with machines. But, the success of America's manufacturing industries has always been dependent on the skill and hard work of its laborers.

must produce necessities such as food and clothing for their citizens. Many industries in developed countries produce luxuries and products for leisure enjoyment. Manufacturing companies in developed companies often buy raw materials from developing countries to make their products.

Increased manufacturing has made life easier in general. However, there are problems connected to the growth of manufacturing. Factories sometimes pollute the air and water with their waste products. Manufacturing uses up huge amounts of energy. Factories use much petroleum and natural gas, which cannot be replaced.

Services

If you walk down the street in your town or city, you might pass a restaurant, a video arcade, a bank, a doctor's office, or a gas station. These are all **service industries**. Service industries do not make products. They supply services. Some of the categories of service industries are health care, education, automobile services, household services, and recreation.

In the United States, service industries make up about two-thirds of the GDP. (See pages 70–71 for information on GDP.)

In the city of Rhodes, Greece, tourists outnumber the local population by four to one in the summer.

Services have become more important to our economy since the mid–1900s. A country usually develops large agricultural and manufacturing industries then develops its service industries.

Fast-food restaurants are a rapidly growing service industry. Others that continue to grow are computer services, legal services, and health care. Service industries that have decreased in recent years include gas stations and house-cleaning services.

Some countries, such as Greece, base a large part of their economy on the tourist industry. This includes the service industries of hotels and restaurants. Thanks to the booming tourist business, other industries in Greece have also done well. For example, the construction industry is helped by the need to build hotels and restaurants.

Technological Change

Technology means the ways people use inventions and discoveries to make their lives better and easier. Technology increases production and reduces the amount of labor needed. People have always used technology, but technology has changed a lot in the past 50 years. For example, in the United States in the 1800s, animals and people did about 65 percent of the work on farms while machines did 35 percent. Today, machines do 98 percent of farm work. Factory work has changed also. One hundred years ago, people did factory work by hand or with hand-operated machines. They worked up to 96 hours per week. Today, with modern machinery, most factory workers work 40 hours per week.

If you ever play video games, you have seen electronic technology in action. Electronic science is less than 100 years old. Electronic devices are used in televisions, radios, DVD players, computers, robots, X-ray machines, and lasers. The possibilities for these tools seem endless. They help people communicate and get work done. Electronic technology helped create the quaternary economic sector (see page 72). The Internet is a good example of computer technology that is quickly changing the way people communicate, do business, and gather information.

Plow

Tractor

Telephone, c. 1876

Telephone and Answering Machine

Typewriter

Computer and Copier

Horse and buggy

Airplane

Technology has improved methods of farming, communication, printing, and transportation.

Transportation

Transportation is the movement of people and things from one place to another. Transportation may take us to our jobs or school. It makes it possible for the people of the world to trade with one another. It makes the world seem smaller by taking us to many different places. Modern transportation has brought people closer together in ways people living 200 years ago could only imagine. Trade between countries has become much easier. Because of modern transportation, you can use goods from all parts of the planet.

The first transportation was by foot. People transported themselves and their goods, carrying them on their heads or backs. By about 4000 B.C., people used animals to transport goods. The wheel was invented in Mesopotamia around 3500 B.C. (Mesopotamia is now the country of Iraq.) The wheel transformed transportation. It enabled people to use four-wheeled carts pulled by animals to transport goods. Ancient peoples also used sailing ships. Since they did not have navigation

A Transportation Timeline

Around 3500 B.C.: The first vehicles with wheels are built in Mesopotamia.

About 300 B.C. to A.D. 300: The Romans build the first large network of paved roads.

1700s: The first steam engine is developed by British inventors.

Around 3200 B.C.: The Egyptians first use sails and make sailboats.

1490s: Better ships and navigation make it possible for ships to travel across the oceans.

instruments, they had to stay within sight of land. In the 1400s, new navigation instruments made it possible for ships to travel farther. Transportation improved in the 1700s and 1800s. People built good roads for horse-driven wagons. Canals also made transporting goods easier.

Many of the greatest leaps in transportation occurred in the last 200 years. The steamboat, the locomotive, the automobile, and the airplane opened the door to modern transportation. Today, automobiles are the most popular form of private transportation. Within and between cities, buses and trains provide **public transportation:** an organized passenger service used by the general public.

Airplanes also provide public transportation. They are also used to transport goods. However, the cheapest way to transport goods is by water. The next cheapest forms are train and truck. Another form of transportation is pipelines. Pipelines carry natural gas and petroleum over long distances.

1903: Orville and Wilbur Wright's airplane makes the first powered flight.

1950s: Passenger airlines begin using jet airplanes regularly.

1890s: The French build the first gasoline-powered automobile.

1920s: Cars become a major means of transportation in the United States.

1981: The first space shuttle is launched.

Communication

Communication is the exchange of information between people through the use of symbols, signs, or behavior. Communication may be spoken or written. One main kind of communication is **interpersonal communication**: face-to-face discussions, telephone conversations, and letters written from one person to another. The second main kind of communication is **mass communication**: messages that are sent out to a large audience through books, magazines, newspapers, radio, and television.

Thousands of years ago people used drumbeats, smoke signals, and fire to send messages in code. With spoken languages, people could speak face-to-face or send runners with verbal messages. Later, horses could speed message-sending.

Picture-writing was invented by the Sumerians in West Asia around 4000 to 3000 B.C. It was a huge advance in communication. It let people preserve messages and communicate without relying on the memory of a messenger. The first writing is called **cuneiform**. It was composed of wedge-shaped characters that stood for syllables.

A Communications Timeline

20,000 B.C.: People painted animals on cave walls.

Around 1040: The Chinese use movable type to make books. This makes it possible to produce books in large numbers.

1600s: Printed newspapers begin to appear in many European cities.

A.D. 105: Paper is invented in China.

Mid–1400s: Johannes Gutenberg introduces movable type in Europe.

In Europe in the 1400s, mass communication became possible. Books, newspapers, and magazines became increasingly common. However, these could spread through the world only as fast as the day's travel would allow. In the 1700s, news from Washington, D.C., could take up to 44 hours to travel by stagecoach to New York City. When Samuel F. B. Morse invented the telegraph, it was a giant step forward. Messages could arrive in minutes instead of weeks. Alexander Graham Bell's invention transformed communication in the late 1800s. Today the telephone is an important form of interpersonal communication.

Mass communication made great leaps with the invention of radio. The first radio broadcast was made in 1920 in Pittsburgh, Pennsylvania. Radio provided news and entertainment more quickly and more often than the newspapers. When television broadcast the first moon landing in 1969, the wonders of modern mass communication were clear. Television helps people all over the world share the same experiences at the same time.

The computer continues to make communication faster and easier for people everywhere. Information can be shared instantly. This new ability to share information instantly has been called the "Information Revolution."

1936: In Great Britain, the first public television service begins.

1980s: Computers make it possible to transmit messages immediately to any part of the world.

1876: Alexander Graham Bell patents the telephone.

1844: Samuel F. B. Morse sends the first telegraphic message, using the machine he invented.

1901: Guglielmo Marconi, an Italian, transmits a signal in Morse code across the Atlantic Ocean.

1962: The first telecommunications satellite is launched by the United States.

Global Interdependence

"It's a small world." You might use that saying when you meet an old friend in an unexpected place. But with today's advanced transportation and communication, the world seems to be getting smaller and smaller.

The nations of the world have traded with one another throughout history. In the 1400s and 1500s, Europeans traveled to the East to buy silks and spices. Traders made long trips over land or by sea. Today's fast transportation and communications methods make it possible for countries to trade many more goods than ever before.

No one country can produce all the goods people need at reasonable prices. Each country has the resources to produce some goods better than other countries can. For example, the United States grows and produces large amounts of cotton. The cotton is sold to many other countries. However, the United States does not produce enough coffee beans for its citizens. So we buy large amounts of coffee from Brazil and other coffee-producing nations. Every country depends on other countries of the world to provide goods it needs. Each country also needs other countries to buy the goods it produces.

The Legend of Saint Ursula was painted between 1490 and 1495 by Vittore Carpaccio. Ten beautiful ships in the painting reflect the importance of that mode of transportation during that time. In the 1400s and 1500s, Europeans traveled by ship to the East to buy the silks and spices that they needed.

International trade makes it possible for the people of each country to have more of what they want and need. They can **import,** or bring in, goods they cannot produce efficiently. They can **export,** or send out, goods they can produce well. Sometimes a country imposes a **trade barrier** on imports or exports. A trade barrier limits the amount of a particular product that can be imported. Or it taxes that product. A trade barrier may make a product more scarce or more expensive. A country may impose a trade barrier to protect its own industries. For example, a country that makes automobiles may put up a trade barrier on cars imported from other countries.

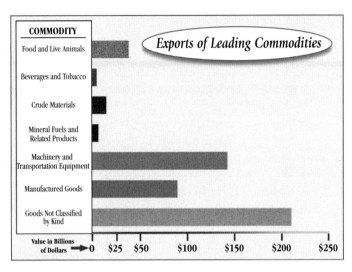

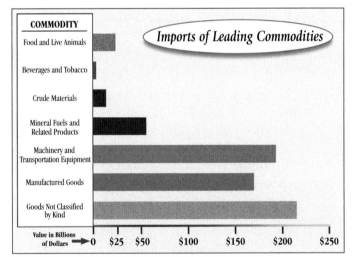

The United States exports and imports billions of dollars worth of goods. (Information provided by *Encyclopedia Brittanica.*)

Today, both transportation and communication keep becoming faster and faster. It is easier and easier to connect people and goods across the globe. As trade increases, the world's countries become more **interdependent:** They rely on each other for many things.

Culture

When you wake up each morning, you probably don't think twice about eating your breakfast cereal, putting on blue jeans, and going to school in a large brick building. But if you visited a country in Africa or Asia, you would find that people do some of these things very differently. All these aspects of your life are a result of your culture. **Culture** is the entire way of life shared by a group of people. It includes language, food, housing, ceremonies, and customs. A part of a population that has ancestry and culture in common is called an **ethnic group.**

Culture includes language, ceremonies, customs, and manner of dress. This woman of the Masai people of Africa wears the traditional dress of that group.

Language is an important aspect of culture. People in every culture use language to communicate. About 3,000 languages are spoken today. The kinds of food people eat, how they eat, and when they eat are also elements of culture. For example, people in many parts of Africa eat only one main meal every

Typical regional clothing of Rajasthan, India.

day. In many societies, males and females generally eat separately. Environmental factors also influence many aspects of culture. For example, people who live in tropical areas may wear one or two pieces of cloth draped around their body. People who live in colder climates need to wear warmer clothing.

Religion is a very important aspect of culture. Often,

most of the people in a geographical area may practice the same religion. For example, Christianity is the major religion in North America, while Islam is the major religion in northern Africa and the Middle East. Religion affects not only people's beliefs but many of their customs.

The culture of a people can change over time. Sometimes changes in science and technology bring changes in culture. When different cultures come into contact, both may be affected. People from one culture might want to adopt some customs of the other. This can cause conflict within a society between those who want to change and those who do not.

World Regions

Culture is one way to define **regions** of the world. A region is an area with one or more common features. Geographers use regions to help them study world patterns. There are many ways to define a region. A geographer might divide the world into regions based on climate or soils. When the post office divided the United States into zip codes, it was creating a kind of region to help make its job easier. Regions are a very useful idea that helps people learn about the world or do their jobs.

When geographers define a region, they consider culture, physical environment, and people's history. Within each geographic region, the people share some aspects of their culture and have some shared history. Sometimes there are disagreements about the exact boundaries of a region.

Canada and the United States are considered one region. The two countries have many aspects of culture in common: ancestry, language, housing, food, and customs. Mexico is also in the continent of North America, but it is not considered part of the same region. That's because Mexico is different from the United States and Canada in important ways. Mexico has more in common with the countries of Central America and South America. Mexico, Central America, and South America are considered a region: Latin America. They share elements of culture, language, and history.

United States and Canada

The North American countries of Canada and the United States have many similarities. They are both wealthy nations. The wealth comes in part from their rich natural resources and farm lands. Both countries were colonized in the 1600s by the English and French, so many aspects of their cultures are similar. Both countries have excellent school systems for their citizens. Both have many museums and libraries.

Canadians and Americans have similar diets. People in both countries eat plenty of beef, pork, and chicken and a wide variety of vegetables. Many citizens of both countries can afford to eat out at restaurants often and have much leisure time. One popular activity is playing and watching sports. In the United States, baseball, football, and basketball are popular. In Canada, hockey is the most popular sport.

There are differences between the two nations. Immigrants from many parts of the world have had a great effect on the cultures of both the United States and Canada. But people from different parts of the world have brought different aspects of their cultures to their new countries. For example, African Americans developed jazz music and other art forms in the United States. Hispanic Americans have added many interesting foods and

At 3,851,809 square miles (10,014,703 square kilometers), Canada is the largest country in North America.

architectural styles to United States culture. Canada has been influenced by immigrants from other cultures. Right now, Canada receives a large number of immigrants from Asia.

Canada and the United States are the largest countries in North America. They also make up a large **culture region.** A culture region is an area in which the people share ways of life that are more alike than different. The people in a culture region often have similar customs, languages, religions, history, and economic development. Both the United States and Canada have a British heritage. English is a dominant language in both countries. Canada actually has two official languages—English and French. One of Canada's provinces, Quebec, is mainly French-speaking. Both countries have advanced technology and developed economies.

Latin America

The region of Latin America includes South America, Mexico, Central America, and the islands of the West Indies. Latin America has people of many ethnic backgrounds. The original inhabitants were Native American. These people had been in the area since about 6000 B.C. Europeans settled here in the

late 1400s. They brought African slaves with them. The people of Latin America are mostly whites, blacks, Native Americans, and those of mixed Indian and white descent or of mixed black and white descent. Most Latin Americans are Christians. Most of these are Roman Catholics.

Nearly two thirds of Latin Americans speak Spanish. About one third speak Portuguese. Portuguese is Brazil's official language. Small numbers of people speak French, Dutch, English, or a traditional Indian language. Seventy percent of Latin Americans live in cities. In most countries, more and

Rio de Janeiro shows the gap between rich and poor.

more people in the cities can afford good housing, a car, and good clothing. But many urban residents still live in poor slums. The 30 percent who live in rural areas have a poorer standard of living than the urban middle class. Many work for poor wages on sugar, banana, coffee, or cotton plantations.

In many Latin American nations the governments are working to improve education. However, some poorer countries have a **literacy rate** of less than 50 percent. The literacy rate is the percentage of people over the age of 15 who can read. Many areas cannot afford enough schools for their populations. In addition, many poor students must leave school to earn money.

Latin America is famous for its festive carnivals. Carnival time is especially spectacular in Rio de Janeiro.

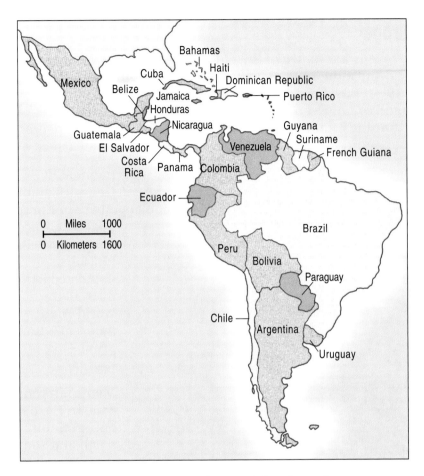

Many Latin American nations have rich mineral resources. The economies of most of the nations have relied on exporting these mineral resources and farm products. More and more, the nations are building factories. As this happens, more people are moving from rural areas to the cities, looking for work.

In Latin America, city populations are growing rapidly. The cities are struggling to meet the housing needs of the people. They are working to provide electricity, water, sewers, and roadways. But the cities cannot keep up with the rapid growth. As a result, many people live in poor conditions. The nations of Latin America face the challenge of growth. They are working to meet the needs of their people and to become industrial nations.

Europe

Europe is a mixture of the old and the new. It has been civilized since the time of ancient Greece, beginning in 3000 B.C. In the 1700s, Europe started the Industrial Revolution (see page 72–73). Even today, reminders of Europe's ancient beginnings stand alongside modern factories. The ancient Colosseum in Rome is in the middle of a busy modern city.

Europe is a continent connected to the Asian continent. It includes part of Russia, the largest country in the world, on the east. About one eighth of the world's population lives in Europe.

Together, Europe and Asia are the most densely populated landmass in the world. Many different ethnic groups live in Europe.

Many differences exist in Europe between the north and south, the east and the west, and the rural and urban areas. Northern Europe contains more industry. The south has more farms.

For many years, Western Europe enjoyed more political and economic freedom than Eastern Europe. During those years, Communist governments in some eastern nations strictly regulated people's lives. From 1989 to 1991, these governments fell. Now these countries are working to develop industries and their economies.

The countries of Europe are very diverse. Each has its own history, language, customs, government, and economy. Even regions within a country may differ vastly from one another. For example, northern Italy has more factories and cities than southern Italy. Yet, the countries of Europe are working to cooperate with one another. They have

A street vendor sells homemade shoes in the heart of Moscow, Russia. Russia is the largest country in the world.

formed the European Union. The Union is an organization of Western European countries that work together in such areas as economic development, security, justice, and foreign policy. It has grown from an earlier organization called the European Economic Community. Members of the European Union include both large and small nations. Some members are the United Kingdom, France, Italy, and Germany. Smaller countries that belong include Belgium and Luxembourg.

Member nations work together to encourage economic growth and development. The nations have adopted common policies and rules in transportation, agriculture, health, immigration, and safety.

Africa

Africa is the second largest continent in area. One eighth of the earth's people live there. Two thirds of Africans live in rural areas. Africa's economy is the least developed of any populated continent.

Many people in Africa speak Arabic or Swahili. However, more than 1,000 languages are spoken in Africa. Most ethnic groups have their own language. Many educated Africans speak English, French, or Portuguese as well as their ethnic language. European languages were brought to Africa when European countries colonized the continent in the 1800s.

Most of the people in northern Africa follow the Islam religion. This Muslim place of worship, called a **mosque**, is located in Cairo, Egypt.

The culture of countries in northern Africa differs from the culture of the countries south of the Sahara. Most of the people in the north are Arabs and follow the Islam religion. (Followers of the Islam religion are called Muslims.) About half the people in these countries live in rural areas. They raise livestock or grow crops. These people often live in houses with mud walls that keep out heat. They rarely leave their villages. Life in a city is more like modern American life. But many cities are crowded and have problems with electricity and water.

Most people south of the Sahara are black Africans. Seventy-five percent of them live in rural areas. In Nigeria, in west Africa, people in rural areas live in houses made of grass, dried wood, or mud. The houses are grouped together in compounds within villages. As in northern Africa, many people in southern Africa are moving to big cities. These cities have a more modern lifestyle, but they also have problems with overcrowding.

Most African nations only gained their independence from European rule after 1960. When Europeans colonized Africa, they sometimes drew borders that separated a single ethnic group into different countries or placed ethnic groups that were enemies in the same country. This caused problems between the countries. It also created problems within countries. When the African nations gained independence, many had weak or harsh governments. People became unhappy with their governments. Some were enemies with other ethnic groups within their countries. These problems have led to civil wars in many countries. A **civil war** is a war between groups inside a country.

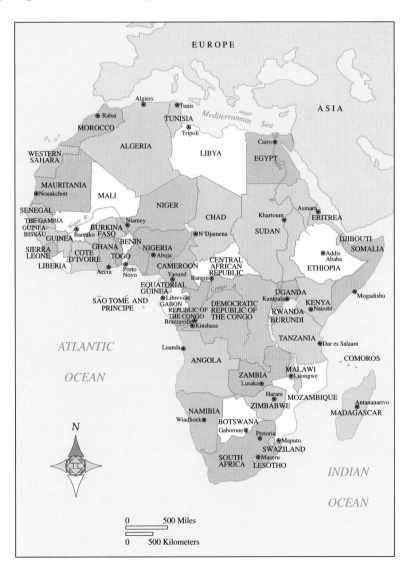

West Asia

West Asia was the birthplace of three of the world's main religions: Christianity, Islam, and Judaism. Except for two nations, most people in West Asian countries practice Islam. In Cyprus, Christianity is the main religion. Most people of Israel practice Judaism.

West Asia contains many of the countries often known as the Middle East. Although West Asia is covered with desert, about half of the region's people work on farms. Most of them do not own their own land. They rent land to grow barley, wheat, dates, or olives. They live in villages with dried mud houses. Men gather in a village's bathhouse or teahouse or mosque. A **mosque** is a Muslim place of worship.

Another form of traditional rural life is that of the nomad. The Bedouins of Saudi Arabia are nomads. These herders travel through the deserts with their camels, sheep, or goats. They live in tents made of animal hides. Wherever they find water or grazing lands, the Bedouins set up their tents.

Black Sea

Caspian Sea

GEORGIA
Tbilisi⊛
ARMENIA   AZERBAIJAN
Yerevan⊛   ⊛Baku
⊛ Ankara
TURKEY   TURKMENISTAN
⊛ Ashgabat

Tehran ⊛

CYPRUS
LEBANON
Beirut⊛   SYRIA
ISRAEL ⊛Damascus
⊛ Amman
Jerusalem JORDAN   IRAQ
⊛ Baghdad
IRAN

KUWAIT

Persian Gulf

SAUDI
ARABIA   BAHRAIN
QATAR
Doha⊛ ⊛   Abu Dhabi ⊛
⊛ Riyadh   UNITED ARAB EMIRATES   Muscat ⊛

Red Sea

OMAN

YEMEN
⊛ Sanaa

AFRICA   Arabian Sea

N

0   500 Miles
0   500 Kilometers

Nomads of the Shammar tribe of Saudi Arabia have a meal inside their large tent.

Islam has an important role in most countries of the Middle East. Some countries are ruled by religious leaders. Iran is one of these countries. Others have strict rules based on the Islam faith. Saudi Arabia has such rules. In several countries, Muslim women have been required to wear a long robe and a face-covering veil when they go out in public. They have not been allowed to drive a car or work with men. The Muslim governments recognize the rights of girls to get an education, but families often do not allow their daughters to go to school. This is especially true in rural areas. Some Muslim women are trying to gain more freedom.

Life in Israel differs in many ways from life in other West Asian countries. Israel was founded in 1948 as a home for Jews from all over the world. Ninety percent of Israelis live in cities.

The way of life in some West Asian countries has changed because of the oil industry. Many of the nations have vast oil reservoirs. Most of these countries are located on the Persian Gulf. They export the oil throughout the world. As a result, the nations have become very wealthy.

The oil industry is a major source of wealth around the Persian Gulf.

South Asia

Perhaps you have practiced the exercise called yoga. Maybe you have heard sitar music or have seen pictures of the Taj Mahal. These are all parts of the culture of India, the country that occupies three fourths of South Asia. Pakistan and Bangladesh are also part of South Asia. South Asia is separated from the rest of Asia by mountains and deserts. About one fifth of the world's people live in South Asia.

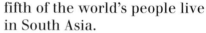

Most of the people of this region belong to one of two major religions: Hinduism or Islam. More than 95 percent of the people in Pakistan are Muslims, and Islam is the official religion of Bangladesh. In India, 83 percent of the people are Hindu. India is also home to many Christians, Buddhists, Muslims, and Sikhs.

Top: Children learn in an open-air school in the village of Dalbandin in Baluchistan, Pakistan.
Above: A village in Fatehabad in the northern state of Haryana in India flooded in 1993. These children take advantage of the situation to have a little fun in the flood waters with some friendly water buffalo.

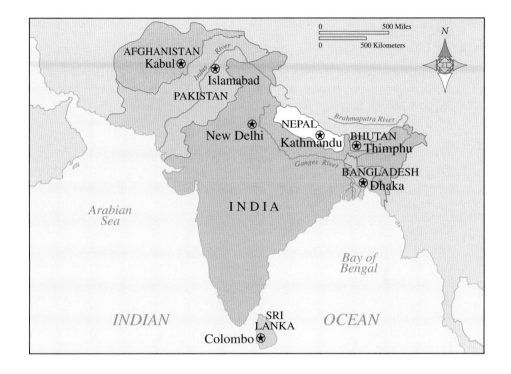

The chief language of India is Hindi. But 16 other major languages and 1,000 minor ones are also spoken. Indian states are organized so that they are populated by people who speak the same language. The Hindu religion plays a big role in people's lives. Each person in a Hindu family is born into a certain **caste,** or social group. Several thousand castes exist. A person's caste determines the jobs he or she will choose. It also determines who the person's friends will be. The caste system is traditional, but it is loosening up. The current government is against the system.

Less than 30 percent of the people in Pakistan, Bangladesh, and India live in cities. The cities in India are very crowded. Many people live behind and above the shops that line the streets. The streets are also full of homeless people because the country's population has grown rapidly, and there is much poverty. Many children must help support their families, so educating everyone is difficult. Literacy is increasing, though. About one third of the adults in the region can read and write.

East Asia

Like the rest of the Asian continent, East Asia is one of the most densely populated regions in the world. One quarter of all the people in the world live in East Asia. It includes China, Japan, North Korea, South Korea, and Taiwan. China is the country with the world's largest population.

The traditional religions of East Asia are Confucianism, Taoism, Shintoism, and Buddhism. These religions influence people's way of life. In East Asia, great importance is placed on respect for one's ancestors and on getting an education.

The two largest countries in East Asia, China and Japan, are very different from one another. China is one of the world's poorest nations. About three fourths of the people work on farms. A Communist government came into power in China in 1949. The new government improved rural life, but the rural standard of living is still low. Japan is wealthier and more modern than other countries in East Asia. About three

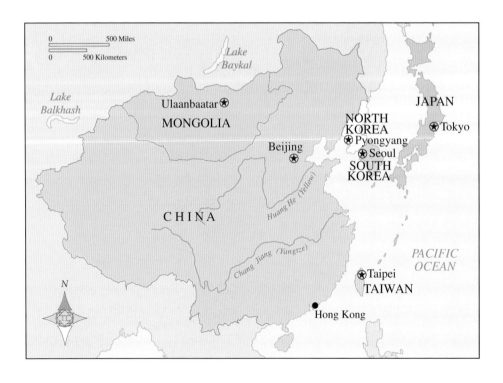

fourths of Japan's population lives in cities, and almost everyone can find a job. Japan has a very strong economy. It is one of the leading industrial nations of the world.

The economic situation could change. China's economy is developing very rapidly. China now exports many products to other nations. With its growing economy and huge population, China is one of the world's largest and most important economies. Taiwan and South Korea, too, have been developing industries and exporting goods.

In China, the Communists have tried to improve the country's education. Although 95 percent of Chinese children attend elementary school, most drop out of middle school. In Japan, students compete for good educations in the country's best schools. Even in grade school, students compete to get into the best schools and to be the best students.

Natural disasters are a serious problem in East Asia. It is a densely populated region located in an area that has many earthquakes and volcanoes. Flooding is

Top: Tokyo is the capital of Japan. *Above:* Bicycles are the major form of transportation in China.

another threat. A strong earthquake destroyed the city of Kobe, Japan, in 1995. Some countries are working to protect their people from natural disasters. For example, in Japan, buildings are built so that they are less likely to topple during earthquakes.

Southeast Asia

Southeast Asia includes the countries of Brunei, Malaysia, Burma, Cambodia, Laos, Thailand, Vietnam, Singapore, Indonesia, and the Philippines. It has gone through many changes in the last 60 years. Most of these countries gained their independence from Europe after 1945. As the countries became independent, different groups fought to control the governments. The result was civil wars and uprisings in many nations. Within the last 10 years, the governments have become more stable.

Most Southeast Asians are traditionally farmers. Here, a man dries rice near Ho Chi Minh City in Vietnam. Rice is the major crop of Southeast Asia.

The Southeast Asian countries have rich resources. These include minerals, forests, good fishing, and fertile soil. Most Southeast Asians are traditionally farmers. For thousands of years, they have lived in small villages and farmed. The major crop is rice.

Many countries in Southeast Asia have large populations for their size. But they have not had to import food. That's because the rice crops have been able to feed the people. The rice is cultivated during monsoon season, May to July. A **monsoon** is a strong storm that follows the dry season in South Asia and Southeast Asia. Monsoons bring heavy rains that flood the land. They make it possible to grow important crops. The lives of many people in Southeast Asia and South Asia depend on the monsoons.

Although farming is still a most important industry, more and more Southeast Asian countries are changing to an industrial economy. Lower-cost labor has led many international busi-

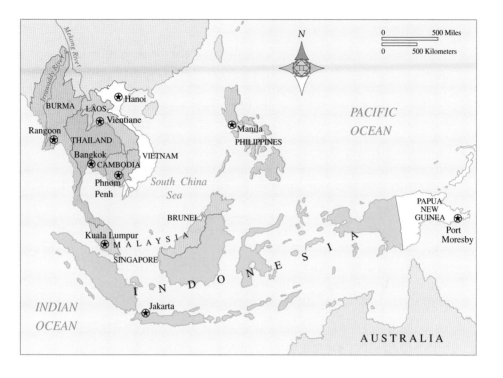

nesses to set up factories in Southeast Asia. Thailand is a good example of a country that is becoming more industrial. Thailand is working to build factories that use its many natural resources. For instance, the country is expanding its oil-refining industry.

The main religion of Thailand and other parts of Southeast Asia is Buddhism. It teaches that true peace is obtained by getting rid of desires for wealth. Young Buddhists are urged to become monks for at least a short time. About 40 percent of them do become monks. On the other hand, young people in Thailand are influenced by American and European lifestyles, too. And, Islam is another major religion in the region.

A powerful earthquake erupted under the Indian Ocean off the northwestern tip of Indonesia on December 26, 2004. It caused giant, deadly waves called **tsunamis** to crash ashore, hitting nearly a dozen countries, killing thousands.

Oceania

Oceania is the name geographers give to a group of thousands of islands in the Pacific Ocean. The region includes small and large Pacific islands. New Guinea and New Zealand are part of Oceania. Although Australia is itself a continent, it is grouped geographically with these islands.

For a long time, Oceania was very diverse and cut off from the rest of the world. Today, good communication and transportation systems put most of the area in better touch with the rest of the world.

Most of the Pacific islands are small and have small populations. The people lead different ways of life. Some have been strongly influenced by European cultures. Others live in much the same way as their ancestors did. Still others combine traditional and more modern ways of life.

New Zealand and Australia were settled by the British in the 1700s. They became independent countries at the beginning of the twentieth century. They have modern economies, and

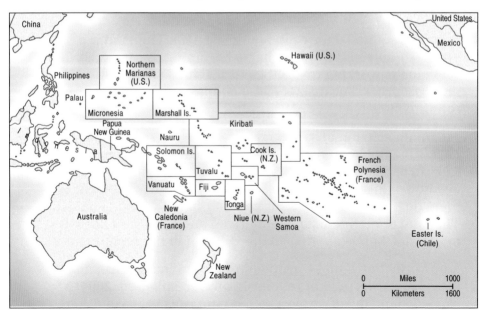

Oceania is known for its unique plant and animal life. This mother kangaroo and her cute baby live in Australia.

most of the people have European ancestors. Many other Oceanian islands were still colonies of European countries or the United States until the 1970s or later. These countries are still developing.

Agriculture is the largest economic activity in the area. But the countries export their crops to the world. You will probably find fruit produced in Oceania in your grocery store. In addition, mining, manufacturing, and tourism have become major industries.

Many Pacific Islanders and some Australians live in small rural communities and villages. More live in major towns and cities. More than four fifths of Australians live in cities and towns. Seventy percent of those people live in cities with more than 100,000 people.

Oceania's long isolation has resulted in a natural environment filled with unique plants and animals. This is the only place you can find kangaroos, wombats, koala bears, platypuses, dingoes, and Tasmanian devils. These interesting and unusual animals have helped the travel industry. Tourists and scientists come to see the animals in their natural habitats.

Australia is considered a part of Oceania, though it is also a continent.

Cultural Change

Do we live in a "world culture"? Some geographers think that everyone in the world is quickly becoming the same. We're wearing the same clothes, eating the same foods, and listening to the same music. These changes are made possible because of modern transportation and communication.

Contact between two cultures causes changes in both of them. Each culture borrows cultural traits that seem useful

These children of Rwanda, Africa, wear Western-style clothing instead of their traditional attire. This is an example of **diffusion**.

or interesting from the other. The process of a cultural trait spreading from its original society is called **diffusion**. For example, corn was a crop originally grown in North America. It quickly spread to Europe and then all around the world. Another example of cultural diffusion is jazz music. Jazz was first played in the southern United States in the late 1800s. The music spread around the world in the mid-twentieth century. The spread of jazz was due to radio, recordings, and international travel by jazz musicians.

Another cause of cultural change is **assimilation.** Assimilation happens when a person takes on the traits of a different culture. Some fear that their culture's distinctive traits are being lost as people adopt the traits of other cultures. For example,

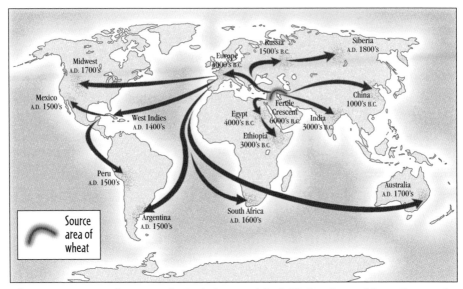

Wheat was a crop originally grown in the Fertile Crescent of the Middle East. It spread first to Europe and northern Africa, then eventually throughout the world.

people in France have used more and more American slang in recent years. Some French people have tried to stop the use of English words and phrases in France. They are afraid of los-

A McDonald's restaurant opened in Beijing, China, in 1992. As China attracts more American businesses, the Chinese people may take on the traits of Western culture.

ing the French language. Likewise, in parts of Asia, many people have left their traditional dress and values. They have adopted the clothing and values of Western countries. Other people in those societies are against these changes. This is especially true in Islamic countries.

Interacting with the Environment

Modification and Adaptation

Humans must live in their environment on earth. Whether they live on the frigid Arctic tundra or in the tropical rain forest, people have a relationship with their natural surroundings. Geographers are very interested in how people interact with their environment. We interact with the environment in two ways: by **adaptation** and by **modification.**

The Inuit people of the Arctic have adapted to their harsh environment.

People **adapt** to their environment in many ways. That is, they change their habits to make it easier to live in their surroundings. In cold climates, people build houses that keep out the frigid weather. They also wear clothes that keep them warm. For example, the Inuit people of Arctic areas built sod or snow houses with thick walls to protect them from the snow and cold, and they made warm clothing from animal skins.

When we use electric air conditioning to cool the air, we are **modifying,** or changing, the environment. Farmers modify their environment by irrigating their land, fertilizing the soil, and planting certain crops. Using chemicals to kill insects is also a form of environmental modification. When workers clear a natural wooded area, they are modifying the environment. When miners take coal or other minerals from the earth, they are changing the environment. When people create industries or drive cars, the pollutants they create can change the environment.

Modification can have both good and bad results. The modifications farmers make to produce crops help feed earth's population. The modifications brought about by pollution cause dangers to humans and animals alike. Building a dam on a river can have both good and bad results. The dam might provide electricity for millions of people. It could also endanger the survival of plants and animals that rely on the river for food.

A dam is a form of environmental modification. This is the Roosevelt Dam on the Salt River in Arizona. The lake behind the dam is called Roosevelt Lake.

Natural Resources

We enjoy the things the earth offers every day. Sunshine, trees, and cool water give us pleasure. More important, they are necessary to life. These parts of nature and many others are our **natural resources**. Earth's natural resources include air, plants and animals, iron, and petroleum. Natural resources can be renewable or nonrenewable.

A **renewable** resource can be replaced after it has been used. Renewable resources include sunlight, air, and water. These resources are necessary to life for people and all living things. Soil, trees and other plants, and animals are also renewable resources. Soil is essential for growing crops for foods. Plants and animals provide food and other products such as medicines.

Earth contains an abundance of all these resources. Some renewable resources are limitless. Sunlight is a good example of this kind of resource. But others must be conserved properly. If the air is polluted by chemicals from factories and cars, plant and animal life will be harmed. If forests are destroyed carelessly, other plant and animal life can suffer or

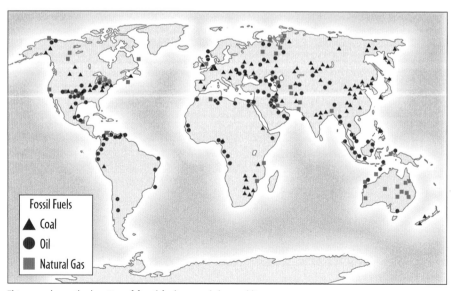

This map shows the location of fossil fuels around the world.

Lettuce is an example of a renewable resource because more lettuce can be grown after this has been used.

die out. If farmers misuse soil, it can take hundreds of years to replace. Unless these renewable resources are conserved carefully, they will be used up faster than earth's natural processes can replace them.

A **nonrenewable** resource cannot be replaced once it is used up. Minerals are one kind of nonrenewable resource. They take thousands or millions of years to form. Right now, they are being taken out of the earth faster than they are forming. Fortunately, some of these resources are **recyclable**. After they have been used for one product, they can be processed and used again. Copper and aluminum are often recycled. Other resources, such as iron, are mined but are stored for later use. Another kind of nonrenewable resource is fossil fuel: coal, oil, and natural gas.

The countries of the world have different natural resources. They extract them from the earth and use them differently, too. Often, the wealthiest countries are those with rich natural resources. For example, the United States and Canada have abundant natural resources. They have used these resources to provide many comforts for their citizens. In other places, this is not always the case. Many countries in Southeast Asia have rich mineral resources. They are beginning to develop these more, so that their people can enjoy a higher standard of living. Countries that do not have important natural resources must buy them from other countries.

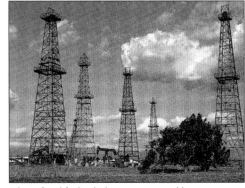

Oil is a fossil fuel, which is a nonrenewable source.

Energy Resources

Did you know that the energy used to heat and light your home may have come from plants and animals that died millions of years ago? **Fossil fuels** come from the remains of plants and animals that died long ago. Coal, oil, and natural gas are fossil fuels. When the organisms died, they were buried by layers of rock and soil. Gradually, they turned into substances we use for fuel. Fossil fuels provide three quarters of the world's energy. Energy is needed for everyday life in the home and office, industry, and transportation.

The world has enough coal to use for several hundred years. Unfortunately, using coal releases large amounts of pollutants into the air. Also, coal mining can damage the land. For these reasons, oil and gas are preferred fuels for heating and transportation. Oil and gas are also easier to transport than coal. However, the known reserves of oil and gas are getting smaller. They will last for only one or two more centuries. In addition, oil and gas also release harmful pollutants into the air.

Because fossil fuels are polluting and nonrenewable, scientists are exploring many other energy sources. **Wind energy** has been used for thousands of years to power sailing ships

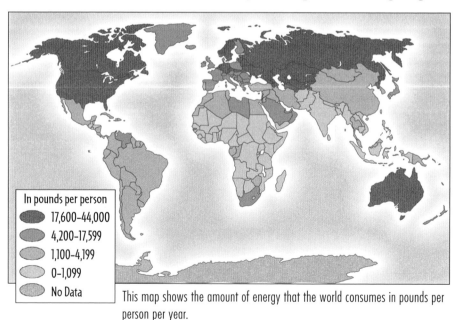

In pounds per person

- 17,600–44,000
- 4,200–17,599
- 1,100–4,199
- 0–1,099
- No Data

This map shows the amount of energy that the world consumes in pounds per person per year.

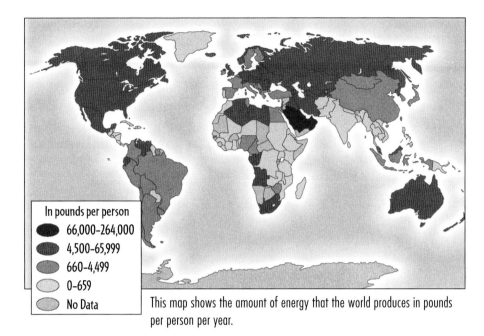

In pounds per person

- 66,000–264,000
- 4,500–65,999
- 660–4,499
- 0–659
- No Data

This map shows the amount of energy that the world produces in pounds per person per year.

and windmills. Today, wind turbines (engines) provide power in places where the wind blows fairly regularly. **Geothermal energy** is another kind of energy. It can be used in places where hot water deep in the earth is released through springs.

Hydroelectric power plants are housed in dams on rivers or other water sources. They provide power from moving water. **Nuclear energy** is released by splitting the nucleus of an atom. It can provide huge amounts of power. All these alternative energy sources have their advantages and disadvantages. For example, nuclear power plants create dangerous radioactive wastes. Getting energy from sunlight and wind can cost a lot of money. Scientists are working to improve the technology for making alternative energy sources more usable for everyone.

This nuclear power plant produces a huge amount of power. Unfortunately, nuclear power plants create dangerous radioactive wastes.

Environmental Pollution

If you have ever flown near a big city in an airplane, you may have seen a dark haze hanging over the city's skyline. If you live near a factory, you may have smelled fumes or seen smoke produced by industry. If you live near a river or lake, you may have seen water dirtied by an oil slick or garbage. All of these are forms of **pollution**: releasing harmful materials into the environment.

The effects of **air pollution** show up in stone buildings in large cities. Polluted air blackens the stone and eats away at it. If dirty air can damage buildings, imagine what it does to people! Burning eyes, headaches, and lung diseases such as asthma and lung cancer can be caused or worsened by air pollution. Air pollution is caused mainly by burning fossil fuels to power cars, trucks, and factories. Burning gasoline produces dangerous amounts of pollutants. When they mix with moisture in the air, these chemicals cause acid rain. Acid rain can damage forests and bodies of water far from the source of the pollution.

How many causes of air pollution can you find in this illustration?

One dangerous result of air pollution has been the thinning of the earth's **ozone layer.** This protective layer in earth's atmosphere keeps out the sun's harmful ultraviolet rays. These rays can cause skin cancer in people and also harm other living things. Chemicals used in aerosol sprays, refrigeration, and foam products are destroying the ozone layer. Chemicals released by burning fossil fuels also trap heat in the earth's atmosphere. Scientists believe this could cause global warming that would affect ecosystems all over the world.

Not only the air but the water and the land are being polluted. Sources of the pollution are hazardous wastes from industries, solid garbage, and pesticides. Polluted water has far-reaching effects. Eating fish that have consumed chemicals such as pesticides may be harmful to people.

Top: The oil tanker *Exxon Valdez* spilled millions of gallons of oil along the coast of Alaska in 1989, polluting the water and destroying many birds. *Bottom:* Other results of water pollution include dead fish and destroyed marshlands.

Fortunately, the problem of pollution is recognized worldwide. People are trying to reduce pollution from vehicles and industry. However, everyone needs to contribute to the effort to keep the earth clean.

Conservation

In the past, people have taken natural resources for granted. They thought clean water, healthy forests, and fertile soil would always exist. Since the Industrial Revolution, there are many more people in the world. More people consume more natural resources. We now realize that earth's resources must be carefully cared for. The careful use of natural resources is called **conservation.**

Scientists have learned that the earth's ecosystems are closely connected. If a forest is destroyed, many other plants and animals lose their habitats. Their existence is threatened. Also, destroying forests causes imbalances in the amounts of oxygen and carbon dioxide in the air.

People now realize that they must plan carefully in clearing forests to make way for farmland or buildings. However, it's not always easy to control the clearing of land for farming. In some parts of the world, people need new farmland to feed

Gold
Zinc
Lead
Copper
Tin
Nickel
Chromium
Manganese
Iron
Bauxite

Petroleum
Natural Gas
Coal

Year 2000   2050   2100   2150   2200   2250   2300

This chart indicates how long our fossil fuels and some natural resources will last at current rates of usage. By the year 2300, everything will be depleted unless we find alternatives or learn to conserve.

Some cities and towns provide recycling bins in neighborhood parking lots.

themselves and their families. The challenge is to find ways to produce more food and improve people's lives while protecting the environment and natural resources. Governments and people all over the world are working toward this goal.

Forests are one natural resource that people are trying to conserve. Another is soil. Soil loses its nutrients when farmers plant the same crop over and over again. Water and wind erode soil when it is plowed carelessly. Another dangerous practice is **clear-cutting** of trees: cutting down all the trees in a large area. Clear-cutting increases soil erosion. Since soil is needed for growing the food people need, farmers and builders must help conserve it.

Fossil fuels burned for energy are being used up fast. In addition, these fuels cause air pollution that harms people and other living things. While scientists look for new, clean energy sources, people must conserve the fuel they use.

Animals and fish are also natural resources that people must conserve. Many kinds of animals have become extinct because they have been hunted carelessly.

Everyone must help conserve earth's resources. How can you help? Recycling newspapers helps save forests. Recycling aluminum cans and automobiles helps conserve minerals. Cutting down on car and electricity use cleans the air and conserves fossil fuels. Cutting down on water use conserves the supply of freshwater.

Recycling everything from aluminum cans to automobiles will help conserve earth's resources. Please do your part.

Natural Hazards

Suppose you are sleeping in your bed and your whole house begins to shake. Or imagine you are walking to the town market when hot volcanic lava flows down a hillside. What if you are playing outside when a huge swirling wind appears on the horizon? Everyone has seen some of nature's dangerous surprises in movies and on television. Earthquakes, volcanoes, and tornadoes are scary even when you are watching them on a screen. To people in various parts of the world, these emergencies are very real. Adapting to our environment includes responding to natural hazards.

An **earthquake** is a sudden shaking in the earth. It is caused by energy released by shifting rock. Geologists have a theory called **plate tectonics**. According to the theory, earth's surface is made up of seven large plates and many smaller ones. These huge pieces are constantly shifting. Most earthquakes occur near a **fault**: the place where two plates come together. As the plates push or grind against each other, energy is stored inside the earth's crust. When the energy stored inside the rock becomes too great, the rock shifts, causing an earthquake.

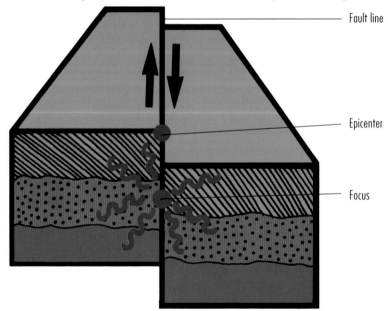

Fault line

Epicenter

Focus

This is an illustration of an earthquake. The break below the surface is the **focus**, and the point on earth's surface where the quake is felt is the **epicenter**.

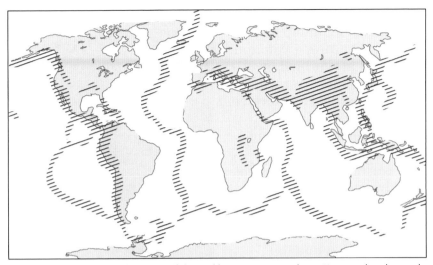

This map indicates the boundary areas of the world's major tectonic plates. Major earthquakes tend to occur along the red lines, though quakes can occur anywhere.

In a strong earthquake, much damage can occur. Buildings and roads can collapse. Water pipes can break. Electric wires and gas mains can break, causing fires. Earthquakes can also cause powerful ocean waves called tsunamis.

The places that most often suffer earthquake damage are located near faults. One famous fault is the San Andreas Fault in California. On the other side of the Pacific, many earthquakes also happen in Japan. In fact, there are faults all along the edges of the Pacific Ocean. Near these faults there are more earthquakes, and also more volcanoes, than in other parts of the world. That's why these fault zones are known as the Ring of Fire.

The scientists who study earthquakes are called **seismologists.** They have invented instruments to measure earthquakes and learned much about how they happen. But it is still not possible to predict earthquakes or to prevent them. People who live near faults must adapt to their environment. In fault areas, buildings are built to withstand the strong shaking of earthquakes. People learn about the best ways to stay safe when an earthquake hits.

Tectonic plates are also responsible for another kind of natural hazard, a **volcano**. Volcanoes are formed by eruptions of molten rock from beneath earth's surface. When a volcano erupts, ashes, lava, hot gases, and rock fragments come out. Like earthquakes, volcanoes usually occur near places where tectonic plates meet.

A volcano erupts in Hawaii, spewing lava and hot gases into the sky.

Most volcanoes are located along a belt around the Pacific Ocean. Some volcanoes erupt constantly and are called **active volcanoes.** **Dormant volcanoes** have been inactive for a while but may erupt again. **Extinct volcanoes** have not erupted in recorded history and probably will not erupt again. The lava, gases, and rocks from an erupting volcano can be extremely destructive. When Mount St. Helens in Washington erupted in 1980, 60 people were killed. Many trees, houses, and roads were destroyed.

Other types of natural hazards are related to the weather. Floods, hurricanes, and tornadoes are examples of this kind of hazard. A **flood** happens when water overflows onto land that is normally dry. A flood may be caused by heavy rains, melting snows, or hurricanes. If several inches of rain fall in a short period, water can overflow the banks of streams and rivers and cause a flash flood. Because a flash flood is sudden and unexpected, it can cause death and destroy property.

Heavy summer rains caused this mighty river to overflow its banks. Floods can cause major damage to towns located near rivers and creeks.

People can prevent floods by controlling bodies of water. For example, they can build levees to hold back water. Or they can deepen channels in rivers so they do not overflow onto land. Conserving soil and forests is also helpful. It helps prevent too much water from running off the land into streams.

Tropical storms are another weather-related hazard. These storms form over warm ocean waters. They are called hurricanes, cyclones, or typhoons. A tropical storm brings huge amounts of rain as it travels from water onto land. It can also cause enormous, damaging waves. Tropical storms can bring floods to coastal areas.

A **tornado** is a dangerous storm that starts on land. It is a powerful, twisting column of air that can touch ground during a thunderstorm. A tornado is more powerful than any other kind of storm. It can lift cars and buildings in its path. The United States has more tornadoes than any other place on earth. Fortunately, weather forecasters are often able to predict tornadoes. They can warn people to seek shelter.

Natural disasters are a part of our environment that we cannot modify. But we can adapt to them. Learning more about earthquakes, volcanoes, floods, and storms is our best defense against these hazards.

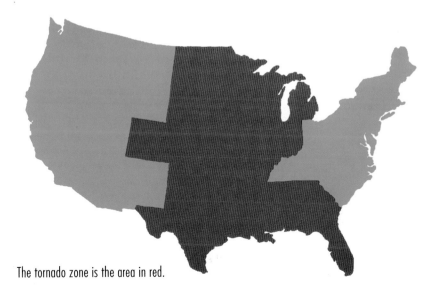

The tornado zone is the area in red.

Geography Is...

Faraway places? Maps and globes? The Aborigines of Australia or the Zen Buddhists of Southeast Asia?

You have seen that geography is all this and more. The student of geography discovers the magnificent plant life of the tropical rain forest and the nomads who wander the barren deserts of Saudi Arabia. A geographer may study the GDP of developing countries and the population densities of the 50 states. Geographers are interested in the deepest part of the ocean and the highest mountain on the earth. They want to know about the oxcarts of Thailand and the space shuttles of the United States.

When you study geography you may find you have much in common with people who seem to live a very different kind of life. You might try harder to conserve the earth's resources. You might develop a new fascination for the plants, birds, and animals of the world.

If you are interested in the world outside your front door, you are interested in geography. Perhaps you have found that learning about geography helps you learn about yourself.

Index

handy homework helper

Improve Your Grades with the World Wide Web

Karen Cangero, M.S.

Consultant:
Marc Alan Rosner

Publications International, Ltd.

Karen Cangero has a masters degree in education and writes about the Internet, education, and children.

Marc Alan Rosner is an education technology support specialist and an educational consultant to *Scientific American* magazine. His published books include *Teaching Science with the Internet, Teaching Mathematics with the Internet,* and *Science Fair Success Using the Internet.* Mr. Rosner has been awarded fellowships for excellence in education by The Joseph Klingenstein Institute, The New York Times Foundation, and the Charles Edison Fund.

Illustrations: Dave Garbot, Chris Reed

Manufactured in China.

8 7 6 5 4 3 2 1

ISBN: 0-7853-3489-0

Contents

A Message to Parents

In the last few years, we have seen the World Wide Web rapidly develop into an important educational tool. And with each passing year, the number of school districts throughout the country that are introducing or expanding their educational technology facilities, curriculum, and overall expectations grows.

However, letting your child loose on the "Information Super-highway" can be frightening. Technology is vastly different today than it was just ten years ago, not to mention when you were in school. Today's kids will need to be able to utilize the online world in order to compete in school—and eventually the job market—in the twenty-first century.

The goal of this book is to help kids use the World Wide Web to improve their grades in school. Knowing how to search for information is the key to using the Web successfully. A large portion of *Handy Homework Helper: Improve Your Grades with the World Wide Web* is devoted to explaining and demonstrating how to perform various types of searches. This includes how to use the Web as a brainstorming tool for activities that kids get involved in when they step away from the computer. We will discuss using the Web to help with test-taking, homework, writing reports, and other school projects. This book puts these important scholastic features into the overall context of your child becoming the best student possible.

The Web is an amazing place, where children can see images from half a world away—or even another planet—and have access to limitless educational materials. However, not everything that exists on the Web is appropriate for children. Close parental supervision and guidance are essential in making your children's online journeys safe, educational, and fun. These steps can help keep your children away from inappropriate sites.

- Discuss with your children what sorts of Web sites they may visit.

- Explain what to do if they accidentally stumble upon an inappropriate site.

- Encourage them to come to you with questions if any material puzzles or disturbs them.

- Be sure they come to you for permission and assistance before spending money on the Internet.

- Put the computer in a "public" room. Keeping the computer in the family room, living room, or den makes it easier for you to monitor their computer use.

- Use software and online services that filter inappropriate material.

- Discuss when they should and when they should not use e-mail and chat rooms.

Windows 98, 2000, and XP include options to screen Web sites based on the renowned Internet Content Rating Association (ICRA) rating system for the Internet. ICRA is the World Wide Web's most prevalent ratings system. It lets you control access to content on the Web. Not every site out there is rated, but many are. Most online service providers also let you restrict your child's access to the Web, chat rooms, and other online features. There are a number of software packages available that try to keep kids safer on the Web. Some popular software packages include CYBERsitter, Net Nanny, and CyberPatrol. For more information on kids' safety and the World Wide Web visit http://www.zen.org/~brendan/kids-safe.html.

Partners in Your Child's Education

Parents play an important role in their children's scholastic success. Research has proven that parents' involvement is much more important to student success than whether the family is rich or poor or whether or not parents have finished high school. This applies throughout your kids' education—from elementary through high school.

To focus more attention on this important subject, the United States Congress added an eighth point to their list of seven National Education Goals, which states: "Every school will promote partnerships that will increase parental involvement and participation in promoting the social, emotional, and academic growth of children."

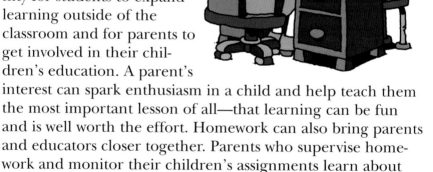

Homework is an opportunity for students to expand learning outside of the classroom and for parents to get involved in their children's education. A parent's interest can spark enthusiasm in a child and help teach them the most important lesson of all—that learning can be fun and is well worth the effort. Homework can also bring parents and educators closer together. Parents who supervise homework and monitor their children's assignments learn about their children's education and school.

Teachers assign homework for many reasons. Homework can help children:

- Review and practice what they've learned.

- Get ready for the next day's class.

- Learn to use resources, such as libraries, online materials, reference materials, and encyclopedias.

- Explore subjects more fully than time permits in the classroom.

Homework can also help children develop good habits and attitudes. It can:

- Teach children to work independently.

- Encourage self-discipline and responsibility.

- Provide young students with their first chance to manage time and meet deadlines.

- Foster a love of learning.

Show Your Child That Education and Homework Are Important

The U.S. Department of Education has some specific guidelines for helping your children with their homework. Children need to know that their parents and adults close to them think homework is important. If they know that their parents care, children have a good reason to always try to complete assignments and turn them in on time. There is a lot that you can do as parents to show that you value education and homework.

- Set a regular study time and place.

- Remove distractions from the study area.

- Provide study supplies and, if possible, any available resource materials.

- Set a good example by spending your time reading and writing, and by limiting your television time.

- Show interest by talking about school and related projects, and by taking family trips to the library and other learning locations.

Monitor Assignments

Children are more likely to complete assignments successfully when parents monitor homework. How closely you need to monitor depends upon the age of your child, how independent they are, and how well they do in school. Whatever the age of your child, if assignments are not being satisfactorily completed, more supervision is needed. Be sure to:

- Ask about the teacher's homework policy at the beginning of the school year.

- Be available to provide assistance and to answer questions during homework time.

- Read over completed assignments and provide constructive criticism.

In addition to helping with homework, there are other ways that parents can assist in their children's learning process.

- Encourage children to spend more leisure time reading than watching television.

- Talk with your children in order to communicate positive behavior and character traits.

- Keep in touch with the school and other organizations your children are associated with.

- Encourage your children's efforts to achieve.

Working with your children as they learn more about education and the world can be one of the most rewarding times of development. And learning about the Web is an activity that will continue for years. Good luck and remember to make learning fun!

What Is the World Wide Web?

Fasten your seat belts. Keep your arms inside the vehicle. We are currently speeding up the ramp to the "Information Superhighway." Accessing information. Logging on. Successful. Welcome to the wonderful world of the World Wide Web!

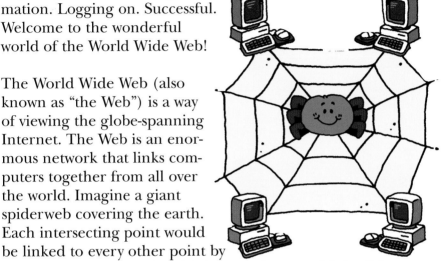

The World Wide Web (also known as "the Web") is a way of viewing the globe-spanning Internet. The Web is an enormous network that links computers together from all over the world. Imagine a giant spiderweb covering the earth. Each intersecting point would be linked to every other point by the spiderweb's threads. This is a good way to think of the Web. Computers all over the world are connected to telephone and communication lines to form the Web. And the computer in your home, when it is connected to the Web, can then communicate with any other computer connected to the World Wide Web.

Many people think that the Web and the Internet are the same thing. They're not.

The Internet is a worldwide collection of computer networks that allows people to find and use information and communicate. It was started in the 1960s by the U.S. Department of Defense. Soon researchers and university professors began to use it, too. It made communicating and exchanging information faster and easier.

The World Wide Web is a way of viewing the Internet. The Web uses mostly pictures to communicate. However, words as well as videos, animations, and sounds are also used. All of these parts of the Web work together to make it a truly multimedia experience!

What makes the World Wide Web truly a "Web," separating it from the rest of the Internet, are hyperlinks (also just called "links"). A link can be a word, a picture, or an icon (such as the pictures you click on your computer desktop), or even a group of words or part of a picture. Links refer to other pages—either within that same Web site or anywhere else on the Web. Clicking on a link brings up its corresponding page. Thanks to hyperlinks, you can easily surf from page to page and site to site—just by clicking your mouse!

Important Web Words

First, let's define some important words that we will be using (if any other words in this book are confusing, check their definitions in the Glossary, on pages 122–125).

Web Site and Web Page. The Web consists of an ever-growing number of Web pages. A Web page is a document created with HTML (HyperText Markup Language). Collectively, a bunch of Web pages found at the same Web address create a Web site. If this confuses you, think of a household. A family with many people sharing one house is a household. But so is one person living alone. It's the same with Web sites—you will find sites that have only one page and sites that have a lot of pages.

Need an ISP?

If you don't have an Internet Service Provider yet, go to the library with your parents and use a public computer there (or use a friend's computer) to check out a list of local ISPs at http://www.thelist.com. If you don't have access to a computer connected to the Internet, check your local yellow pages.

Home Page. A site's home page is the page that shows up on your computer screen when you first arrive at the site. It's like looking at the cover of a book. Usually, a home page will tell you a bit about the site and have links that you can follow. These links may lead you to other pages on that site or to other sites on the Web.

Web Server. Web pages and sites are stored on computers called Web servers. These servers store information and send requested pages to browsers. The Web is actually a worldwide network of Web servers.

Internet Service Provider (ISP). Internet Service Providers, sometimes called online services, are the gatekeepers of the Internet. Your ISP provides you with the software and the telephone connection you need to get online. To get onto the Internet, your computer must call up your ISP. Then, the ISP connects your computer to the Internet and the Web. Many people use their online service—such as America Online or Microsoft Network—as their ISP. Others use a local ISP.

Browser. A browser is software that lets computers display Web sites and pages, including any text, sound clips, pictures, videos, or animation on a Web page. Most computers come with a preinstalled browser, but if your computer didn't, you probably received one from your ISP. Browsers also let you use hyperlinks. Most people use Netscape Navigator or Microsoft Internet Explorer as their browser. A complete discussion of browsers is on pages 21–25.

URL. Uniform Resource Locator. That's a fancy way of saying Web address. Every Web page has its own address. No other page has the same URL. At first, URLs may look like a jumble of letters, numbers, periods, and slashes, but there is a system to how they work. When typing in the URL on your browser's address bar, make sure you type it correctly. One wrong letter, number, or piece of punctuation will change the URL, and you will receive an error message or be directed to a different site. See pages 25–27 for more information on Web addresses.

Bookmark. A bookmark is a saved link. They are called Favorites in Microsoft Internet Explorer and Bookmarks in Netscape Navigator. They are usually stored in a folder in the browser. These links make returning to favorite sites easy. Simply click on the bookmark. Your browser will take you to the saved page. That way, you don't have to locate and retype the URL each time you visit a favorite Web page.

Web Uses

People who use the Web have access to research materials, news, shopping, entertainment, tons of information, and all kinds of other stuff. We will explore the Web's educational resources in later chapters. Here are some other ways people use the Web.

E-mail. Electronic mail (e-mail) is the most popular part of the Internet. It's like regular mail, but it lets you send and receive "letters" with your computer. You can usually get free e-mail software from your ISP or browser. In addition to sending a simple e-mail message, you can include attachments. An attachment can be a picture, video or sound clip, or another letter. Any file on your hard drive can be attached to e-mail. However, not all e-mail programs are set up to send and receive some attachments (such as sounds, videos, or pictures).

Warning!

Viruses can be attached to e-mail messages. If you aren't sure that an e-mail file attachment is safe, *do not download it!* Downloading a virus can cause a lot of trouble for your computer (it can even erase your hard drive!). However, just opening and reading an e-mail message cannot activate a virus or harm your computer.

Message Boards. Message boards, also called discussion boards, are huge groups involving people from all over the world. These are basically electronic bulletin boards where people post messages for each other. Others may come by and post responses to the original message or post their own message. Each board focuses on a particular topic. The messages can be read by anyone visiting the bulletin board, and anyone can post a message.

Weblogs. Weblogs or blogs are similar to message boards. They are personal Web sites that contain dated entries in chronological order starting with the most recent. A Weblog allows you to publish a variety of stuff, such as essays, documents, pictures, and so much more! It's almost like an online diary. Weblogs provide a way for you to post information about a subject and keep it updated. Some blogs invite feedback and comments from visitors in the form of a guest book.

Because Weblogs were built to make it easy to put information on the Web, you can do all your publishing through a WYSIWYG (what you see is what you get) editor. This is a simple browser-based editing environment. You don't need to be a programmer to use a Weblog since all management is done through a point-and-click menu.

Chat. "Let your fingers do the talking!" Of course, kids' computers do the talking, not their mouths. Messages are typed back and forth. That's what chatting is all about. Chatting is a great way to meet different people. Chatting is done in "chat rooms." Everyone in the chat room can read and respond to the message. Many Web sites provide chat rooms for kids on a variety of topics.

Web safety is a big issue today. Several companies provide kids-only chat rooms that are closely monitored. Still, kids shouldn't log into a new chat room without their parents' permission. Be sure to read the Web safety rules (see pages 43–45) before going into a chat room.

Kids Only!

Here are some kid-friendly chat rooms:

- **KidChatters** (http://www.kidchatters.com) Fully monitored chat rooms for kids ages 9 through 13. Chat rooms, instant messaging, and e-mail.
- **Headbone Zone Chat for Kids** (http://www.headbone.com/friends/chat) Fully monitored kids-only chat. Chat rooms, e-mail, games, and activities.
- **KidsCom Chat & Buzz** (http://www.kidscom.com/chat/chat.html) Fully monitored kids-only chat. Polls, chat rooms, and activities.

Instant Messaging. Instant messaging (IM) is a way for two people to have a conversation by themselves while logged onto the Internet. IM only works if you both have the software needed and are both online. It comes in handy if you are sending multiple e-mails back and forth with the same person. With IM, you can quickly see the other person's response. And unlike message boards and Weblogs, you and your friend are the only ones who can see what you write, unless someone is looking over your shoulder!

Information Gathering. The Web can be considered the biggest reference library in the world. Much of this book discusses research on the Web. Besides research, you can use the Web to get news and information. Millions of people log onto the Web daily to check the news, weather, and sports scores. These sites will keep you up-to-the-minute (and give you something to talk about during current events at school!):

- **The Associated Press** (http://www.ap.org) The world's oldest and largest news organization. Check out AP news in all formats: photo, video, and audio.

- **Intellicast.com** (http://www.intellicast.com) Great weather site. Check out your forecast and take a look at interactive maps, almanac facts, and more.

- **The Sports Network** (http://www.sportsnetwork.com)
  Check out scores, stats, and stories.

Shopping. Web shopping has become a multi-billion dollar industry. You can find anything on the Web. Virtual stores are never closed. Some of these stores only exist on the Web—such as Amazon.com. Always be sure to ask your parents for permission before purchasing anything on the Web.

Entertainment. The Web has more information than you could read in a lifetime. Thankfully, it has outlets for fun, too. Want to try some new computer games? Need to know which new movies are good? Want to find out the latest gossip on the hippest new bands or TV shows? The Web has it all—plus more! Dig into online games, contests, jokes, screensavers, movies, TV, music, and more.

There's a lot of free stuff on the Web, too. If you know how to get it, it's yours! In Chapter 8 (see page 95), we'll discuss downloading files to your computer. Downloading means copying a file from another computer. Many sites gather files—such as photos, maps, and games—for downloading.

An Educational Web?

Now we know that the Web is part of a huge, linked computer network. You can use it to locate lots of information, to communicate, even to shop. But, can using the Web really improve grades? Yes! By using the Web wisely, students can:

- Get homework help. Online reference materials, such as encyclopedias and dictionaries, provide access to a multitude of information.

- Communicate with other students, educators, and experts.

- Research topics for papers and other projects. Search engines and directories find information on any subject.

- Improve problem-solving skills. Good searches require thought and analysis.

- Discover places around the world and learn about other cultures.

- Gain technology skills. Obtain hands-on experience with skills needed in education and the workplace.

- Have fun! The Web offers lots of interactive chances for combining learning and entertainment.

It's important to remember that the Web doesn't have a boss or a principal. Everyone who posts information on the Web helps build it. Of course, some sources are more reliable than others. When you're gathering research for a report or other project, make sure you think about your sources. Which is a more reliable reference for a report on butterflies: an encyclopedia or your neighbor's little brother Bobby? Go with the encyclopedia. It's possible that Bobby is a well-known butterfly expert, but the information in an encyclopedia is double- and even tripled-checked for correctness; butterfly-lovin' Bobby isn't.

The Web works the same way. While some butterfly buffs may have home pages devoted to butterflies, you can't be sure that they're accurate. It is always better to use established reference materials. Using good reference sources is covered in depth on pages 40–43.

When to Use the Web

The Web is an important information source. But remember that it is just one part of your study routine. Traditional study and research skills are still very important. Search the Web for information. But also check your school and local libraries for resources. And of course your school textbooks and class handouts are other places to find information. Use the Web as an extra library to find facts. It isn't meant to replace the encyclopedia at the library or the notes you take in class.

One cool part of the Web is its speed. The Web is a great place to look for information if you don't have much time for research. Doing a search takes time, but the Web is never closed. Sundays, evenings, holidays—you can always browse the Web.

Of course, the Web isn't just for schoolwork. It's a place to find games, make friends, read about a hobby or interest, and more. However, just like TV time, Web time should be limited too. Be sure to plan time for other activities besides surfing the Web. Playing outside, reading a book, talking with your friends, doing your chores and homework, and spending time with your family are all important, too.

How to Get to the Web

Now that we have most of the Web basics under our belts, let's get surfing! Your parents should have already done the following steps in order to connect to the Internet. (An exception is logging on through a cable modem or DSL; see page 21.)

Dial-up

To get on the Web from a dial-up connection, you will need:

1. A computer. A Macintosh or PC (personal computer) with at least 64 MB of RAM.

2. A modem. Modems let computers talk to each other. They connect to telephone lines. There are both internal and external modems. Popular modems today are 28.8 kbps, 33.6 kbps, and 56.6 kbps. "Kbps" stands for kilobits per second. This is the speed of the modem (like miles per hour in the car). These speeds tell how fast the computer can get information from other computers. Very few computers still have 14.4 kbps modems, since the Web is getting too big and fast for these to work very well.

3. An Internet Service Provider. See page 13 for more information on ISPs.

4. A browser. See pages 21–25 for more on browsers.

Connecting to the Web is pretty painless.

- First, turn on the computer.

- Once the computer has warmed up, select the ISP or browser icon (usually by double clicking on it).

- Select connect. (Not always necessary, depending on software.)

- Enter your username and password. (All ISPs require these, although sometimes they are stored in the computer and don't need to be entered each time. If that is the case, the connection will be automatic.)

If this has been done correctly, two things should happen:

- The modem makes beeps, dings, and static noises as your computer connects with the ISP's computer.

- The browser's home page will then be displayed.

Cable or DSL Connection

Another kind of connection is through a cable modem. This lets a computer attach to high-speed Internet cable services offered by many cable TV companies. You would need the same items listed on pages 19–20 (computer, modem, ISP, and browser), except the modem is a specific cable modem, which can download in speeds around 30 mbps (megabits per second). Your cable company will provide your modem.

The fastest connections available use special modems for superhigh-speed telephone connections called DSL (short for digital subscriber line). The speed for DSL is between 128 kbps to 1.544 mbps. Although it may seem that cable is faster, cable connects with other people in a certain area while DSL is completely independent from other users.

To connect to the Web, follow the steps listed on page 20. The difference between cable and DSL vs. dial-up is your phone line won't be tied up since you're connected through a cable line and not the phone line. So you won't hear any beeping, dinging, or static noises. But don't worry! Just because you can't hear those noises, it doesn't mean you're not connected. Once the browser's home page opens, it means you're logged onto the Web.

There is no right or wrong connection to the Web. Cable and DSL offer the benefit of an always-on connection capability. That means that you could stay logged onto the Web indefinitely if you wanted without tying up the phone line. That is, of course, with your parents' permission.

The Browser Window

Microsoft Internet Explorer (Explorer for short) and Netscape Navigator (Netscape) are the most popular Web browsers. They both do very similar things, but they also have some differences.

The address location box is your ticket to visiting Web sites.

Menu Bar. Just like all computer programs, your browser will have a menu bar. Every available function is on the menu bar. Many of the menu functions will be familiar to you from other programs. For example, using the menu bar, you can open files; cut, copy, and paste; and get help.

Toolbar. The toolbar is located just below the menu bar. It is also called a button bar. Toolbar buttons help you navigate Web pages.

Some buttons are found in both Netscape and Explorer:

Back. Your browser keeps track of where you've been on the Web. It remembers every page you visit. This feature is helpful because after a few minutes of following links you can be far away from where you started. Clicking the Back button on the toolbar takes you back, with each click, page by page to where you started.

Forward. If you go back too far, click Forward. This button moves you up one page at a time in your Web history. This

---

Get Current! Update!

Want to get the latest copy of Netscape Navigator or Microsoft Internet Explorer? Download them from the Web! For Navigator, go to http://channels.netscape.com/ns/browsers/default.jsp; for Explorer go to http://www.microsoft.com/downloads/search.aspx?displaylang=en. Make sure you have your parents' permission if you want to download the most recent version of these free browsers.

only works if you have used your Back or Home buttons to revisit previous pages.

Home. Displays your home page. This is the page that you tell your browser to show when you log on. By default (that means automatically), the home page is usually your browser's home page. Other choices you might consider are a search engine or other favorite Web site. This is usually set up in the Preferences (or Options) section of your browser.

Reload/Refresh. Redisplays the current page. Your browser checks the current page against the one in your history. If there are changes, the new page is loaded. If not, the same page is loaded again. This function is useful when visiting any Web site that updates information often, such as checking ESPN.com for sports scores.

Stop. Stops the current transmission. As soon as you begin loading a page, the Stop button becomes active. Use the Stop button when you have accidentally asked for the wrong page or the page that you have requested hasn't loaded after a long wait (when this happens, it usually means that there is a problem with that page).

Print. Lets you print the current window. Make sure that the window you want to print is the one that you are currently on.

Other buttons on Explorer and Netscape's toolbars let you:

- **Open** a Web page by typing its URL.
- **Find** a word or phrase on the current page.
- **Search** for information on the Web.
- Collect and visit your personal Web **Favorites** or **Bookmarks.**
- Read and write **Mail.**

Address Location Box. Below the toolbar on Explorer or next to the toolbar on Netscape, you will find the address location box. This feature serves two functions.

1. It displays the address of the page your browser is currently showing or downloading.

2. It instructs the browser to retrieve any address you type into the box. (Hit Enter on your keyboard after typing the desired address to begin loading the new page.)

Explorer and Netscape have a nice feature called Auto-Complete. As you begin typing a URL in the address box, it automatically searches your history. If it finds a match, the browser suggests the site. That way, you can get to a Web site after typing only a few letters in the address location box. You can turn this on and off in Netscape under Preferences and Smart Browsing. In Explorer, it's located under Preferences and Forms AutoComplete.

Logo Box. To the right of the toolbar or the address locator box you will find the logo box. This box contains the logo for the browser you use. Netscape's logo box is an "N" on a teal-and-black background. Explorer's logo box features a lower-case "e" that rotates into a globe. Besides advertising the browser's company, the logo box is a status gauge. When the logo is animated (the picture is moving), it means that a transfer is in progress.

Here's a Tip

If a download seems endless, check your logo box. If it stays animated for a long time, this usually means that something is wrong with the requested page (like it is under construction or just not working at the moment). You may want to click the Stop or Reload/Refresh buttons on your toolbar.

Scroll bars. These may appear on the right side and/or bottom of your browser window. Depending on the size of the window that you are viewing, you may need to scroll to see the entire page. The scroll bars work just like the ones you have in almost all other programs. Your browser window can sometimes be adjusted to make the page fit on the screen by clicking the boxes at the corners of your screen.

Status bar. The status bar is usually along the bottom of your browser screen and provides important information about what your browser is doing. As a page is downloading, the status bar sometimes displays the name of the page it is retrieving. It keeps you informed of the browser's progress as it contacts, retrieves, and loads a page. When downloading a file, the status bar tells you how many items are waiting to download or the percentage of the file left to download. When you position your cursor over a link, the status bar displays the URL of that link's Web page.

World Wide Web Addresses

Just like the houses in your town, every Web site has an address. These are also known as Uniform Resource Locators or URLs. There is a system (called a protocol) to naming Web sites. Knowing this protocol's rules can help you understand and remember a Web site's address.

Nearly all URLs begin with **http://.** This tells your computer that the address points to a hypertext document—a Web page. "HTTP" stands for "HyperText Transfer Protocol."

Next, in most Web page addresses, comes **www.** This lets you know that the site is on the World Wide Web.

The next part of the URL is usually the name of the site's organization. This portion of the URL may be the organization's name spelled out, an abbreviation of the name, or a different name altogether. This part of the address is called the domain. For example, the domain name for the Public Broadcasting System's Web site is **pbs.** Think of the domain name as the name of the city in your street address.

Finally, the last part of the URL (or the "suffix") provides information about the type of organization maintaining the site. Common suffixes are:

- .com. This is for companies and other commercial Web sites.

- .edu. For educational facilities, such as colleges, school districts, and some research facilities.

- .org. For nonprofit organizations.

- .gov. For government organizations.

- .mil. For military branches and facilities.

- .net. For a network of computers linked together, such as Internet Service Providers.

By knowing this system, you can often guess a Web site's address. For example, if you were trying to locate Yale University's home page, you might type **http://www.yale.edu** into your address location box. (And you would be correct!)

Sometimes slashes separate parts of longer Web addresses. Each directory, subdirectory, and file name follow a slash. Your browser knows that a slash means that the address is getting more specific.

For example, the National Aeronautics and Space Administration (NASA) site has a section for kids. At NASA Kids, you can find games, activities, and even ten things you should know about comets. If you wanted to find out about those interesting comet facts, it is possible that you would be able to follow the links from NASA's home page. But if you know the full address, you can go there right away!

The first part of the address directs you to NASA's Web site, **http://www.nasa.gov.** But that's not the entire address for the comet facts!

The NASA Kids site is in the **audience/forkids/home** directory at NASA's site. You need to add this directory to the address: **http://www.nasa.gov/audience/forkids/home.** That's the official Web site for NASA Kids. If you want to find more fun stuff about NASA, check with the main NASA Kids site once you've looked at the cool facts about comets.

We're almost there! To check out the ten comet facts, the last part of the address is **CS_Ten_Facts_About_Comets.html.** Add that to the end of the address for NASA Kids, and you'll have **http://www.nasa.gov/audience/forkids/home/CS_Ten_Facts _About_Comets.html.** That's quite a mouthful!

Enough Stretching! Let's Surf!

You should be pretty stretched out by now and ready to jump into the ocean of the World Wide Web. With the basics and safety tips under your belt, you will be able to work wonders with the Web. The following chapters will open up a new world of possibility for your school activities, homework assignments, reports, projects, hobbies, and other interests. And, chances are that by the time you are through, you will have learned something new. Maybe you will find new interests along the way. One thing is for sure: You will never look at your computer the same way again. But enough already! Let's start surfing!

Getting Started

Victoria's third grade class has been learning about computers and the Internet. She has a computer at home. She mostly uses it to write letters, play games, and paint pictures. And she had never been on the Internet or the World Wide Web before. But last week, Victoria's class learned about some of the things that people can do on the Web. Victoria and her class recently visited the library computer room and went online for the first time. Here's what they did.

Each student sat down at a computer and turned on the power. Victoria's teacher, Ms. Moore, said that this is called "booting up." Then Ms. Moore gave the class these instructions.

1. Find the "My Computer" icon in the top left corner of your desktop. Double-click on it.

2. In the My Computer window (which you just opened), find the "Dial-up Networking" icon. Double-click on it.

3. In the Dial-up Networking window, find the "Internet Connection" icon. Double-click on it.

4. In the Internet Connection window, click just once on "Connect" at the bottom of the window.

5. A new kind of window, called a "status" window, will open. The status window, and the status bar in the window, let you know that the computer is busy getting you online.

6. The status bar will disappear once you have been connected to the Internet.

Victoria followed Ms. Moore's instructions carefully. She had a little trouble finding the "Connect" button, but Ms. Moore helped her. Then Victoria watched the status window. First, it said "Dialing." After a minute it said, "Establishing Network Connection." Then the window let Victoria know that the computer was "Verifying User Name and Password." Finally, it said "Logging onto Network." Then it suddenly disappeared! Victoria was online!

Your software at school or home may be set up so that your browser automatically opens when an Internet connection is made. If you need some help getting online, ask a grown-up.

Victoria's class connected to the Internet using their school's Internet Service Provider (ISP). Now they need to connect to their browser in order to go anywhere on the Web. Remember that a browser is software that brings up Web pages on your computer.

Once a Web connection has been made, double-click on your browser icon. Icons are little pictures that represent the programs on your computer. They are usually displayed somewhere on the screen (called the "desktop"). The position of your icons depends upon your computer and how it is set up.

Get Connected!

The steps for connecting to the Internet may be different for you. It depends on how your computer and software are set up. Some ways you might connect to the Internet are by:
• Double-clicking on your browser icon.
• Double-clicking on your online service icon.
• Double-clicking on your Internet Service Provider (ISP) icon.

Victoria double-clicked on the Netscape Navigator icon on the left side of her desktop. Then the browser window opened. Ms. Moore explained that the logo box and status bar show that the browser is loading a page. Victoria watched the stars fly in the Netscape logo box. The status bar slowly filled up, from left to right, as the page loaded. When it is first started, a browser loads its designated home page.

After the browser's home page had loaded, Ms. Moore handed out a list of the week's vocabulary words. But instead of looking up the words in the classroom dictionaries as the students usually would, they were instructed to use an online dictionary. Ms. Moore then explained how to get to Merriam-Webster Online.

1. Click on the address location box. The address will become highlighted and a blinking cursor will appear.

2. Type "http://www.m-w.com" in the address location box. The old home address should disappear as soon as you start typing.

3. Hit "Enter" or "Return."

Personalize Your Browser

A browser's home page is different from a Web site's home page. You can set your browser to open any Web page you like whenever your browser is opened. By default (that means automatically), that page will be your browser's home page. For example, Netscape Navigator's default home page is Netscape's home page. You can change which page the browser goes to when you type it in your browser's menu. Select Preferences under Edit, then enter in the address of the home page you want. For Microsoft Internet Explorer, click on Edit, Preferences, then Browser Display. Type any Web address you wish: your favorite search engine, homework help page, and so on.

Look It Up!

Merriam-Webster Online (http://www.m-w.com) is much more than a dictionary. It's a free language center. Just like the regular dictionary, each word is followed by the pronunciation, part of speech, definitions, and some historical information. However, the online M-W dictionary uses the word in a sentence or phrase and gives you more information about the word's history. There are also word games, a thesaurus, detailed descriptions of "cool words," and lots of other useful features. If you really want to get smart, check out the word of the day, every day!

Victoria watched as the Merriam-Webster Web site appeared on her screen. She did it! She was on the Web. She carefully typed her vocabulary words one at a time in the "Merriam-Webster Dictionary" box and searched for their definitions. The site gave her lots of helpful information, including an audible pronunciation with the sound on her computer.

Next, Ms. Moore showed the class how to save the Merriam-Webster Web site as a "Bookmark." Bookmarks are saved links to your favorite pages. Then, in the future, when you want to return to that site, you can do so with a simple click. That way you don't have to remember and retype the site's address every time you visit!

To save the Merriam-Webster site as a bookmark, Victoria followed these instructions.

1. Make sure you are on the home page of the Merriam-Webster Web site. If not, use the "Back" button to return to the site's home page.

2. Go to the "Bookmarks" (also called "Favorites" in Microsoft Internet Explorer) menu and pull it down.

3. Select "Bookmark This Page" or "Add Page to Favorites."

Working with Bookmarks

Bookmarks make using the Web much easier. Using bookmarks, you can return to favorite or helpful pages again and again with little effort. There are several ways to bookmark a page. The first thing you need to do is make sure that the page you want to bookmark is the one currently shown on your browser.

To add a bookmark in Netscape Navigator (or "Netscape" for short):

Make sure you are on the exact page you want to bookmark.

Pull down the "Bookmarks" menu.

Select "Bookmark This Page."

Other ways to add a bookmark are to hold down the "CTRL" (or "Command," known as the "Apple Key" on Macintosh computers) key and then hit the "D" key, or click your right-hand mouse button and select "Bookmark This Page."

To add a bookmark in Microsoft Internet Explorer (or "Explorer" for short):

Make sure you are on the exact page you want to bookmark.

Pull down the "Favorites" menu.

Select "Add Page to Favorites" or click your right-hand mouse button and select "Add Page to Favorites."

Other ways to add a bookmark are to hold down the "CTRL" (or "Command," known as the "Apple Key" on Macintosh computers) key and then hit the "D" key, or click your right-hand mouse button and select "Add Page to Favorites."

When you add a Web page to the Favorites in Explorer, you need to decide if you want to "subscribe" to that site. Subscribing means that Explorer will check those Web sites every so often for new content. You can tell Explorer to check your subscribed sites for new material daily, weekly, or monthly.

Then you can choose either to be notified that there is new content available on one of your subscribed sites or to have the updated content automatically downloaded (see page 95) to your hard drive. This type of subscription isn't like paying for a regular magazine or newspaper delivery—this doesn't cost anything.

If you choose to have new stuff from your "subscriptions" automatically downloaded to your hard drive, you can then check out your favorite Web sites offline at your leisure. However, subscribing can take up a lot of space on your hard drive. Make sure you talk with your parents about this Explorer option.

Organizing Your Bookmarks

Victoria is starting to feel more comfortable on the Web. She's been doing some online stuff for school (such as a report on the weather) and some just for fun. But her list of bookmarks is getting too long. She sometimes has trouble finding a specific site.

Luckily, both Netscape and Explorer have features to let Victoria organize her bookmarked links. She can put similar bookmarks in handy folders (such as putting all of her homework help bookmarks together) to organize her bookmark list. Then she can give the new folder a name. Here's how she organized her bookmarks for the Web sites she is using to do her report for school.

1. In the Bookmarks menu, Victoria selected "Manage Bookmarks" and then "New Folder."

2. Then, the "Create New Folder" window opened.

3. In the text box, Victoria typed "Weather Report."

4. Victoria then clicked "OK" to close the Bookmark Properties window.

To move the bookmarks into this folder, Victoria simply clicked and dragged each bookmark onto the folder. She needed to be in the "Manage Bookmarks" section in order to do this—the same section she's in when setting her bookmarks. When she held the set bookmark over the designated folder, the folder was highlighted, signaling the bookmark was almost in the folder. She let go of her mouse button and the bookmark was now filed.

Victoria repeated the same steps to create other folders for school and fun sites. The next time Victoria opens her bookmarks, instead of a long, confusing list of links, she will see her neat list of folders. Now she'll quickly know where to find any site she is looking for!

Megadirectories and Search Engines

The Web grows constantly—every day, every hour, every minute. It has more information than any library in the world. Anyone can put information on the Web. It's easy and free! This is both good and bad.

The good news is that whatever you are looking for is probably on the Web—somewhere. The bad news is that you're going to have to search through an amazing amount of information to find what you're looking for.

Luckily, some Web services exist just to help you find what you need. Megadirectories help Web users by sorting Web sites into categories (just like Victoria, when she created folders for her list of bookmarks). Then you can search through the categories, and their many levels, to find the sites that you are looking for.

Bookmark Bonuses

You'll notice that when you pull down the Bookmarks menu that no actual Web addresses are listed. For example, instead of seeing "http://www.mlb.com" you'll see "Major League Baseball" listed. These titles describe the book-marked Web page. That way you don't need to remember all of the letters, dots, or slashes in Web addresses. Bookmarks make browsing much easier!

Search engines, on the other hand, do the looking for you. You type in words that describe what you're looking for. These words are called keywords. Hit "Start Search" or some similar command, and the search engine quickly looks all over the Web and returns a list of links to sites that match your keywords. Both megadirectories and search engines help you find what you need, but they work very differently.  Many search tools today act as both megadirectories and search engines. This lets you perform a search in whatever way is best for you.

Megadirectories

Megadirectories have many levels. The top level is the largest. This level sorts Web sites into general categories; then come the subcategories, sub-subcategories, and so on. Unfortunately, no one megadirectory can list every Web site out there. Why not? Because the Web is growing all the time, even changing from one second to the next. Megadirectories try to keep up with the growing World Wide Web, but the Web always seems to have a jump on them. Plus, there is no central Web registry. Anyone can put a Web page or site out there, but sometimes nobody knows about that page or site. Sometimes the designer of the page has to list the site with one of these directories. Plus, with so many sites out there, you can see why a lot of them just kind of float around in cyberspace without being listed in a directory.

Not all directories want to index the entire Web anyway. Some directories only index sites related to a certain topic. A directory that just indexes sites about sports wouldn't be the place to search for the history of the United States. Others only want to index what they think are the best Web sites, and not all Web sites make the cut.

Nearly all directories offer a keyword search option. At these sites, you can search category levels to find the topic you are looking for or even search the whole Web using your keywords. Some directories let you choose a category or subcategory first and then search only within that section. This is a great way to narrow your search so you don't get too many unrelated sites listed from your search.

Search Engines

If you know exactly what you are looking for, a search engine may be for you. Instead of browsing through layer after layer in a megadirectory, keyword searches in search engines take you right to your information.

We'll take a close look at how to make good searches on pages 46–61. First, let's get the basics on some of the Web's most popular megadirectories and search engines.

AltaVista. Imagine searching through more than 200 hard drives to find a file...in less than one second! That's what an AltaVista search does. AltaVista is a search engine that lets you search with one word, a few words, or a question. Just type the words you want to search for and click "Find" to get results.

Your results (also called "hits") are ranked so that your closest matches appear at the top of the list. You can also browse through categories at AltaVista if you want to. AltaVista's address is **http://www.altavista.com.** (For more on AltaVista, see page 54.)

Ask Jeeves for Kids. This is a search engine hosted by an Internet butler named Jeeves. Ask Jeeves for Kids is a natural-language search engine, which means you can ask a question just the way you'd ask your teacher. There are links on the side of the home page where you can find homework help and research for school projects, but there are also fun games and activities to enjoy. One fun thing to do is to watch the Peek screen to see what sort of questions other kids are asking. Ask away at Ask Jeeves for Kids at **http://www.ajkids.com.** (For more on Ask Jeeves for Kids, see pages 54–55.)

Excite. This search engine is very easy to use. Excite only goes three levels deep, so you won't need to dig through an endless pile of levels to find an answer. Excite reviews each site within its directory, so you receive a short description of each. Excite doesn't try to index all the sites on the Web— only the ones that they think are the best. Most keyword searches return only sites that contain the words that you requested. However, Excite also finds related terms. For example, if you search for "dog care," you will get a list of sites that feature those two words in their descriptions. But Excite will also bring you pages about "pet grooming," even if the words "dog" and "care" aren't on the page. Get excited by Excite at **http://www.excite.com.** (For more on Excite, see pages 55–56.)

Google. One of the largest, most famous Web megadirectories is Google. By searching more than eight billion Web sites, Google lists several subcategories, allowing you to check out results in images, groups, news, and froogle. Froogle is a search engine to look for items for sale. Move on over to Google at **http://www.google.com.** (For more on Google, see page 56–57.)

Kaboose. Kaboose is a family-friendly search engine. On the home page are links to all sorts of information, from homework, entertainment, or even dinosaurs! You can also jump to other Kaboose-related sites such as FunSchool for Kids, Zeeks for Teens, and KidsDomain for Families. Climb on board the Kaboose at **http://www.kaboose.com.** (For more on Kaboose, see page 57–58.)

KidsClick! KidsClick! is a search engine designed by librarians to give kids information right at their fingertips. There are more than 600 subjects where you can find information on spacecraft, art museums, jokes, and aliens, just to name a few. There are tons of sub-menus to locate whatever topic interests you. Click on over to KidsClick! at **http://www.kidsclick.org.** (For more on KidsClick!, see page 58–59.)

MetaCrawler. MetaCrawler is a little different from other search services. This one doesn't have a database. When you search MetaCrawler, it may send your request to several different search engines. MetaCrawler uses most of the search tools listed here, including Ask Jeeves, Google, LookSmart, and Yahoo! MetaCrawler takes your search results and organizes and ranks them for you. Crawl (or run) to MetaCrawler at **http://www.metacrawler.com.** (For more on MetaCrawler, see pages 59–60.)

Yahoo! Yahoo! is also one of the largest, most famous Web megadirectories. It has many categories and a ton of subcategories. Chances are, you can find anything you are looking for here. Yahoo! also lets you perform keyword searches. Yahoo! is waiting for you at **http://www.yahoo.com.** (For more on Yahoo!, see page 60.)

Yahooligans! Yahooligans! is Yahoo! for kids. Its categories are designed for kids, with choices such as School Bell, Around the World, and Arts & Entertainment. It also has a keyword search feature. Every link in Yahooligans! has been checked out and found to be safe for kids. This is a great starting point for homework and project help, research, and fun. Hang out

Super Searchers

How do directories and search engines find their sites? These services use Web hunters—sometimes called spiders, worms, or robots—to search the Web for new or updated pages. Each directory has different ways they use to gather information. Sometimes, the same search in different directories will give you identical results. And sometimes the results will be different.

Some categories that seem to pop up in nearly every megadirectory are:

Computers. Hardware and software, downloads, the Internet and Web, computer games...pretty much anything related to computers!

Education. K–12 information (look here for homework help), colleges, and other school stuff.

Entertainment. The world of TV, music, movies, and celebrities.

Health. Fitness, nutrition, therapy, medicine, and all kinds of ideas to keep you in (or get you into) tip-top shape!

News. Headlines and full coverage of world, national, and local stories and weather. Features newspapers, magazines, and other news services.

Sports (or Recreation & Sports). Pro and minor-league sports events, teams, data, and fan clubs.

with Yahooligans! at **http://www.yahooligans.com.** (For more on Yahooligans!, see page 60–61.)

Most megadirectories and search engines are pretty simple to use. There are some techniques and tips that can really turn you into a Web-searching pro. We'll get into that a little later on pages 46–61.

Doing good searches can help you avoid a lot of unimportant, dumb, or even harmful material that is on the Web, as we will see in the next chapter. So keep reading and you'll be a Web whiz before you know it!

"All the News That's Fit to Print"*

The title of this chapter comes from the slogan of *The New York Times* newspaper. This slogan means that the people who work at that newspaper say that they are going to try to print all of the important information that they want people to know about. It also means that if something is not important, untrue, or offensive to the readers, that they won't print it. That's the "Fit" part. That way, people who read the newspaper won't be offended or misled.

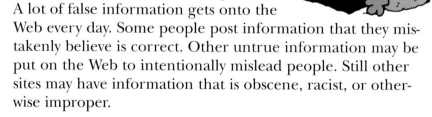

However, the World Wide Web does not limit what is put online. Traveling on the Web isn't always a smooth ride. And not all of the information out there is fit to print. Remember that the Web doesn't have anyone overseeing it. A lot of false information gets onto the Web every day. Some people post information that they mistakenly believe is correct. Other untrue information may be put on the Web to intentionally mislead people. Still other sites may have information that is obscene, racist, or otherwise improper.

When using the Web to find information for homework, a project, or for fun, you need to be careful. How can you be sure that the information you find is accurate? The easiest way is to use only respected sites. On the next page you will read about how to tell where a site comes from. The best clue is from a site's title. The site's suffix (.com, .edu, .gov, etc.) tells you a lot about a site. Often, its domain name does, too.

*Copyright © The New York Times. *Permission granted for use.*

You can usually trust information that you get from:

- Educational facilities (.edu).

- Non-profit organizations (.org).

- Sites hosted by established reference materials. For example, Encyclopædia Britannica and Merriam-Webster Dictionary.

- Sites hosted by respected or professional organizations. For example, the National Geographic Society for cultural and wildlife topics or Major League Baseball and the Baseball Hall of Fame for information on baseball history, players, and teams.

- Sites from trusted newspapers and magazines. For example, *Time, Newsweek,* or *The New York Times.* However, keep in mind that some publications may have strong opinions, especially about politics. Sometimes these opinions are written as facts. Read carefully!

When doing projects for school, it is always a good idea to get your information from several sources. Don't get facts from just one place and leave it at that. Check out the same information at several respected sites. That's the way real Web research pros do it!

Using Multiple Sources

Taylor is in the fourth grade. His class is learning about biographies. They've already read some biographical books in class. Now, Taylor has to write a biography of a famous athlete. He decides to write about first baseman Albert Pujols. He goes online to search for information about Albert Pujols. His search returns several different Web pages and sites that have information on Pujols.

They are:

- Major League Baseball site: Albert Pujols biography.

- *Sports Illustrated* site: articles, a biography, and statistics on Albert Pujols.

- ESPN.com: Albert Pujols statistics, comments, and facts.

- Sports Reference, Inc.: statistics, salaries, and transactions of Albert Pujols.

- Jimmy's tribute to Albert Pujols.

- Paul's Albert Pujols home page.

After checking out all of these pages, Taylor finds that a lot of the information about Pujols is the same at each site. Basic information, such as Pujols's height, weight, birth date, and baseball statistics (including the batting title he won in 2003) is the same on each site.

However, some of the sites list some personal things about Pujols. Jimmy's site says that Pujols is nervous about public speaking. He may be. But no other site claims this. Taylor can't be sure if public speaking really does make Albert Pujols nervous. This type of information may not be very important to the biography. Jimmy might have gotten that information from a friend, a magazine article, or maybe heard it during a baseball game. Maybe public speaking makes Jimmy nervous or he just made it up. It's impossible to tell.

Therefore, Taylor should not use that information in his biography of Albert Pujols. Taylor should look to the Major League Baseball, *Sports Illustrated,* and ESPN.com Web sites as sources for his report. Personal sites, such as those put on the Web by Jimmy and Paul, can't be trusted and may not be reliable. They don't have the same responsibility to the truth that professional sites do. Jimmy and Paul may have done great jobs in creating home pages about Albert Pujols. But information on their sites may be incorrect. It may be hard to check as well.

Disinformation

Merriam-Webster Online (http://www.m-w.com) defines disinformation as: *false information deliberately and often covertly spread (as by the planting of rumors) in order to influence public opinion or obscure the truth.*

Sometimes, people will post data to the Web for their, or their organization's, gain. Sometimes, even respected sources, such as popular magazines and newspapers, will publish disinformation without knowing it. Sometimes the truth is hard to find.

You know that lying is wrong. However, some advertisers and organizations do not have a problem with lying to people. That's why it is very important to know the sources you use online.

When doing research for school projects or reports, the best way for you to make sure that you are getting honest facts is to use several sources. When Taylor was doing his biography on Albert Pujols, he didn't just use one resource to gather his information. He went to three different respected sources of information and compared what they had to say about Pujols. The more sources you use to compare information, the better your chances are that the data you use is true.

Web Safety and Cautions

Your parents have taught you to be careful when you're out exploring the neighborhood. They tell you to "Look both

ways before you cross the street"; "Only go where you're supposed to"; and "Don't talk to strangers." Some of these wise
warnings apply to the Web as well. The Web is just like the
real world in a lot of ways. You need to be just as
careful in the online world as you are in
your neighborhood.

You and your parents will probably
want to set some of your own rules
about World Wide Web use. Here are
some rules that everyone on the Web
should follow.

Never give out any personal information. Don't
tell anyone your real name, address (street or
e-mail), passwords, or telephone number.
And don't ever send anyone your picture.
Just like in everyday life, some people can
harm kids. Some grown-ups pretend to be kids when they are
online, so you have to be extra careful. If you have developed
a friendship with someone on the Web, and want to get to
know them better, discuss it with your parents first.

**Never meet anyone in person who you met on the Web
without your parents' permission.** If you have developed
a friendship with someone on the Web, and you want to
meet in person, have your parents go with you and always
meet in a public place. On the Web it is easy for anyone to
pretend to be someone they're not. It is always better to be
safe than sorry.

Never send or respond to nasty messages. If you receive a
message that makes you uncomfortable, show it to your parents. Don't feel bad about reading something upsetting. It
wasn't your fault. Just show it to your parents. Nasty messages
can be traced to their sender. Of course, you don't want to
upset anyone (or get in big trouble), so make sure that you
don't send any nasty messages of your own.

Never download a file without your parents' permission.
Don't download anything that comes to you by e-mail or pops
up in a chat area. It might be a virus. If you're not sure what
to do, you can always check with your parents. Some Web sites
require you to have certain software to view a file. If you need
to download that software, again, check with your parents
before doing anything.

Never go where you're not supposed to. The Web can be a
magical place. You can see a video of the surface of Mars, talk
to kids in other countries, learn about all kinds of fascinating
facts, and play games too. Unfortunately, you can also find all
sorts of nasty information. Racist, hateful, obscene, and dis-
turbing information is posted on the World Wide Web. If you
just go where you are supposed to, every Web experience
should be a good one.

You and your parents may talk about some other rules for
using the Web. Some rules may include:

- What types of sites you are and are not allowed to visit.

- Time limits for using the computer and going online.

- Participating (or not) in chats.

- Going online (or not) when adults are not home.

All of these **Don'ts** and **Nevers** can be pretty scary. But (here
we go again) *don't* worry. Sure, rules aren't meant to be fun.
These rules are meant to try and help keep the Web fun—
and safe—for you. There are millions of great, safe Web sites
out there for you to explore. The Web is a magical open door
that is always ready to take you someplace that you've never
been to before.

And now that the door is open, let's take a look inside and
see what we can find!

Digging Deeper: Search Techniques

Making good searches on the World Wide Web takes some practice. Just browsing around the Web doesn't require good search skills—and can be a lot of fun. But, when it's time to get to work, you need to know how to find what you need—or at least know how to find the map to get you where you're going! Then it's time to use a search service.

In Chapter 2, we discussed the basics of megadirectories and search engines. We listed the names and main features of some of the most popular ones. Now it's time to really take a look at how to do a good search on the Web. We'll also take a closer look at these megadirectories and search engines.

But first things first. Let's take a look at what might happen during a typical search.

Samantha's fourth grade class went on a field trip to the zoo earlier today. They had a lot of fun looking at and learning about all of the different animals (Samantha especially liked the beautiful, long-necked giraffes). Now, Samantha's teacher, Mr. Myers, has assigned reports on "Your Favorite Animal From the Zoo" for homework. Samantha decided to write her report about giraffes. Mr. Myers told the class that their reports should include important facts about the animal, such as its size, appearance, habitat, and diet. Samantha decides to search the World Wide Web for information about giraffes.

The first step in conducting a Web search is getting to the search engine (see pages 54–61). Once Samantha has logged onto her ISP and brought up her search feature, she is ready to enter some keywords to start her search.

This step in the search is very important. The search engine actually hunts through the Web looking for the keywords that you type. Any pages that it finds with that word on it will be part of Samantha's search results.

Samantha enters "giraffe" in the box next to the search button (this box is called the "search field") and clicks "Search." After the computer chugs for a few moments, Samantha sees her results—more than 6,000 documents! The results displayed include a gift catalog and a page of giraffe jokes. There are just too many pages listed to go through all of them. Samantha needs to figure out how to make her search more precise in order to get the information she needs to write her report for school.

Samantha's search was too broad. There are a lot of documents on the Web that contain the word "giraffe," but might not have any real, factual information about the animal. Samantha needs to "refine" her search.

Refining a search means that you are trying to be more specific. You don't have time to look through 6,000 Web pages to find a few pieces of information! That would take a really long time. You'd be turning in your homework weeks after it was due and your eyes would be as big as saucers from staring at the computer screen for so long! There's got to be a better way to get exactly the information that you need. Fortunately, there is!

Keywords Solve the Mystery

Keyword searching is quick and easy. Just type a word and hit "Search." But it is best when you know—or have a good idea—exactly what you're looking for. Sometimes it takes a couple of tries, using different keywords, to find the correct information.

It's kind of like fishing. You are looking to catch a catfish. So you set the hook up with some bait and throw it in the water. A few moments later the bobber stirs! You have a fish! But it's a tiny goldfish. No good. You take the fish off the hook and throw it back into the water. Maybe next time, you'll use different bait or a lure to attract the catfish. Then, once you use the right bait and fishing technique and catch a catfish, you might decide that this fish is too small. You need to catch a three-pound catfish.

In Samantha's search, the keyword "giraffe" was too broad. With keyword searching, you can tailor the search so you get exactly what you want. Samantha doesn't want just any information about giraffes. She wants to get information about the animal's size, appearance, habitat, and diet.

When a search engine goes to work, it compares exactly what you type to its entire index of Web sites. As smart as computers are, they can only do just what you tell them. A search engine couldn't possibly know that Samantha meant that she just wanted information about giraffes' size, appearance, habitat, and diet.

Choose your keywords carefully. Before you even sit down at the computer, think about your topic. Write some words on a piece of paper that describe what you're trying to find. Then, when you do your search, don't freak out if at first you get a ton of hits. Take a look at your list and use some specific words to make your search better. You can also use words and symbols known as "operators" to make more specific searches.

Operators

Operators are words and symbols that tell a search engine how to treat your keywords. They are sometimes called qualifiers or Boolean operators (see page 50 to read about George Boole, for whom this term is named). Operators are very simple, everyday words such as *and, or,* and *not.* Using these words along with your keywords can make Web searches even more specific.

And. Using "and" joins your keywords at the hip. You won't get any hits unless both keywords are on the Web site. Some search engines let you use the plus sign (+) for "and." The "and" operator is a great way to narrow your search results. In Samantha's case, she could narrow her search by trying the keywords "giraffe and habitat." The next time you get way too many hits for a search, add "and" plus another keyword.

Or. Using "or" between two keywords tells a search engine to find everything that contains either word. Suppose you are studying holidays in school and need to find some information about Chanukah. You know from the lesson at school that Chanukah can be spelled either as "Chanukah" or "Hanukkah." You want to be sure that you get all sites about the holiday in your search results. Therefore, you should type "Hanukkah or Chanukah" in the search field. Usually "or" makes for a very broad search—and a lot of hits. However, if you are having trouble finding any hits, using "or" between a few keywords might do the trick.

Not. Using "not" between two keywords tells the search engine to look for the first word but specifically *not* the second one, such as "giraffe not jokes." The search engine will reject any Web sites or pages containing that second keyword. Some search engines let you use the subtraction symbol (-) to mean "not." Using "not" is another way to narrow your search when you get too many hits.

Boolean Searches

Sometimes, World Wide Web searches are called Boolean searches. Why? What does Boolean mean anyway? Is it some kind of skinny ghost?

A Boolean search is one that combines keywords with words called operators such as "and" and "or." The name for these types of Web searches comes from George Boole. He was a mathematician who lived in England in the 1800s. He developed a type of thinking called symbolic logic, which led to a lot of modern math. Symbolic logic used mathematical symbols, such as + and -, in logic. Using these symbols made the equations easier to understand. They helped to get rid of any confusion. Boolean searches use operators the same way. That's why his name is used to describe this way of searching on the Web.

Quotes (""). Putting quotes around any keywords tells the search engine to look for these words exactly as you typed them. Using quotes helps when you're searching for a specific name or phrase because it keeps the words together. For example, if you're looking for information about the American Cancer Society, type "American Cancer Society" in the search box. This way only sites specifically mentioning the American Cancer Society will be in your results. Otherwise, you'll have to sift through millions of sites that have either the words American, cancer, or society in them.

Asterisk (*). An asterisk used in a keyword search is called a "wildcard." You can put the wildcard at the front or end of any word. Use the wildcard if you aren't sure about the spelling of a word in your search. However, try to get as close to the spelling of the word as you can. Don't oversimplify! Say you're looking for information on the Internal Revenue Service. However, you don't know how to spell it correctly. So you type "inter*" into the search field. Wow! That returned millions of hits! It would take a long time to find the Internal Revenue Service in that list. A better way to use the asterisk would be to enter all of the words you do know how to spell into the search field. Then use the wildcard with any word that you are unsure about, such as "internal reven* service."

Parentheses (). These work in searches just like in math. Keywords in parenthesis are kept together and handled before any keywords not in parentheses. Any keywords that you put in parentheses will be considered more important than other keywords you use.

Another helpful hint is to always use capital letters when using operators. That's how search engines know that they are operators and not just other keywords. Most search engines, but not all, understand keyword operators. Some build any usable operators into drop-down menus for easy use. Others will have search "options" or "advanced search" listed next to the search field box. All of these ways to make a search more specific will help you use your time on the Web more wisely.

Search engines have been getting easier to use in the last few years. Some can even answer actual questions. In the future, operators might become outdated. However, for now they're an easy way to make better searches. Look at each search engine's Help features for information and help on searching. We'll discuss the features of each search engine in detail later in this chapter.

Digging Through the Megadirectories

As we pointed out in Chapter 2, nearly all search services have directories. Use directories when you are just browsing through a topic. Some of the information that you find will not surprise you. However, the fun part of using directories is taking a look at the stuff that you didn't expect.

Digging through the levels of a megadirectory is like following clues to buried treasure. Suppose that you are taking the President's Physical Fitness Test in gym class. This national program takes a look at the benefits of exercise. You get interested in this topic and decide to look for more information online. If you decide to look in a megadirectory, your search would go like this.

1. Open your search service. You will probably want to use a service that has a good directory such as AltaVista, Ask Jeeves for Kids, Excite, Google, Kaboose, KidsClick!, MetaCrawler, Yahoo!, or Yahooligans!

2. You will see a list of topics. Look them over and pick a few that might have information on the benefits of exercise. Your first choice should probably be Health. Other possibilities might be Lifestyle, Kids & Family, Sports & Recreation, or Hobbies & Interests.

3. Click on Health. A new list of topics—the entries on this second list are called "subcategories"— appears. In each megadirectory, there will be different subcategories under each main heading. If one directory doesn't give you the information you need, try another.

4. Scroll to the bottom of the subcategories. Under this list you might find links to some related Web sites. The pages that these links take you to could have the information that you need. However, not all subcategory lists will include links.

5. Look at the subcategories. Look for topics that will have information on the benefits of exercise. Good choices might be Exercise, Fitness, or General Health. Think about your treasure hunt. Are any of these topics clues that will lead you to the treasure?

6. Choose Fitness. Under this subcategory, there might be a lot of sites for gyms and personal trainers that won't help you in your hunt. However, some of the Web sites here look an awful lot like treasure:

What Are These Percentages?

Many search engines rank the sites that they list by using percentile scores. These numbers mean something a little different at each search engine. Generally, if the keyword that you are searching for is in the page's title or comes up often on the page, it will get a high score. However, this number usually doesn't mean very much. A good hit for your search may be around 30 percent. At other times, the 99 percent rating might be right on the money. Don't worry too much about these ratings.

Guidelines for Personal Exercise Programs. This was developed by the President's Council on Physical Fitness and Sports.

Fitness Online. This site brings you continually updated features on nutrition, training, health, fitness, and more.

Shape Up America! Provides the latest information about safe weight management and physical fitness by Dr. C. Everett Koop.

If it turned out that the Fitness subcategory wasn't a good choice, you could have used your Back button to move back to the Health level. Each directory keeps track of the path you follow through its levels. You can see where you've been by looking at this history in one of the pull-down menus at the top of each page (sometimes called "History" in the "Go" menu).

Search Fruitfully

The following megadirectories and search engines were originally mentioned in Chapter 2. These are some of the most popular, useful sites to use when searching for information. Each search service has neat features that make it different from the others. Try them all to find out which ones you like to use the best. Remember that different sites provide different links, so you may want to use more than one when doing your research.

AltaVista. This site is a powerful search engine with some interesting features. AltaVista also has a searchable index. You can search for Web sites, Images, MP3s, Videos, Directories, and News. AltaVista was the first to launch Image, Audio, and Video search capabilities.

Here are some of the top features you'll see at AltaVista.

- The settings are interchangeable. You can choose to have a detailed description, the URL listed, the size and language provided, and translations of useful links or the site. You can also choose to have AltaVista highlight the search term in the results or provide a different number of results per page (the fewer, the faster). This might come in handy if you're using a dial-up modem.

- You can search for images rather than Web sites. If you're doing a report on the Eiffel Tower and are looking for black-and-white pictures of the tower, you can easily find them at AltaVista. Select Images at the top of the page and choose Black and White under the Color option. You can also pick what size you want the image to be and where AltaVista should try to find the image (you can choose from a variety of options, such as the Movies, News, and the Web).

Ask Jeeves for Kids. Ask Jeeves for Kids is a natural-language search engine. This means you can simply type in a question rather than try to find specific keywords. You don't have to struggle with finding the right words to find whatever it is you're searching for.

Here are some of the site's top features.

- There's a link to a Fun & Games area on the left-hand side where you can find answers to questions such as "Where can I play crossword puzzles?" or "How do video games work?" You don't even have to type in a question.

- There's a big pile of books on the right side of the home page that links you to places where you can find common homework help. Choose from such topics as science, astronomy, or history.

- One fun thing to do is to watch the Peek screen to see what kinds of questions other kids are asking. If you see something that interests you, click on the Ask button. You'll get the same answer as the kid who asked the question.

Excite. This site's home page sure offers a lot of services. The search engine and directory indexes are found at the top of the page. Other features include news, computers, sports, and even your local weather forecast. You can personalize Excite so that when you open it, you'll see only the news and information that you want to see. This benefit is free, but make sure to check with your parents before signing up. Excite will even find you local events such as concerts, sports events, and shows. Sign up as an Excite member to take advantage of these services.

Here are some of this site's exciting features.

- The Excite directory lists more than 20 popular categories of Web sites. Clicking on each category brings up a list of subcategories—which Excite calls departments—and more. You'll also find news headlines, chat rooms, bulletin boards, and related readings on your topic. Check out the Travel category. You'll find links to areas all over the world, including the Caribbean, Europe, even Antarctica!

- Excite uses several search engines to find what it is you are looking for. It examines search engines such as Google, Yahoo!, Ask Jeeves, and Overture to find Web sites for you. After you type in your keywords, you can choose to have Excite list the results according to each individual search engine or by relevance.

- The Advanced Search and Preference features offer you a variety of search options. Some of these options are in pull-down menus while others require you to type in your preferences. Without ever typing a Boolean operator you can include and exclude words and phrases.

- Ever wonder what other people in the world are searching for? Excite offers an interesting feature called SearchSpy where you can do just that. Select the Filtered option, and you can see a running list of all keywords people are searching for. You can also click on these words to view Excite's results.

Google. Google is a favorite search engine for a lot of people. And for good reason. Most of the time, you can find the best sites fastest with Google. That's because of the way Google ranks the Web sites it presents. The top sites are the ones that have the most other sites linking to them.

Here are some top features you can find at Google.

- Using the search engine feature is very simple. All you need to do is type in your keywords. Click on Google Search, and you'll receive a list of all the sites they can find, rated from most to least popular. Or, you can click on the I'm Feeling Lucky button. That will take you directly to whatever site is rated number one.

- If pictures are what you're looking for, click on the Images tab, and put in your keywords. Google will find a bunch of online pictures with your words in their titles.

- Google ignores common words such as *where, the,* and *how* that slow down your search without improving the results.

- If you want to search for synonyms in addition to your search term, place the tilde sign (~) immediately in front of your search term.

Kaboose. Kaboose is a kid-friendly search engine where you can find links to anything from ecards, brainteasers, even entertainment gossip! There are also links at the top of the page to other Kaboose-sponsored sites such as FunSchool for Kids, Zeeks for Teens, and KidsDomain for Families.

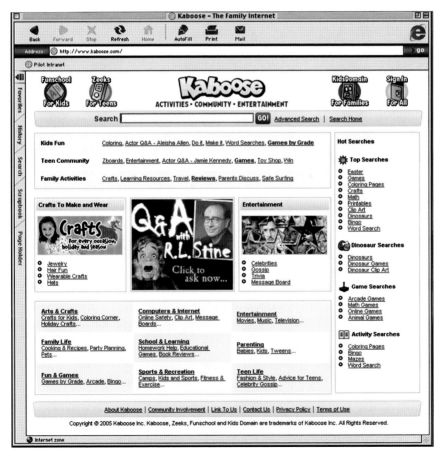

Kaboose's home page has loads of search options.

Climb on board these features at Kaboose.

- The Advanced Search feature is very basic: You can search for all of these words, the exact phrase, or any of these words.

- There are nine main categories called Arts & Crafts, Computers & Internet, Entertainment, Family Life, School & Learning, Shopping, Fun & Games, Sports & Recreation, and Teenstyle. There are also broader sections at the top including Kids Fun, Teen Community, and Family Activities.

- When you want to read reviews of some kid-oriented toys, books, video games, and DVDs, you are taken to another Web site that is part of the Kaboose Network. This Web site is called Kids Domain, and you can find reviews submitted by kids just like you! There are also more than 10,000 pages of games, crafts, and holiday activities.

KidsClick! KidsClick! is a Web site designed entirely by librarians. This search engine will come in handy when you're working on reports and need to find information. The more than 600 subjects are listed by category, or if you know what you're looking for, you can search alphabetically.

Here are some features found at KidsClick!

- If you're familiar with the Dewey decimal system (a way to classify books designated by a three-digit number usually found in libraries), you can search for your subjects that way. Simply click the link at the bottom of the page that says, "What does this page look like through a Librarian's Eyes?"

- If you're confused on the many search options out there, KidsClick! offers a search lesson. Click on the link at the top of the page to go to the KidsClick!

What Are We Searching Here?

Where are search engines really searching? Do they search the *whole* Web? Not really. Each engine has its own list of sites. When you ask for a search, you are only searching that list. Some services, such as Yahoo!, try to have the largest, most complete list. Others, such as Excite, only list the sites that they think are the best. On the other hand, MetaCrawler uses the lists from other services as their list. Sometimes the Web sites overlap.

But most search services have their own list of Web sites that they search in. That's why the same search on different search engines will get you different results. Even searching for the same thing on different days using the same search engine can get different results. (Remember that the Web is changing all the time!)

So, when you tell a search engine to search the Web, you're really telling it to search its index of the Web.

World of Word Searching. Here you'll learn about operators, spelling, and using pictures or numbers to find what you're searching for.

MetaCrawler. Unlike some search engines, MetaCrawler does not have its own index of the Web. It sends your search to several other search services such as About, Ask Jeeves, Google, LookSmart, Yahoo!, and others. MetaCrawler asks these other engines to find hits and then organizes them for you. This makes MetaCrawler a little slower than other search engines. But the way that it is set up gives you a very complete search.

- Since MetaCrawler uses several search engines to find your information, you may receive many suggestions. In order to organize these results, you can have Meta-Crawler list your results by relevance or by search engine.

- There is a list of the top six most popular searches on MetaCrawler. If any of the words interest you, simply click on the keyword and you're taken to a number of links where you can find out more information.

Yahoo! This is one of the most widely used search engines with more than 345 million users worldwide as of January 2005. Yahoo! is also growing every day! This is both good news and bad news. The good news is that you can find almost anything you want in Yahoo! The bad news is that you may need to dig through a lot of junk to find it. Use these Yahoo! tips to help you dig faster.

Here are some tips when searching with Yahoo!

- Look under each main category link on the Yahoo! home page. See those links? Those are shortcuts links. They link to the most popular subcategories in Yahoo! Clicking on these links takes you directly to that subcategory page. That way, you save clicks and get to browse third-level categories and links right away.

- After entering keywords and selecting Search, you'll see the Yahoo! search results page. The first items Yahoo! returns to you are matches to its sponsors. You'll find the real results starting after the links listed in the light-blue box. The URL where you can find your keyword at is also listed after the description of the site.

Yahooligans! The cool part about Yahooligans! is that it's especially designed for kids! All of the stuff in Yahooligans! has been checked out and approved especially for young Web users. That way you will get a manageable number of sites to explore in each topic, and you don't have to worry about stumbling onto a site that wasn't meant for kids.

Here's what you can find at Yahooligans!

- There's a directory listing Web sites about almost anything that interests you. But you don't always have to dig through the directory. On the left side of the home page you'll see a lot of favorite areas for fun and learning, such as games, jokes, and a list of cool sites.

- In the Ask Earl section, you can ask questions of Earl, the Yahooligans! answer guy, and see what interesting questions other kids have asked.

- For fun, answer the Yahooligans! poll at the right on the home page and let other kids know what you think. You can also check out their answers.

Keep on Seeking!

Searching the Web can be hard. The more you work with these search services, the better you will get. At first you may think that you are on a wild goose chase. But if you follow these easy hints and tips, and keep at it, you'll be a super Web sleuth sooner than you expect! Sometimes people really can find a needle in a haystack—if they have the knack and a plan of attack.

In the next chapter we will take a look at how to become a better student in general. Now that we have the Web basics down, we need to make sure our study habits and school skills are up to par. Then we will finally be able to put all of our new Web skills to good use. Using the World Wide Web to help with schoolwork really can be fun. After a while, you might even forget that you're actually doing schoolwork!

Study Skills and Test Taking

Learning to study is a lot like learning how to ride a bike. It takes a while and a lot of practice. And sometimes you fall down and scrape your knee. But don't get discouraged. Once you're a good bike rider—or student—you just keep getting better. A good bike rider, like a good Web surfer, can go a lot of places and learn new things. The same is true of learning how to study and take tests.

This chapter doesn't have much to do with the Web, but it will help you become a better student. Just like you can't put a roof on a house before the walls are up, you can't use the Web to help you in your schoolwork until you know the basics of being the best student that you can be! Learning how to be a good student, just like working on the World Wide Web, is best taken one step at a time.

Learning Styles

Being aware of how you learn best will help you study, and eventually, take tests better. We don't all learn the same way! Which way do you think that you learn things?

Visual learners. These types of students learn something by seeing it. If you're a visual learner, once you see or read information, you'll probably know and remember it.

Aural learners. "Aural" means "of or related to the ear." This type of student learns things best by hearing them. If you're an aural learner, once you hear information, you'll probably remember it. Aural learners can listen to a teacher's lecture and remember and understand what they have said.

Verbal learners. These people need to say information out loud to remember it. Reciting homework and lessons is very helpful to verbal learners.

Lexicographic learners. Boy, that sounds fancy! Don't worry— it's not that complicated. These people are drawn to written language. They need to write down stuff in order to learn and should always take really detailed notes.

Try to pay attention and see how you learn best. Think about your vocabulary words. Do you need to read the words and definitions to learn them? Can you remember them after you or the teacher has read them out loud? Maybe you need to write them down in order to understand them.

Being aware of how you learn best can make studying easier. Try these styles and see how they work for you. One style might be just right, or you might try a combination of styles.

Getting Organized

You can't learn to ride a bike without the right equipment. It's the same with studying. For bike riding, you need a bicycle, a helmet, pads, patience, and so on. You need to have the right tools for studying success, too.

Organization is important. It will be pretty hard to do your homework if:

- You forgot what the assignment is.

- You leave your books at school.

- You aren't sure about what you should do for the assignment.

- You brought home the wrong papers.

- Your books or other materials have been misplaced.

Let's look at some simple organization tools and tips that will help improve your study habits.

Go-Home Folder. Keeping a "Go-Home Folder" will help you keep your assignments organized. Use a sturdy, two-pocket folder—plastic is best so that it won't be ruined if it gets wet. Mark the left-side pocket as the "To Do" pocket. Put any homework worksheets there. You'll also keep your "Assignment Log" there. (We'll talk about that in a minute.) Put anything that needs to go home in your To Do pocket: permission slips, notices for Mom and Dad, or anything else that needs to go home with you. That way, before you leave school, you only need to check one place to see that you have everything. Label the right side of the folder "Done." Put finished homework, signed permission slips and tests, and anything that has to go back to school in the Done pocket.

Assignment Log. Keep a small notepad in your Go-Home Folder to serve as your "Assignment Log." In each class, write down any homework assignments in your Assignment Log. Before you go home, check your Assignment Log to make sure that you have all of the materials that you need for each task in your folder or book bag.

Assignments Calendar. Keep this in your study place at home. Or, you might want to keep this reminder in a family-use area, such as the kitchen, where both you and your parents will see it. Mark down any long-term projects—such as reports—in your "Assignments Calendar." Then, break up the assignment into chunks. For instance, you could divide the project into steps such as "research," "rough draft," and "final draft." Mark due dates for those steps on your assignments calendar. That way, these jobs will become part of your homework routine. You won't be pressured at the last minute to do the whole thing (which isn't any fun).

Kory is a sixth grader. She is a smart girl, but her grades aren't very good. Kory and her parents and teachers are sure that she could easily earn better grades. When she does her homework, it is usually done well. However, she forgets to bring some of her assignments home almost every day. Last week, she didn't hand in a social studies report on time because she forgot that it was due. Her locker and backpack are really messy. Often, she loses papers and can't find anything quickly. Her guidance counselor suggested using a Go-Home Folder, an Assignment Log, and an Assignments Calendar to help her keep track of her homework.

Kory and her mom bought a folder, an assignment pad, and a calendar. They set up the Go-Home Folder and put the Assignment Log in it. They hung the Assignments Calendar in the kitchen on the refrigerator.

After two weeks of using her new organization system, Kory made a lot of progress. Every school day, she wrote her homework for each subject on her pad. Then she put any handouts in the folder to bring home. At home, long-term assignments, such as her science project on the water cycle, were listed on the calendar. Kory didn't become a perfect student overnight, though. Sometimes she would forget to bring the Go-Home Folder home. But that doesn't happen very often anymore. And her grades are getting better already! Kory says she feels as if school is easier now.

Study Environment

Some kids think that they can (and too often, do) study anywhere: on the floor of their bedroom with music blasting; at the kitchen table, surrounded by brothers and sisters scarfing snacks and talking on the telephone; or sprawled out in the living room with the TV on.... Sorry kids—it doesn't work. Research shows that a good study environment is very important to your success in school.

Let's take a look at your study environment. Do you:

- Study in one regular location designed for studying?

- Study in a place free from noise and interference (TV, loud music, talking, people doing other things)?

- Study in a well-lit place free from visual distractions (posters, TV, pictures, or hobbies)?

- Study in a comfortable (but not too relaxed) place?

- Have all of your study materials in your study location?

You should answer "yes" to all of these questions. Studying in one set place helps you work. Just like your mind knows that it's time to sleep when you're in bed, if you have a usual study spot, your mind will get into a "study mode" when you are there. You will be able to study better.

Noise and visual distractions hurt your studying. If you study in your room, close the door to block out noise. Leave the TV and your brothers and sisters on the other side. Make a "Do Not Disturb" sign and hang it on your doorknob. Visual distractions should be moved out of sight. You don't want to be looking right at anything that might take your attention away from your studies. Your chair, desk (or table), and light should be just right, so that you are comfortable and can see well, but so that you don't really notice them. Your study area should sort of blend into the rest of the room and feel natural—  no distractions—so that you can focus on your work.

Keeping your study area organized means that you can get right to work—and finish faster. You should always have just what you need when you are studying.

Keep these important supplies on hand:

- Paper (wide-ruled)
- Pens and pencils
- Ruler
- School notebooks
- School folders
- Reference materials (such as a dictionary, thesaurus, and encyclopedia)
- Calculator

Set goals for yourself to improve your study environment. Remember that nobody can become a perfect student overnight. Just take it one step at a time. If you really try to improve your study area and start studying better, you will see an improvement at school.

Kory used to study on the living room floor. She liked to watch her after-school television program and have a snack while doing her homework. Sometimes, Kory would get too interested in what was on TV, and she would just stop studying. Other days, she would keep working while she watched TV, but it would take a long time—too long.

The TV and her brother and sister constantly interrupted her. Kory was tired of spending so much time on her homework. She began to really dislike schoolwork. And Kory's teacher didn't like the crumpled pages Kory was handing in for homework. Sometimes they had doodles on them. Sometimes they even had crumbs and spills from Kory's snack.

Kory's parents decided that her desk in her room was a better place for doing homework. Now, after school, Kory comes home, eats her snack in the kitchen, and then goes to her room to do homework. She and her parents have set up a good study area in her room. And, since Kory doesn't want to miss her television program, she sets up the VCR to tape it while she studies. Then she watches the program later, after her homework has been finished (and she can fast-forward through those annoying commercials!).

Her desk is against a wall that doesn't have any posters or pictures on it. She tries to keep her desk neat and stocked with supplies. She also decided to move her Assignments Calendar from the kitchen to her new study area. And she is only allowed to listen to quiet music during study time (she likes to listen to soft music that doesn't have any words while she studies—sometimes she even forgets that it is playing). Kory has found that it takes her a lot less time to do her homework. And it seems easier, too, now that she can concentrate better. Best of all, Kory's grades are continuing to go up!

Taking Good Notes

When sitting in class or reading a book for school, it is very important to know how to take good notes. That way, you have a record of important ideas that you can look at later to help in studying. Or, if you forget something that the teacher said, you can always look at your notes to see what you forgot.

We take notes in order to:

- Have a written record to review.

- Force us to pay attention.

- Organize the speaker's words or the text you are reading.

- Have a summary of a classroom discussion or book and to practice lexicographic learning (see page 63).

It's a fact that most people forget half of what they hear or read within one hour! Taking notes is important.

Taking notes is a skill you will probably use for the rest of your life. You will need to take notes throughout high school and college. Plus, when you grow up, you may want to take notes at a meeting during work, for a community organization, or a club. The note-taking skills that you develop now will last a lifetime.

So, how do you take good notes? There are several techniques for taking notes. One of them may work well for you. It is important to remember to take notes in a way that works for you—don't just take notes the way your best friend does. You might even come up with a method of your own!

Outlining

When you use an outline to take notes, you list main ideas and put details under them. This breaks up important points so that you can look at them more closely.

Mapping

Mapping is a graphic way of taking notes. It is making a picture to explain the topic. For example, if your map was an apple tree, the trunk would have the topic, the branches would be the main ideas, and the apples hanging from the branches would be the supporting details. Lots of pictures can be used for mapping. See if you can think of any.

Venn Diagram

This is named after John Venn, the English mathematician who came up with the idea. A Venn diagram is used to compare and contrast information. Use it to study any two people, places, or things. A Venn diagram is made of two (sometimes more) intersecting circles. Label each circle for one

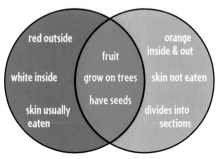

red outside
white inside
skin usually eaten

fruit
grow on trees
have seeds

orange inside & out
skin not eaten
divides into sections

Apples   **Oranges**

of the two things you are comparing. Any information that both things have in common goes in the center section, where both circles meet. The characteristics that describe only one of the things that you are comparing or contrasting go on the side labeled for that one.

Clues

Always listen closely to what the speaker is saying. These clues will let you know when something important is coming.

- Anything the teacher tells you to write down should be in your notes.

- Anything the teacher writes on the board during a lesson should be in your notes.

- Anything the teacher repeats should be in your notes. Listen for words such as "again," "in other words," and "to repeat."

- Anything the teacher emphasizes should be included in your notes. Listen for words such as "the most important," "remember that," "pay particular attention to," and "the main idea is."

- Examples should be included in your notes to explain a point. Listen for words such as "for example," "such as," "like," and "for instance."

- During the summary, make sure that you have noted all of the important points. Listen for words such as "in conclusion," "to sum up," and "as a result."

Reading Effectively

Reading your textbooks can be hard. With pages and pages to read, sometimes you can forget the beginning before you get to the end. A method called SQ3R can help you get the most out of your reading time. SQ3R stands for Skim, Question, Read, Recite, and Review.

Let's take a look at how SQ3R works.

Skim. First, skim what you are going to read. This means that before reading the assigned text, you should go through it and take a quick look at what you will be reading about. This gives you an overview of the reading. Pay attention to:

- Chapter and section headings
- Introductions
- Sidebars
- Charts and tables
- Picture captions
- Summaries
- End of chapter questions

Question. It is a good idea to question what you read. As you read, make each chapter title and heading into a question. Jot down the question in your notes. As you read, look for the answers to your questions. Pay careful attention to the main points and ideas as you read. The questions will give you a good idea what to look for.

Read. As you read, make sure to look for the answers to any questions you had. Make a note of anything that you don't understand as you are reading. Look up unfamiliar words in your dictionary. And when in class, never be afraid to ask questions. Chances are that you aren't the only one in the class who doesn't understand a difficult concept. By asking questions, you not only help yourself to learn, but the rest of the class as well!

Recite. Try to say the answers to the questions you had from memory (without looking at the answers!). Think about other examples of similar topics related to your question. This will help you remember the answers in the future.

Note Taking Dos and Don'ts

Do have two pens for taking notes. Ink is easier to read than pencil. You'll have an extra pen if one runs out of ink.

Do use wide-ruled paper and skip a line between each point. This leaves plenty of room to add details later (so have plenty of paper on hand).

Do label the page with the subject and date.

Do tune in to the speaker.

Do ask questions if you don't understand.

Do write down main ideas.

Don't try to write every word your teacher says.

Don't worry about handwriting—as long as you can read it.

Review. When you are finished, review what you have read. Go over it either in your mind, out loud, or on paper. Try to summarize the material (list all of the main points). Review the questions you wrote down and be sure that you know the answers. Go back and reread any points that aren't clear.

Active Study Strategies

How do you usually study? If you're like most students, you look over your notes or reread the textbook. Unfortunately, these study strategies often lead to boredom and daydreaming—even dozing! Study strategies that require action also require attention. Don't let studying be a bore! Some active study strategies include:

Reciting

- Explain the topic out loud and in your own words.

- Teach a lesson on the topic to someone else.

- Ask and answer questions that might be on a test about the topic out loud.

Writing and Remembering

Make and use a set of flash cards for anything that you
need help remembering

- Write the question on one side of the card and the
  answer on the other.

- Try to answer the questions out loud.

- As you go, make two piles of cards: one for the
  answers you know and one for the answers you don't
  know yet.

- Keep going over the cards you don't know, saying the
  answers out loud.

- Go through the entire pile again to make sure you
  know them all.

Visualizing

- Close your eyes and picture what you are trying to
  learn.

- Create pictures and charts to describe what you are
  learning.

- Go online and visit Web sites about the topic you are
  studying. You can find pictures, maps, charts, and
  more online.

Try all of these techniques and see what works for you.
Different people need to study differently. The trick is to
keep trying until you find a system that works for you.

Test Preparation

Taking tests can make some kids tense. They worry about
knowing the answers to the questions. Even kids who study a
lot get worried about tests. But by taking good notes, doing
your homework, and reviewing material that will be on the
test, you will do fine. And remember: Relax!

To help prepare for tests:

- Listen to what the teacher reviews, and ask what you should study.

- Review your class notes.

- Look over your homework assignments.

- Look at the textbook again, and check out the summaries and important points.

Once you know what to study, get ready for the test!

- Use your study area.

- Hang your Do Not Disturb sign.

- Organize your notes and materials.

Then get to work!

- Review, visualize, and recite your material.

- Test yourself to see what you know.

- Make and use flash cards.

- Study with a friend and test each other.

Test-Taking Pointers

Tests are a fact of life in school. Spelling and math tests, essay exams, college entrance exams—these are all important tests that you will have to take. While preparation and studying are the best ways to get ready for tests, there is more you can do. There are some techniques that will help you score better. Think of this as learning how to take a test. Here are some general guidelines that you can use when taking any test.

1. As soon as the test papers are distributed, jot down any words, facts, or formulas that you might not remember (on scratch paper if you are allowed to use it).

2. Read the directions very carefully.

3. Skim over the entire test.

4. Now read the test. Answer questions that you know the answers to right away. Circle any questions that you are leaving blank.

5. Go through the test again. This time, work on questions that you left blank the first time.

6. *Do not* change any answers you marked unless you are *absolutely sure* they are wrong. Your first impulse is usually the correct one.

7. If wrong and blank answers are counted the same, guess the answers for any questions that you don't know. However, sometimes wrong answers are penalized. If a blank answer is zero points, but a wrong one is minus one, don't guess.

8. Use any remaining time to review your answers.

Not all tests are the same. Some different types of tests are: true/false, matching, multiple choice, and essay.

True/False Tests

This type of a test can be tricky. Typically, sentences will be listed about topics that you have been studying, and you have to figure out if the sentence is true or false. Use these guidelines when taking true/false tests:

- Mark "true" only if a statement is completely true.

- Mark "false" if any part of a statement is false.

- Words such as "all," "always," "never," "none," "only," "best," and "worst" *usually* make a statement false.

- Words such as "often," "probably," "sometimes," and "usually" *often* make a statement true.

- Do not change your first answer unless you're positive it was wrong.

Matching Tests

This type of test asks you to match the correct word with a sentence or to match two ideas that are similar. When taking matching tests remember to:

- Match the ones you know first and cross them out.

- Go through the others. Eliminate any that are obviously wrong. (Sometimes there are more answers than questions. Remember to count to make sure.)

- See if the last step left you with only one answer. If so, make that match.

- When you have eliminated all of your options, guess.

- Use each item only once unless the directions tell you otherwise.

Multiple Choice

These tests list several answers for one question. Your job is to mark the correct answer. Sometimes this can be tricky! Read each question and answer closely. Keep these points in mind:

- After reading the question, first try to answer it in your head without reading any of the listed choices. Then check to see if one of the listed choices matches your answer; if so, mark it.

- If you don't know the answer, eliminate any that you know are wrong. Also eliminate any silly answers to any of the questions.

- Pick the best answer from the remaining ones.

Essay Tests

Some people really dislike essay tests. Writing your own answer, instead of choosing the answer from a list, can be scary. However, if you have done your studying and stay calm while taking the test, you will do fine. Remember to:

- Read all of the questions and mark the ones that you know the answers to—if you have a choice. Sometimes, for example, you will be asked to write essays for three out of five questions.

- Make an outline or map of the main idea and supporting details.

- Check the clock to make sure you have enough time. Don't use up all of your time on the first question.

- Cover only the points asked for in the question. (Don't write about George Washington as President if the question asks about his role in the Revolutionary War, which happened before he was elected President.)

- Start with a good topic sentence.

- End with a good summary sentence.

Learning how to take tests well doesn't have to stop after the test is over. After you get a test back, read over any comments carefully. Try to understand any mistakes that you made. Ask your teacher if you have any questions.

Keep at It

Putting together successful study strategies takes time—and some work. Try some of these and see what works for you. The right strategy will make studying easier for you and help your grades and understanding of your schoolwork. And at the same time you will develop good skills that will help you in all kinds of things in your life—including using the World Wide Web!

Research and Report Writing

Writing a good report requires getting your act together. First, you may need to pick a topic (unless one has been assigned to you). Then you'll have to gather information and make an outline. Writing the rough draft and editing it comes next. Then the final draft can be composed. Also, you may want to find some pictures, charts, maps, or other visual information to jazz up your report. The Web can be a great resource for report writing in several ways.

- You can use the Web to help you pinpoint a topic that interests you.

- Researching on the Web gives you immediate access to a lot of information.

- Hunting on the Web for extra resources will lead you to great clip art, graphics, maps, charts, video and audio clips, and more.

Follow these steps for report-writing success.

1. Choose a topic. First, you will probably select a general topic. Usually, this will be something related to the unit you're studying in class. Your general topic might be the American Revolution, space travel, or energy. Many students try to write their reports using these broad subjects. However, a successful report needs to have more of a narrow focus. Better topics would be: the Boston Tea Party or General George Washington, the history of the space shuttle program or *Apollo 11*'s voyage to the moon, or solar energy or making your home more energy efficient.

2. Locate resources. A big part of writing reports is doing research. You need to find good information to include in your report. Of course, the library is a great place to find books, reference materials, and periodicals. Use the Web, too. It will give you access to publications your library might not stock. Plus, you get to visit sites for agencies and organizations. What would a report on the history of the space shuttle be like without a visit to NASA and the Smithsonian National Air and Space Museum? Let the Web broaden your horizons. And the information you can find online is often much more current than information in books printed years ago (very appropriate for the space shuttle report!). Remember to mark sites you might want to use in your report as Bookmarks. Make a special folder just for this report and put all your links there. Then you'll be able to find them easily when you're ready to take notes. Plus, if you need to write a bibliography, you'll have a good record of your sources.

3. Take notes. Use the reading techniques we discussed on pages 68–72 to gather information about your topic. Take a lot of notes. It's always easier to leave extra things out later than to try to stretch a skimpy report.

4. Develop an outline. This forces you to organize your notes. You can use any of the other techniques we talked about on pages 69–70. Try to find four to seven main points to write about under your main topic. These will be your subtopics. Then, your notes should fit under the subtopics. Make sure each subtopic is just a word or two—a phrase at most. Under the subtopics, write the supporting details and other information. If you're using mapping, make a new map for each subtopic and fill in details from your online and traditional (library) research. If you have some blank spots in your outline, go back online or to the library. (For detailed online search techniques, see pages 46–54.)

5. Write a rough copy. After your teacher has said that you have enough information, sharpen your pencil—or boot up the computer. It's time to write. Your first paragraph is called

How the Web Can Help

If you have a general topic in mind—energy, for example—see if the Web can help narrow it down. Use a Web site that has a big directory—such as Yahoo! or Excite. Type "energy" into the search field box or click on its category link. You'll probably see dozens of subcategories there. Some will have information on things that you know about, such as solar power, wind power, or energy efficiency. Other topics may sound pretty weird, such as sonoluminescence, which is—as strange as this sounds—the release of light by bubbles in a liquid that has been excited by sound! (There are several Web sites on this topic, if you're interested.) Browsing around these categories is a great way to find a topic.

the introduction. This is where you tell your readers what the report is going to be about. The main part of the report is called the body. This is where you write about the subtopics. Use each subtopic or map to write a new paragraph. Make sure that you follow your outline. If at any time you think that you need more information, go back online or to the library. The final paragraph is called the conclusion. This should sum up the report and restate why your topic is important.

As you write the rough draft, don't worry about spelling, grammar, or handwriting. Just keep writing. Keep your concentration. Skip lines (or make the copy double-spaced on the computer) so you have room for corrections.

6. Edit the rough copy. As you look over your report, ask yourself these questions:

- Is the title of my report interesting?

- Does the introduction explain the title and what the report will be about?

- Does the introduction make readers want to read on?

- Does the body of the report provide detailed information on my topic?

- Does the body do what the introduction said it would?

- Does the report give factual information?

- Does the conclusion briefly sum up the report?

- Does the report give a complete picture of my topic?

You should answer "yes" to each of these questions. If not, go back and make changes to the report. Then reread and check for spelling, punctuation, and grammar.

7. Write your final copy. Be sure to double-check spelling, punctuation, and grammar. Make sure you have included all required parts of the report, such as a title page, charts, bibliography, and anything else that was required. Check neatness! Teachers don't like to read sloppy assignments.

Space Is the Place

Tyrone's fifth grade class has been studying space exploration. Now he needs to write a report on that topic. The class has discussed a lot of different things about outer space. They have learned about the Soviet space program, Alan Shepard's journey into space, the space shuttle program, and even the space station already in outer space. There is so much that Tyrone could write about that he's having a hard time deciding!

Step 1: Choose a topic. Tyrone's general topic is space exploration. At first, Tyrone was thinking about writing on the Soviet space program, astronaut training, or *Voyager*'s journey to Mars. Finally, Tyrone decided to do a biography on legendary astronaut John Glenn. When Glenn joined the crew of the Space

Shuttle *Discovery* at the age of 77, he was in the news a lot. Tyrone watched the *Discovery*'s liftoff and landing, and he followed the details of the voyage on television and the Web.

Step 2: Locate resources. First, Tyrone did some brainstorming. He thought of places where he might find information and biographies about John Glenn. After thinking a bit and writing some notes, his list included the library, NASA, and the Smithsonian National Air and Space Museum. Then Tyrone logged onto the Internet and began his initial search for information on John Glenn. His first stop was to the search engine Yahooligans! Tyrone typed in "John Glenn" in the search field box and hit Search.

Yahooligans! listed several hits for his search: a biography from World Almanac, a speech from the History Channel Glenn made after his first trip to space, transcripts from interviews with former astronauts about Glenn from Scholastic, and the home page to Glenn's political Web site.

Tyrone found a neat site from NASA where kids just like you were able to ask John Glenn questions about what it's like to be in space. These questions were asked in October 1998 while Glenn and other astronauts were aboard the space shuttle *Discovery*.

Some of the other sites looked helpful as well. The Smithsonian National Air and Space Museum had lots of information on Glenn's shuttle mission. Tyrone was learning a lot about John Glenn. For instance, Tyrone knew that Glenn was an astronaut. But he also learned that Glenn had served in World War II and had also been a U.S. senator! Some Web sites that Tyrone visited included:

- NASA Astronaut Biographies (http://www.jsc.nasa.gov/Bios)

- STS-95 Educational Downlink (http://spaceflight.nasa. gov/shuttle/archives/sts-95/eduevent.html)

- Smithsonian National Air and Space Museum
  (http://www.nasm.si.edu)

Step 3: Take notes. Tyrone printed out a lot of the pages he found. That way he could make notes right on the pages. First, he skimmed the material quickly. Then, he jotted down headings and subheadings to start making his outline.

Step 4: Develop an outline. Tyrone used the headings and subheadings to create main topics for his outline. He used the following topics, in this order, as his main points.

1. Personal Information and Education

2. Military Experience

3. Mercury Space Program

4. Senator John Glenn

5. STS-95 Mission

Then Tyrone found important points to list under each of these headings. These points became subtopics. He listed his research notes under each of these subtopics. Each sub-topic will become a separate paragraph in his report. He checked his many resources for more information whenever he needed to.

For example, under the Senator John Glenn heading, Tyrone listed these subheadings: Elections, Committees, and Sponsored Legislation. Each of these subheadings will be developed into a paragraph in Tyrone's report. In the Committees paragraph, for example, Tyrone will describe each of the four Senate committees that Glenn served on.

Step 5: Write a rough copy. Now it's time to turn those headings into paragraphs. Before writing anything, Tyrone took his outline into class to get his teacher's approval. Then Tyrone wrote his report using his notes and outline. He wrote quickly and didn't worry about spelling or neatness. He skipped lines so he could insert more details and make corrections easily. He referred to his outline a lot while writing.

Step 6: Edit the rough copy. Tyrone looked over his report and decided that *Biography of John H. Glenn, Jr.* wasn't a very interesting title. Borrowing some words from NASA Mission Control on STS-95, he changed the title to *An Astronaut Hero and American Legend: John Glenn.* He continued reading over the report and made a few changes to correct mistakes and make it more interesting. He reread it and corrected spelling and grammar. He even had his mom read the report, and she suggested a few other changes.

Step 7: Write the final copy. Tyrone then typed the final draft of his report on his computer. He was careful not to make mistakes. When he was finished he did a spell-check and read the report again. He double-checked the report's punctuation, spelling, grammar, and vocabulary. He had his dad take a look at the final copy as well. Tyrone was excited about what he had learned and how the report had turned out.

Oral Reports

Suppose Tyrone's teacher had assigned an oral report instead of a written report. What would Tyrone have done differently?

Actually, a lot of his preparation would have been the same. He would still have needed to pick a topic and collect resources. He would have had to take notes and develop an outline. He would have used the outline to write a rough draft and then edited that copy before writing a final copy. But instead of just handing in a printed report, Tyrone may have written notes he could refer to on note cards as he gave his oral report in front of the class. Or, he might have created an extended outline to use during his presentation.

When preparing an oral report, you need to be very familiar with your topic. Tyrone has learned a lot about John Glenn while preparing the report. But Tyrone would have to prepare notes to use while he gave the presentation (either on note cards or in the form of an outline). You can't just read a report, word for word, in front of the class. Everyone would fall asleep! He would practice presenting his oral report to some friends or his parents before getting up in front of the class so that he would be used to speaking about his topic in front of people.

Also, Tyrone would have to get some more materials to help involve his classmates in his presentation. Perhaps he would have wanted to distribute handouts or hang some pictures on the chalkboard. Here the World Wide Web really helps Tyrone. At the Smithsonian National Air and Space Museum, he could have found a picture of John Glenn's original space ship, the *Friendship 7*. At Yahooligans!, he could have found photos that were taken of Earth from the window of *Friendship 7*. Or he could have printed and distributed some of John Glenn's Senate speeches. Remember: Tyrone would have to make sure that all of the visual resources he used from the Web were okay for public use. If you are ever in doubt about the restrictions on a resource, just ask whoever is in charge of the Web site.

The Web is a valuable research tool to use when writing reports and developing presentations. Current information, as well as historical data, is really at your fingertips. And the Web is a great resource for finding cool pictures and other graphics that can dress up your reports. But it is not just a great resource for big projects. It is also a very valuable tool to use when you need help with everyday homework, as we'll see in the next chapter.

Homework and Other Projects

Homework. What is interesting about homework? You get assignments, you go home, you do them, and you hand them in, right? How could the Web help with homework?

You would probably be surprised at all the homework help waiting for you on the Web. You just need to read the signs and find the right exit on the Information Superhighway. We're going to point out those important signs for you, so keep reading and keep your eyes peeled!

Pretty much every teacher assigns homework, so it must be important. Teachers assign homework to help students:

- Practice new skills that were learned in class. Practice helps you remember what you learned.
- Keep old skills fresh.
- Review what you learned in class.
- Learn new things not covered in class.
- Prepare for new lessons.

Did you know that homework helps teachers too? By assigning homework, teachers:

- Check how well you understand their lessons.
- Discover what areas you need help in.
- Identify areas the class needs to review.

Homework Tips

Before we jump back into the Web, let's go over a few general homework hints that will help you.

Pick a set study time. By doing your homework at the same time every day, your brain learns to get into a "homework mode" then. You probably get hungry and sleepy at around the same times each day. You should study at the same time each day, too.

Make your study time a definite period of time. If you know you have to spend at least 45 minutes in your study area, you won't feel the need to rush through your work. You may want to give yourself a little free time when you first get home to relax and have a snack. Don't wait too long to start though. You need plenty of time to do your homework well.

Set up a study area. Remember when we described an ideal study area a few chapters back? Take another look at pages 65–68 to see what a good study area should be like, and compare it to your current study area. Try to make sure your study area is as close to that description as possible. You'll thank yourself (and your teachers and parents will as well!).

Do the hardest stuff first. Early in your homework session, you'll probably have the most energy. This is the time to get the hardest assignments—or ones you like the least—out of the way. Save the assignments you like for last—sort of like homework dessert (like a nice, long-division éclair!).

Take a break. You should take a break from the books every 15–20 minutes (You probably can handle this...). Stand up and give your body a long stretch. Walk around and maybe drink some juice. When you get back to your desk, you'll have more energy. Your concentration will be back, and you'll get more work done.

Ask for help. If you don't understand something, ask your parents or an older sibling to explain it. If that doesn't get you anywhere, check out some of the Web sites that are listed on page 89 and page 91 for help. Sometimes it takes a day or so to get an answer, though. If you get stuck and can't finish your homework on time, don't freak out! Just explain it to your teacher the next day. The most important thing to remember is to really give homework your best shot.

Using the World Wide Web is always fun and interesting. But how can we use it to help with homework assignments? Let's find out! The following sites have all sorts of homework hints and help to give.

Get Responsible!

Even though you're a kid, and you don't really have a "job" (like grown-ups do), going to school and doing homework is kind of like your job. It's something that you have to do every school day and even though you have fun at school, you always do some work. Here are some common excuses and solutions for not handing in homework.

Excuse: "My dog ate my homework."
Solution: Keep your homework in your Go-Home Folder and safely out of the reach of Poochie. Plus, make sure that Poochie has his own food and toys. That way, your vocabulary words won't look so tasty!

Excuse: "I fell asleep before I finished my homework."
Solution: Do your homework shortly after school or early in the evening so you will have enough energy to finish it. You could also do homework at school during any breaks.

Excuse: "I forgot that we had homework."
Solution: Write homework in your Assignment Log and keep it in your Go-Home Folder. Check the Log before you go home to make sure that you have everything you need.

Excuse: "No one reminded me to do it."
Solution: Homework is part of your job. Take responsibility for remembering it yourself.

Multnomah County Library Homework Center
(http://www.multcolib.org/homework) is a subject directory, containing reference sites to answer homework-related questions. The librarians at Multnomah County Library, based in Oregon, operate this site. You can even e-mail a librarian a question at their Ask Us! section. There are also links to more than 50 homework-helper sites with a sentence or two description. This will help you determine if the site will be helpful to your research.

HomeworkSpot.com (http://www.homeworkspot.com) is a homework-related site for grades K through 12 where students can find answers to many different subjects. If you have a question about language arts, math, science, social studies, arts and crafts, health and fitness, and foreign languages, just to name a few, you can find the answers here. The site is divided into elementary, middle, and high school sections to help you better locate the information.

HomeworkSpot.com also features a reference center that provides free, immediate access to many of the world's best libraries (http://www.libraryspot.com) and museums (http://www.museumspot.com). These sites are very similar to HomeworkSpot.com, so if you're familiar with the main site, you will have no problem navigating the library and museum sites.

National Geographic Homework Help (http://www.national geographic.com/homework) is maintained by *National Geographic* magazine, so you know there will be plenty of pictures, information, and homework help available. The categories are listed under subject heads, such as history/culture, animals, maps/geography, photos/art, science/nature, and places. You can click on the links listed under the subjects, or you can search the One-Stop Research area for pictures, articles, maps, and more! There are also links to the *National Geographic Kids* magazine, as well as the GeoBee Challenge, where you can try your hand at geography questions.

Projects

The Web can be a great homework partner. When you're doing projects, you can use the Web for research. You can also use it to get ideas and find stuff—such as maps, clip art, recipes, graphics, quotations, and more—to dress up your projects.

The Franklin Institute Online has a Kids Did This! Web page (http://sln.fi.edu/tfi/hotlists/kids.html). Visit it to see projects produced by kids! It's a great site to get some ideas for projects in all subject areas. Sometimes they even tell you where the kids who did these projects found their information and graphics.

Ask an Expert

Sometimes when kids get stuck they just want to find somebody who really knows their stuff to answer a few questions. When you are looking for a real pro to help you with something, check out these sites. Most let you choose from a variety of topics.

- **Ask an Expert Sites** (http://njnie.dl.stevens-tech.edu/askanexpert.html)

- **Pitsco's Ask an Expert** (http://www.askanexpert.com)

- **AllExperts.com** (http://www.allexperts.com)

There are a ton of other sites with access to experts in a variety of subjects. See pages 94–103 for more on expert information on the Web.

Get Original!

The kids in Zach's fourth grade class are writing books for a language arts unit. Zach has selected Italy as his topic. He did some research in his school library. Then, he logged on to the Internet to do some research online. He found additional

Homework Helper Sites

These are some of the best homework helper sites on the World Wide Web. Pop onto these pages when you are stuck on a homework problem, or even if you are just looking to learn something new!

TeenSpace at The Internet Public Library (http://www.ipl.org/div/teen/browse/gh0000) is a general homework help page that lists a lot of good sites that have links to all kinds of homework help.

Schoolwork Ugh! (http://www.schoolwork.org) is a directory that lists other Web sites by category. It is maintained by a friendly librarian who will answer your questions by e-mail.

B. J. Pinchbeck's Homework Helper (http://school.discovery.com/homeworkhelp/bjpinchbeck/) has more than 700 homework help links and has won many awards. Amazingly, it was put together by 11-year-old B. J. and his dad in 1996. B. J. continues to maintain the Web site and keep the links current. According to B. J., "If you can't find it here, then you just can't find it."

Homeworkhelper.com (http://www.homeworkhelper. com) is a good place to find homework helper information. There's also tutoring help in addition to specific subjects.

information about Italy, its geography, and its history. He also found really great stuff to make his report very original.

Zach started his search at KidsClick! He decided to search for maps of Italy. He opened the Geography/History/Biography directory, and he went to the Maps subdirectory. He decided to look for maps first. A site called Oddens' Bookmarks (http://oddens.geog.uu.nl) provided good information. Another helpful site was World Atlas and World Maps (http://geography.about.com/library/maps/blindex.htm) where many different types of maps were available. Zach downloaded some of the maps (see page 95 for information about downloading) that showed Italy's geography and climate and even a real picture of Italy taken from a satellite!

Next, Zach decided to add some common Italian words and expressions to the back of his book. Searching in Google, Zach was able to locate the Web site Alpha Dictionary (http://www.alphadictionary.com). This site lists almost 1,000 online dictionaries—in more than 280 languages! Zach was pretty sure that he could find an Italian-American dictionary here. The R-O-Matic Italian/English Dictionary (http://www.aromatic.com/itaeng) let Zach type in words and phrases and gave him the Italian translation. Also, if he had Italian words he needed to translate into English, he could do that here. "Cool," thought Zach, "just what I need." Word Reference (http://wordreference.com) was a site that Zach found while using the search engine AltaVista. Zach printed some pages and made some notes to add to his book.

Everyone loves Italian food, so Zach thought that some recipes would spice up his book. Zach went to Yahoo! and tried to find a category for Italian food. He started in the Society heading under the Yahoo! Web Directory and searched through the Food and Drink and Countries and Cultures subheadings until he finally found "Italian." He clicked on the Recipes link, and there he found several recipe sites. After checking through several of them, he found several recipes he thought would provide helpful information. He decided to include some recipes for Italian cookies, spaghetti and meatballs, and stuffed, cheezy calzones. He printed out the recipes to use in his book. He was positive that his teacher and friends would think they were delicious.

Zach also wanted to include some famous Italians in his book, but he wasn't sure where to find them. He tried a few search engines without any luck. He thought that Christopher Columbus was a famous Italian, so he searched directory sites—such as Yahooligans! and Excite—for "Christopher Columbus." He was hoping that one of the hits would lead him to a Web page about famous Italians. No luck there, either. Zach was beginning to get frustrated. Finally, Zach went to The Internet Public Library (http://www.ipl.org/div/askus) and sent an e-mail asking a librarian where to find a list of and information on famous Italians.

The next day, Zach got a response back—from a school librarian in Tokyo! She found some great sites for Zach. First, she told him how she found them. She did a search in AltaVista. She entered "famous + Italian" in the search box. She got three good hits from that search. One was the Italian-American Web site of New York. Another one listed Italian-American celebrities.

Zach visited all of these sites. He learned that two men who signed the Declaration of Independence were of Italian descent: Maryland's William Paca and Delaware's Caesar Rodney. He also learned that the man who supposedly captured Billy the Kid, Angelo "Charlie" Siringo, was of Italian descent. Italian-Americans invented the one-handed basketball layup and the ice cream cone, too. Zach learned about Italian-Americans who fought in the Civil War, wrote famous songs, and founded famous companies. The librarians at The Internet Public Library really came through for Zach! He remembered to send an e-mail message back to the librarian who had helped him to thank her.

Because the World Wide Web has so much information for you to check out, chances are that you will find new stuff all the time. And this will make the research you do interesting— and it will make your work interesting for other people. You can find all kinds of examples to use in projects. This will make the work you do very much your own—chances are, it won't be like any of the other projects in the class!

Online Reference Resources

Access to reference material is important. Sometimes a search of the World Wide Web isn't necessary when working on school projects. You might just want a quick overview of a subject or some important facts. Or maybe you just need to look up a word, find a map, or find synonyms for a word. When this is the case, using reference materials is your best bet.

These resources help you find information on a variety of subjects. Plus, most reference materials are very reliable and comprehensive. They are probably some of the first things to turn to for information.

- Need help with your vocabulary words? Pull out a dictionary.

- Looking for information on DNA for your science report? Grab the encyclopedia.

- Studying the mountains of Australia? Look in an atlas.

- Writing a paper and need another word for "try" (which you've already used 12 times!)? Get out your thesaurus.

There are a lot of uses for reference materials—both for school and everyday questions. Suppose that your mother swears that your baby brother never sleeps if there's a full moon. Your mom might check a calendar for the next full moon. If your dad is an avid gardener, an almanac is a valuable reference for him. And the telephone book is one reference book that people use every day.

But buying all kinds of reference books can be expensive. And sometimes you don't have time to go to the library (or would prefer to get your information from home). Luckily, today a lot of popular reference materials are online.

Downloading

After you have been searching the Web for a while, you suddenly come upon the perfect graphic for your project! After making sure that it is okay to do so, you are ready to download it. On most Web browsers, it is pretty easy to figure out how to download a Web page or graphic. Usually, you will pull down the File menu and choose Save As. In Netscape, the Save As dialog box will automatically figure out what you are trying to save (either text or an image) and will suggest how to save your information.

Then you will just need to choose where on your hard drive you want to keep the file. It is probably a good idea to create "Download" folders for each new project that you work on so you can keep your information organized. And, instead of downloading, you sometimes might want to just print the page that you are on, if you think that you won't need to keep it stored. If that is the case, all you have to do is make sure that you are on the page that you want to print and click the Print button.

Downloading is usually used to save graphics to insert into projects at a later time. Always remember to respect any copyrights that people have assigned to their work. Never take credit for anybody else's work. That's called plagiarism, which is another name for stealing. But don't worry. A lot of people on the Web want to share their work, and you can find a lot of cool, free stuff to download.

Now, let's look at some common—and helpful—reference materials that you can find and use online.

Encyclopedia Answers

An encyclopedia is a comprehensive summary of information. Some encyclopedias focus on specific topics. However, most encyclopedias cover all kinds of general information.

Why use encyclopedias on the Web? Encyclopedia volumes on the Web add bells and whistles that you won't find in the books at the library. Just like regular encyclopedias, online volumes have articles with information, but they also feature such extras as pictures, graphs, and maps. Also, encyclopedias on the Web sometimes feature video and audio clips as well as

links to other related Web sites. An online encyclopedia can really be one-stop shopping for information. Remember how heavy those volumes of reference books are? No more weight lifting! When using an encyclopedia on the Web, you just type, point, and click!

More specific online encyclopedias exist on the Web as well. For example, you can check out the Encyclopaedia of the Orient. This reference material has information about Far Eastern countries, from Algeria to Yemen. In another encyclopedia, The Encyclopedia Mythica, you can search for information on mythology and folklore from all over the world. Another example of a specific reference source is The Stanford Encyclopedia of Philosophy. This resource covers all you might need to know about philosophers and philosophy.

Online encyclopedias exist for all kinds of specific topics. If you can find one that covers your subject, it can be a great discovery. However, general-purpose encyclopedias are usually good enough sources for help with homework, papers, and projects.

Dictionary Details

Dictionaries are alphabetical listings of words or phrases. They contain definitions and sometimes other information, such as pronunciation, synonyms, where the word came from, and sentence usage.

Online Encyclopedias

Encyclopedia.com (http://www. encyclopedia.com) is a free encyclopedia that provides users with more than 57,000 articles from the *Columbia Encyclopedia.* Each article has links to newspaper and magazine articles as well as pictures and maps. Encyclopedia.com also has HighBeam Research, which is a digital archive for information seekers. With this, you can search through 32 million documents.

FREE Internet Encyclopedia (http://www.cam-info.net/enc.html) may not look very cool, but it's totally free and has *tons* of information. Select the MacroReference index to get a list of general topics or MicroReference for detailed, specific subjects. Also, if you're searching several sites for information, you can click on Pocket Encyclopedia for a condensed version of this site.

Encyberpedia (http://www.encyberpedia.com) isn't technically an encyclopedia. It's more like a directory. Click on any of the subjects on the page. Unlike other informational sites, this doesn't give you an article. What Encyberpedia does give you is a staggering list of links. Most have detailed descriptions to find whatever information you need.

MSN Encarta (http://encarta.msn.com) has a condensed version of its encyclopedia that is available for free and gives you good basic information. Most searches will give you several hits. Unfortunately, you have to pay to use the deluxe version of this encyclopedia.

Just like encyclopedias, online dictionaries sometimes jazz up entries. For example, when you look up the word "web" at Merriam-Webster Online, you will find that it is a noun, it came from the Old English word "wefan" (which means "to weave"), and it has various definitions. Sounds a lot like an entry in a regular dictionary, doesn't it? However, this dictionary entry also has links to related words such as "cobweb" and "spiderweb." Learning all about a word can make its spelling and meaning easier to understand—and remember.

Online Dictionaries

Merriam-Webster Online (http://www.m-w.com) is considered *the* online dictionary. And it couldn't be easier to use. Just type your word in the dictionary search field and click Go. Not only do you get the word's meaning, but also included is the word's pronunciation, part of speech, and how to change its form (such as how to make it plural). Also included are links to entries for similar words. This dictionary even gives you the history and date of creation of the word you look up.

OneLook Dictionary (http://www.onelook.com) lets you search more than 990 dictionaries at once. Type in your word and hit Search. Then this search engine goes to work consulting more than 100 general dictionaries, including Merriam-Webster's and WorldNet Vocabulary Helper, and gives you a link to each dictionary's definition. You can also do a reverse dictionary search with OneLook at this site. If you know the description, but can't remember the word, this tool comes in handy.

YourDictionary.com (http://www.yourdictionary.com) provides links to more than 2,500 dictionaries. These dictionaries list words in more than 300 languages! You've probably never heard of most of them, but it's fun to take a look. This Web site also has some helpful links to grammar guides (also in a variety of languages) and thesauruses. And if you need a word translated, you can do that, too!

Thesaurus Sources

A thesaurus is a kind of dictionary. It lists words with their synonyms and antonyms. Do you ever find yourself looking for a word that's on the tip of your tongue? You can think of similar words, but not the right one. Or what about when you've used the same word over and over again in a paper? You need to find some words that mean the same thing, but can't get that one out of your head. At times like this, reach for a thesaurus—or visit one online.

Online thesauruses are simple to use. Just type in your word and then get a list of words with the same meaning. Online thesauruses are helpful because not everyone owns one. It's not the sort of book most people use every day.

Almanacs Anyone?

Almanacs are books of facts about a certain subject. They are updated and published yearly. Almanacs usually have lists, charts, and tables of information.

Almanacs on the Web are really useful. Since almanacs are annual books, they become outdated quickly. The online versions always offer current information and are often updated more than once a year. The almanac on your family bookshelf at home might be from 1993. The library is probably more up to date with almanacs from 2002, 2003, and 2004, but not 2005! Then it's time to go online for some fresh information.

Online Thesauruses

Roget's II: The New Thesaurus (http://www. bartleby.com/62) is a wonder for Web word searchers. Peter Roget spent more than 50 years cataloguing and categorizing words and their synonyms. Type in the word that you are requesting synonyms for. If your word is listed in more than one category, you'll be asked to select the general definition.

Merriam-Webster Online (http://www.m-w.com) is part of the Merriam-Webster dictionary site. In this impressive online thesaurus you'll get the Merriam-Webster word definitions in addition to the requested word's synonyms. It's not as extensive as Roget's, but not as overwhelming either.

Thesaurus.com (http://thesaurus.reference.com) is a bare-bones Web site that is part of Dictionary.com, so you can switch back and forth between the two. You can find a lot of free information here, but there's also a Premium membership for a fee.

Online Almanacs

Infoplease (http://www.infoplease.com) is almost a reference bookshelf in itself. It has a dictionary, encyclopedia, atlas, thesaurus, and almanac. To browse the almanac's categories, use the button bar along the left-hand side of the screen. Use the search feature to look in just the almanac or all the reference sections.

The CIA World Factbook (http://www.odci.gov/cia/publications/factbook) should be your first stop for information about foreign countries. In the Country or Location section, you are given a list to choose from along the left-hand side of the screen. Once you find the area you are looking for, click on it. The first thing you will see is the country's flag and map. Then the country's geography is listed as well as important historical information and current issues. You also get details on the country's people, military, economy, government, communication, transportation, and more. You name it, it's there!

The Old Farmer's Almanac (http://www.almanac.com) has quite a history. The printed version of this online resource has been used since 1792 for weather and planting information. Now you can visit this farmer on the Web. This site is helpful when doing science reports on a variety of topics. Pull down Site Index from the menu on the home page. You'll find a linked list of topics to choose from, or you can just browse from there.

Get the Facts with an Atlas

An atlas is a collection of maps. Most atlases also give you some geographical information. But these maps tell you much more than how to avoid getting lost!

Atlases on the World Wide Web really jump off the screen. Ever find yourself with your nose to a map trying to read the name of some river or city? Forget about looking for a magnifying glass! On the Web you can just point and click to zoom in on whatever you want.

What if you need more information about something you see on a map in a traditional paper atlas? You would have to find somewhere else to look it up. Online, you can just point and click. Links and more give you plenty of information. And with Web atlases, you don't need to wait to buy the next edition for updated data.

Online Atlases

National Atlas (http://www.nationalatlas.gov) is very easy to use. Its maps give you a bunch of pictures of the United States. Here you can find geographical information as well as facts about different cultures and societies from all around the country. You can roam across America and zoom in wherever you want to reveal more description and detail. Just point at map features with your mouse to learn more about them.

U.S. Census Bureau Maps and Cartographic Resources (http://www.census.gov/geo/www/maps) provides high-quality, detailed maps of any place in the country. This easy-to-use atlas is especially good for getting information about cities and towns in the United States.

Worldtime (http://www.worldtime.com) is a service featuring an interactive world atlas. This reference tool also lists sunrise and sunset times for more than 500 cities.

USGS Map-a-Planet (http://pdsmaps.wr.usgs.gov) is really out of this world! Okay, science buffs! How would you like to see an image map of any area on Jupiter? What about Mars or even the moon? Developed by the U.S. Geological Survey (USGS), Map-a-Planet lets you choose from a variety of zoom levels, image sizes, and map projections. These images were created using data from several of NASA's *Viking* space missions.

Complete Research Searching

Oxford Reference Online (http://www.oxford reference.com) is maintained by one of the world's largest reference publishers. This site contains more than 100 dictionary, language-reference, and subject-reference works published by Oxford University Press. Oxford Reference Online, updated three times a year, is a fully-indexed, cross-searchable database of reference books. Also, for a fee, you can subscribe to the Premium Collection, which provides more in-depth information and more titles to choose from.

Refdesk.com (http://www.refdesk.com) must be home to the biggest desk in the world! What *doesn't* this site have? You could get lost clicking on all the fascinating tools here. Like clocks? You can see the USNO (United States Naval Observatory) atomic clock, plus a United States and world population clock. There's a Homework Helper section and Ask the Experts. There's a ton of search engines. And don't forget current news! This part of the desk features hundreds of publications, live television and radio feeds, business news, weather, and sports. And if you need a break, check out comics, crosswords, Fun Stuff, and Free Stuff. If you really just want to get to work, use the Search Resources section. It lets you search this site (and all its tools) or the World Wide Web. Instead of providing articles, this encyclopedia and search engine return lists (long lists) of links related to your topic. Some topics are very well covered but you might occasionally hit a dead end.

The Whole Research Enchilada

Some research sites are like reference book sets. They don't have just a dictionary or an encyclopedia. You can look for information in several research resources. Sites like this may include a dictionary, an encyclopedia, a thesaurus, a news index, an atlas, and so on. Usually, you can use each tool separately or use a "power search" option to quickly look through the entire site for information.

This sort of research tool doesn't exist outside of the Web. You would need to find—and carry—each of the volumes. Think of lugging around just a dictionary and an encyclopedia! That alone would be quite a chore. Plus, online research sites usually have more tools. One search looks for your topic in several reference sources. And these sites usually have links in their articles to help you find even more information.

Still Looking?

Do you want to unearth some cool sites of your own? Where should you start? Good question. Remember the chapter on searching, earlier in the book? (See pages 46–61.) Here's a great way to use those tips: You could use a traditional search engine. Type in "encyclopedia" and start clicking around those hits. It is a good idea to use directory searches here. Many search engines have reference categories built right in!

Search-Engine Reference Resources

Check out the search-engine references below when doing research. But remember: Practice makes perfect! If you don't find what you are looking for right away, keep looking.

Yahooligans! Reference
(http://yahooligans.yahoo.com/reference)

Google Directory Reference
(http://directory.google.com/Top/Reference)

AltaVista Directory (http://www.altavista.com/dir)

Ask Jeeves for Kids Newsroom
(http://www.ajkids.com/news.asp)

KidsClick! Facts/Current Events
(http://www.kidsclick.org/topfact.html)

Yahoo! Reference (http://dir.yahoo.com/Reference)

School Subjects

Your day at school isn't spent doing just one thing. Your class might work on math problems first thing in the morning. Then your teacher might give a lesson in social studies. You might have an art class just before lunch. In the afternoon, your class might work on science experiments. Before you go home, you might spend time reading aloud in groups.

Schoolwork involves a lot of different subjects. In elementary and middle school, these subjects are usually language arts, social studies, science, math, and the arts. And just like the megadirectories on the Web, each of these subjects includes many different topics.

Language Arts

Language arts is the study of language. It includes both reading and writing. The alphabet, spelling, phonics, grammar, and vocabulary are some of the building blocks of language arts. But language arts doesn't only involve studying English. Foreign language is also a language art. If you study a foreign language, you will study its vocabulary, spelling, and grammar. You will also learn how to read, write, and speak it.

The Web can be a fun and useful addition to your schoolwork in language arts. Working on your skills on your own will really help you when it comes time to do work at school.

Some language arts Web sites offer games and quizzes to help you with spelling, grammar, or vocabulary. Others recommend great books for you to read. Still others help you with writing. The Web can help you brainstorm for a topic, find information, and get writing. And don't think that writing is something that should only be done for school. Do some creative writing on your own time. You may find that writing your own stories is a lot more exciting than watching a TV show. Reading and writing go hand in hand. The more you read, the better you will be able to write (and vice versa). These two skills will stay with you throughout your life and they will always come in handy. Get some ideas on how to start working on your language arts skills at these Web sites:

Biography Maker (http://www.bham.wednet.edu/bio/ biomaker.htm) wants "to inspire lively story telling and vivid writing which will make your readers want to know more about your subject." This site walks you through the important steps of writing a biography, which include questioning, learning, and storytelling. Don't forget to look at the Six Traits of Effective Writing. Stop by this site while you're in the early stages of writing a biography. It will help you develop the skills necessary to becoming a better writer, which not only helps you in English class but will also help you in other subjects.

OH! Kids Language Arts (http://www.oplin.org/ohkids/ Homework/langarts.htm) wants to help you learn more about language. This site is published by the Ohio Public Library Information Network. The subject index covers such important topics as grammar, spelling, and writing. Make sure you take a look at the options available under the For Young Authors heading. Improve your writing skills, and take time to read what other kids have been writing.

The Children's Literature Web Guide (http://www.acs. ucalgary.ca/~dkbrown) lists all sorts of resources for eager readers. It guides you to award-winning children's books, reading-related Web sites, book discussions, and lots of other resources. Remember to try to read as much as you can— good readers are better learners. Browse around this site to find a good book. Then head to the library and pick it up!

Grammar Gorillas (http://www.funbrain.com/grammar) will test your grammar skills. This page is part of the great FunBrain site. You can play a beginner or advanced game of Grammar Gorillas. You play by choosing the correct part of speech requested. Win bananas for each right answer! If you really go ape and get all of the questions correct, you can send your score to your parents and brag to them.

Vocabulary Puzzles (http://www.vocabulary.com). You probably know all about vocabulary tests. This site, the home of Vocabulary University, takes a new spin on learning words by having you figure out fun puzzles. Each section of the test features questions that involve similar types of words. New games are posted every so often, and the folks who run this cool online school are always adding new features to the site. Learning new words will help you with your reading, writing, and speaking—and that sure covers a lot! Enroll today and start working your way toward graduating from Vocabulary University!

Social Studies

Social studies is really several subjects in one. Social studies combines the study of history, different cultures, government, current events, and geography.

In social studies, you can learn all about what happened in the past: explorers, discoveries, inventions, times of war, and times of peace. You can learn about how the U.S. government works. Look into the past to see how our government was formed, or study an upcoming presidential (or local) election. You'll also learn about other cultures and their governments. Today's current events become tomorrow's history, and they're all a part of social studies. It can be really interesting to see how our world has developed.

The Web is a great resource for learning more about what is happening every day to change our world. The more you learn about what goes on all around you, the better informed you will be in school when it comes time for social studies.

Geography relates directly to everybody in the world. We all have our own place on the map, whether we live in Portland, Maine; Portland, Oregon; or Portland, Victoria, in Australia! Studying maps helps you understand our world and the people who live in it. There are all kinds of maps on the Web—zoom in on a map of your local area or another country.

Visit the Web and see how it can help you in your social studies: take a virtual tour of the White House, read Congressional bills and Supreme Court decisions, visit a wire service and read up-to-the-minute news, drop by the United Nations and read about human rights and economic development all over the world, learn about famous people, or visit historical museums to get a picture of the past. Learn about your country or see the world at these social studies sites:

Biography.com (http://www.biography.com) is a great resource for kids who are looking to learn the important facts about somebody famous from the past or present. This site features more than 25,000 profiles kids can search for and browse through. Stop here when you are doing research for a report or just to learn more about the people who shape our world. Learning about the past helps us understand the present a little better.

IPL KidSpace: Culture Quest (http://www.ipl.org/youth/cquest) is a great resource for inquisitive kids to visit. This site, posted by The Internet Public Library, celebrates societies around the world. Visit any part of the earth through this site. Culture Quest has broken the world down into eight convenient regions. Get better acquainted with different parts of the world as well as the art, customs, and history of the people who live there. You just might find an interesting topic to write about for an upcoming school report.

Smithsonian Institution (http://www.si.edu) Web site, just like the collection of museums in Washington D.C., is a national treasure. The Smithsonian site features art galleries, museums, and much more. You can find all kinds of information about many topics. Be sure to check out Smithsonian Kids where you can learn fascinating facts about the U.S. Presidents as well as what it was like to walk on the moon. Being well informed about topics will open more doors to learning and experience than you can imagine.

Science

Science can help you explore all kinds of things about our planet Earth—and other worlds, too! Science covers a lot of ground: life, energy, motion, heat, force, space, elements, matter, and more! Science studies everything that makes everything exist and happen the way that it does. Sounds pretty wild, huh? Well, it is!

Science lets you travel to the moon or to another universe. It lets you look into a living human body to see how life works. Learn why some people have blue or brown eyes and why others have one of each! It shows you the power of the earth's wind, water, and weather and the sun's awesome power, too. Science can even explain everyday things, such as why you lean forward if the car you're riding in suddenly slows down (it's called *inertia*, and it's a powerful force). Did you know that color is actually created by light? Or that gravity holds us all onto earth and makes us weigh what we do? On the moon, where gravity is much less of a force, you would be much lighter! And don't forget the power of time—it turns coal into diamonds and moves the continents around like bath toys. Science explains everything—or at least it tries to.

The Web can be an important aid in your science schoolwork. Just like other school subjects, there is so much that you could study, there just isn't enough time in the day to cover everything! Exploring more of what you study in school on your own time will give you the chance to come across subjects that are really out of this world. And then, as you continue to study more in school, you will have plenty of ideas stored up about all sorts of subjects! Visit these super scientific Web sites to see where they can lead you:

Discovery Kids (http://kids.discovery.com) is your ticket to parts of the earth you have probably never seen. Explore by Subject is a good place to start. Topics here cover a lot of ground: animals (such as tigers and sharks), dinosaurs; space (such as Mars and the space station), history, and much more. Dig into some new scientific topics and get a jump on your studies in school. You could easily spend a lot of time browsing around this site. Or just use the Search function to find exactly what you are looking for. Discover a world of information here.

HowStuffWorks (http://www.howstuffworks.com) is full of hundreds of articles on how things work. If you're new to the site, check out The Top Ten. Here you can find the top ten most popular articles, which include how car engines work, how hybrid cars work, and even how cell phones work! HowStuffWorks has several categories at the top of the page, such as computer, auto, electronics, science, health, money, travel, and much more. Check out the Quick Stuff box to learn a few interesting facts. Pass those facts along to your friends and teachers to show them how much cool stuff you really know!

Exploratorium (http://www.exploratorium.edu) is the online home of the Exploratorium Museum in San Francisco, California. Online visitors can dig into science experiments located on more than 15,000 Web sites. This site puts some of the best science exhibits and experiments on the Web for kids to look at and try. Check out the Science of Music with online exhibits, movies, and questions. Spend some time in the Learning Studio trying some different science activities, such as building a solar system or a salt volcano. Working on science in your spare time will really give you an edge in school by giving you firsthand experience with scientific exploration—that's what being a real scientist is all about!

The Franklin Institute Online (http://sln.fi.edu) has loads of online exhibits that cover almost every branch of science. Click on Learn to find all kinds of information. For example, the EARTHFORCE section digs into earth science and Undersea and Oversee is all about the ocean. The exhibits and articles are on cool, fun topics such as robots or the history of flight. Frankly, this site is one of the best on the Web. Spend some time here and brush up on history and science all at once. And come back often—this site is always adding something new for kids to get into.

Math

Math is the study of numbers. That may sound simple at first, but math studies *all about* numbers: how they work; how they are related to each other; how they are combined; how to measure them; how they change—well, you get the idea.

You started learning math as a small child. Your parents and picture books probably helped you learn to count. From there you learned about numbers and what they stand for. Then you learned to add and subtract, multiply and divide. And the process continued through school as you learned about fractions, decimals, and word problems. In the future you will dive into algebra, geometry, trigonometry, and maybe even calculus. All of these math subjects build on one another like bricks in a house. And there is room for the World Wide Web in that house.

One way the Web can help you with math is through homework help. A lot of sites will answer questions that you have through e-mail—your own personal online tutor! But there is much more to these sites than just questions and answers.

Some sites will help you brush-up on math skills while you play a game. Other sites pose mathematical puzzles, riddles, and exercises for you to solve. Another way to explore math on the Web is—get this—by reading stories! These mathematical tales will really tease your brain!

By working on math on your own, with the help of the Web, you will be training yourself to think faster and more clearly. Those skills will not only help you with your math at school, but in all of the other areas of your life. Get cracking on your math skills with the help of these Web sites:

Ask Dr. Math (http://mathforum.org/dr.math) is the ultimate mathematics homework helper. If you are ever stuck on a problem and don't have anybody to turn to for help, don't freak out! Just call the doctor. Helpful folks who can field your math questions online are always only a few moments away. Answers to frequently asked questions (FAQs) are stored in the Archives—check there first for the solution to your problem. And if you can't find an answer, ask Dr. Math. Motivated math maniacs can find links to other sites that feature fun problems to try and solve. Always trying your hardest to figure out difficult problems will help train your mind to work better. There is no limit to how far you can go!

Math Playground (http://www.mathplayground.com) is an educational and fun math site. There are many games and activities to help improve your grades. Try your hand at the Math Hoops, where you practice word problems. If you answer three of the five questions correctly, then you can shoot a basket! Click on the Flashcards link under Do the Math, and test your skills at multiplication, addition, and subtraction. Think you have a tricky math question? You can submit it to Math TV, and maybe your question will be featured on their weekly video. Whatever the math problem, you're bound to have fun finding the answer here!

Math Baseball (http://www.funbrain.com/funbrain/math) lets you take a swing at solving math problems. When you show up at this online ballpark, you choose the style of math to be played. Work with one task, such as multiplication, or try several math skills at once. Then choose a skill level from Easy, Medium, Hard, or Super Brain. The pitcher will throw a problem at you, such as "6×5," and if you answer correctly, you'll get a single, double, triple, or home run depending on how hard the question was. You can have fun and practice math at the same time. Just like playing a sport, you need to practice school skills in order to stay sharp.

The Arts

A lot of your other school subjects are related to one another. In the same way, everything else that you learn can be applied to the arts. Visual arts (such as painting, drawing, sculpture, and crafts) and musical arts (creating and listening to music) are a lot of fun to do and see. Appreciating and creating art is a skill that is developed through study and practice. And it is a great way to express yourself. By doing so, you will be developing a unique way of telling other people what you really think—and it will help make you smarter and a better student. For instance, did you know that more than 80 percent of the people who worked on the *Mars Pathfinder* project studied music or art (or both) as children? (*Mars Pathfinder* was a space mission to Mars.)

Art in elementary school is usually hands-on. You get to do all kinds of projects, such as finger painting, clay sculpture, papier-mâché, mosaic tile, and more. There's more to art than getting your hands dirty, though.

For example, you can learn about different artists from the past, what types of art they created, and what their art meant to other people. This type of art is known as art history. Or you could study all about a certain type of art, such as how to paint pictures of people. Getting really good at any type of art is usually a long process, but it is a lot of fun to work on. And the Web can help you develop your interest in the arts.

Another side of art is music. Some research show that studying music can actually make you smarter. And some studies even show that listening to classical music—especially music by Wolfgang Amadeus Mozart—can help your brain work better and make learning easier. This hasn't been proven yet, but it is interesting. Music is a lot of fun, and if it happens to make you smarter as well, great! Some of the musical things you can do online include taking piano lessons and listening to and learning about all kinds of music.

You can visit world famous museums on the Web, too. Take a look at—and even learn *how* to look at—some of the masterpieces decorating these online halls. Get some help developing an appreciation for the arts, or get some ideas for making some art of your own with these creative sites:

Children's Music Web (http://childrensmusic.org) always has something to tempt your ears. Check out today's words of wisdom, and listen to some seasonal songs. This site also features reviews of music, interviews with musicians, and related articles. Click on over to the Resources for Kids section in order to learn new songs, vote on your favorite songs, find out about upcoming concerts and good radio stations in your area, and learn about other musical news and information. Expand on the music knowledge you have learned in school and take some new information back to your classmates. Chances are, it will be music to their ears!

Instrument Encyclopedia (http://www.si.umich.edu/chico/ instrument) is a great place to start learning about musical instruments from all around the world. Here you can take a tour of various types of instruments listed in four categories: wind, electronic, string, and percussion. Or you can search for each instrument according to geography. Each entry features the instrument's history, how it is made, and how it is played. Find an instrument that looks interesting to you, and then look into possibly playing it for the school band! Creating music is even more fun than listening to it, and you'll be developing a new skill that can last a lifetime.

The Piano Education Page Just for Kids (http://piano education.org/pnokids.html) is a super site for kids who already play the piano, those who are looking to start, and even for those who just want to learn more about composers and the piano. You can also listen to selections of piano music at this site. There are also tips posted monthly about piano playing as well as links to other piano-related sites. The folks at this site encourage you to listen to music as much as possible. Music is a great way to express yourself, both by playing and listening. And, by learning how to read and follow music, you will expand your language skills.

Metropolitan Museum of Art (http://www.metmuseum.org) is a nice way to introduce yourself to the world of art. Even if you can't visit the museum in person in New York (and if you can, make sure you do), this site has a lot to offer. Browse the Permanent Collection section to see some art from around the world. Then pay a visit to the MuseumKids section. There are activities, games, and a lot of information that will help you learn more about art. As you learn more about the art that different people from around the world have created, you'll be learning more than just history. You'll be learning about societies from the past and present and how they have contributed to the world in which we all live.

It All Gets Caught in the Web!

Some Web sites offer a wealth of information on virtually any content area that you wish to explore. They have many topics, even more subtopics, and hundreds of links. These sites take you beyond the basics of language arts, social studies, science, math, and the arts. Visit the worlds of anthropology, nutrition, space biology, the theater, transportation, and more.

Infoplease Homework Central (http://www.infoplease.com/homework) has some great links. You could spend weeks at this site and never get through all of the information. You'll have to see it to believe it.

Kid Info (http://www.kidinfo.com/schoolsubjects.html) lists many links to homework-help sites listed by school subject. Or, if you know what you're researching, you can type in the keywords and search directly. There's a wealth of information here, so spend some time digging through all the subjects, and you'll be set!

Always Explore to Learn More

The sites in this chapter may seem like they can only offer you help with homework and school-related stuff. But they can do a lot more than that.

These sites dig deep into topics that you may have only heard a little bit about. Visiting them may not always help you find the answers to next week's science test, but they might help you find topics and subjects that interest you. They might even encourage you to explore further and learn more. And the more you learn in general, the better you will do in school. Not just because you have to, but because you want to! Follow links that look interesting to you, and a world of information will unfold. Happy exploring!

Get Off the Computer!

Life does not revolve around the World Wide Web. In fact, about 15 years ago, few people had ever heard of it! They certainly hadn't used it. The cool sites that we've talked about didn't exist. There is a lot more to life than the Web. But guess what? The Web can help you find those other things! Then it's time to get up, turn off the computer, and get busy.

Explore Your World

It may be hard to imagine, but this world has more than 6 billion people on it. Some live in neighborhoods a lot like yours. Others live far away—some without running water, electricity, stores, or computers. Many others live in places somewhere in between those two. On the Web, you can learn about other kids from all over the world.

If you can peel your eyes off of the computer screen and look out the window, you might see something interesting. Nature! Sky! Birds and squirrels! Fresh air! On the Web, you can learn all about the outdoors and get some cool ideas for how to spend your time outside.

Open the door to these sites and see if any look inviting:

Help Save Animals and Their Habitat: 101 Things You Can Do! (http://www.oregonzoo.org/ConservationResearch/whatyou.htm) is great for animal lovers. To save endangered species, we need to protect their environments. Learn about ways to help at this wild site. There are tips here for you to use at home, on vacation, and while shopping. There are even some business tips that you can share with your parents.

U.S. Consumer Product Safety Commission (or CPSC) (http://www.cpsc.gov) helps keep families safe. The CPSC wants to try and help prevent unnecessary injuries. At the Especially for Kids page, you'll find out how to protect yourself and your family. Learn how to look for unsafe products and what to do about them. The Brainbusters safety quiz is loaded with tips.

Environmental Kids Club (http://www.epa.gov/kids) is part of the U.S. Environmental Protection Agency. At the Kids Club you can learn all about air, water, animals, and recycling and how you can help the environment. Games, stories, and puzzles teach you hundreds of ways to protect your environment. Check out the Game Room, Art Room, and Science Room for more fun activities.

World Almanac for Kids (http://www.worldalmanacforkids. com/explore) is full of information and statistics about all kinds of stuff! Ever wonder who shares a birthday with you? Check out Historical Birthdays to find out. You can also look through the Did You Know? section to find interesting facts you may not have know. There's so much to explore!

Rainforest Heroes (http://www.rainforestheroes.com/ kidscorner) need your help! Every day, old-growth rainforest trees that are home to millions of animals are being cut down and used as building materials. While it is important to build homes for our families, that doesn't mean it is okay to destroy the homes of rainforest animals in the process. This site from the Rainforest Action Network provides sample letters you can use to send to companies and suggestions for other steps to take. Plus, you can learn all about the rainforests—and the people and animals that live there.

FactFinder Kids' Corner (http://factfinder.census.gov/ home/en/kids/kids.html) is part of the U.S. Census Bureau's

Web site. Here you can find statistics about the states, learn about the U.S. census, and much more! On the home page you'll find the estimated U.S. population at that very minute. You can learn all kinds of facts about the United States here.

Learn a New Skill

One great thing about the Web is that it can help you learn new skills or start a hobby. These skills may make your life more fun or they might be helpful. Some are both. Let's do some browsing and see what new skills we can pick up!

Rescue 411 (http://library.thinkquest.org/10624) is all about first-aid basics. Someday you might be faced with a life-or-death situation that requires quick action. You might be babysitting a child who burns herself with hot water. You may be the only one around when someone falls down and is knocked unconscious. Will you know what to do? Unfortunately, many times the answer is no. Learn important first-aid basics at this site and play You Bet Your Life! This interactive game show lets you see how sharp you are at first aid.

Learning the Compass (http://www.angelfire.com/fl/compless) shows you how to use a compass. Compasses use the earth's magnetic field to point out direction. They look like watches with N, E, S, and W instead of numbers. Take this compass lesson and learn how to use one.

Conjuror Magic! (http://conjuror. com/magictricks) provides instructions for new magicians such as yourself. This site teaches you tricks you can do with items from around your house. Make sure to get help from an adult when you want to try any potentially dangerous tricks. Once you've mastered those, you can move onto the material for advanced magicians.

Gardening for Kids (http://www.geocities.com/enchanted forest/glade/3313). Want to grow a beautiful garden of flowers? Check out this site! Start with basic tips—from soil to water to mulch. You'll get the foundation of gardening. Learn about different plants in the flower archives. These kid-friendly plants are easy to work with and dazzling!

Get Active and Healthy

American kids spend more time in front of the TV—and computer—than they do exercising. Exercise doesn't have to be boring—it can be lots of fun! Riding your bike, playing kickball, or just running around are all great ways to exercise. The Web can give you some ideas for fun exercise, too. Shake your bones after checking out these sites:

Be a Fid Kid (http://www.kidshealth.org/kid/stay_healthy/body/fit_kid.html) from KidsHealth teaches kids that there's always time for exercise. If you're by yourself or with friends, or if it's raining or it's cold, there's some type of exercise you can do. Check out this site to see for yourself.

Bodies in Motion...Minds at Rest (http://library.thinkquest.org/12153)can help you get in shape physically and mentally. Find out how to get in shape and stay that way. Check out the Basics section for a refresher on how to warm up and check your heart rate. You can also find out if you're in shape or not. Get moving, and get in shape!

Crafts

Arts and crafts are great ways to express yourself. Plus, you can make nice things to decorate your room, give as gifts, or for school projects. Get creative after visiting these sites:

Joseph Wu's Origami Page (http://www.origami.vancouver.bc.ca) has a gallery of origami and diagrams on how to make a frog, crane, dragon, and more. Under Articles, you can read about the history of paper folding.

Kid Stuff (http://www.make-stuff.com/kids) is a fantastic site for making crafts. You can find great kid-oriented projects. It includes fun and easy arts and crafts and cooking projects. Although part of the site requires a paid membership, there are still plenty of crafts and recipes you can make for free. Just scroll down the page for all the free stuff.

In the Kitchen

Who doesn't love to eat? Use these sites to learn to make some goodies of your own. Good food can be good for you. These sites provide recipes that you can make in your kitchen (ask a parent for help). You might even learn a little about nutrition along the way. Get hungry, and take a bite out of these sites:

Kids Food CyberClub (http://www. stockportmbc.gov.uk/primary/ ladybrook/nut/WW5.htm) has a food guide, books about food, how to grow veggies and fruits, nutritional information, and activities. Use your online research skills to answer the question of the month. Learn about nutrition with the USDA's Food Guide Pyramid. You can even Rate your Plate by figuring out what a serving size is. Find out what books about food kids like you have recommended. Or even suggest your favorite to other kids. Follow links to other cool kids' sites that feature food, gardening, cooking, crafts, and writing.

Nutrition Café (http://www.exhibits.pacsci.org/nutrition) helps kids figure out if they're getting enough nutrition. Check out the Have-a-Bite Café where you can build your meal with items from several menus. Once you select your meal, the site shows you how it stacks to the Recommended Dietary Allowance (RDA) for calories, fats, proteins, and much more. There are games here, too, so click on Nutrition Sleuth and help Inspector Snarfengood solve the case!

Learn a Language

If you haven't had the chance to learn a foreign language in school, you can give it a try on the Web. Or if you have had some instruction, check out these sites to brush up.

French (http://www.jump-gate.com/languages/french). This site teaches you to read and write French with several lessons. Start with grammar basics. Then, move to common phrases and sentences. Eventually (if you stick with it), you might be able to read an article from Paris's *Le Monde* newspaper that is available at the site.

Spanish (http://www.spanishunlimited.com). This free site teaches you Spanish. You will need to register to have access, though. Be sure you ask your parents before registering at the site.

Chinese (http://www.wku.edu/~yuanh/AudioChinese). This is an audio lesson in Chinese. Listen to and learn hundreds of essential Chinese phrases. Learn how to say "glad to meet you" and "good-bye." Move onto phrases and words you would need for dining and shopping in China.

KidChef (http://www.kidchef.com) is "where kids rule the kitchen." Answer the KidChef Poll on the left-hand side, or browse previous poll questions. You can also see what's happening in the kitchen under Fun Stuff. Here you can even ask a cooking question under Ask the Chief Chef. So get cooking!

As you travel the Web, look for pages and sites that are interesting. You can use the Web to communicate, shop, learn, and study. Perhaps most important, you can use it to expand your horizons. It is hard to believe that a little box on your desk can take you anywhere on this planet—and let you look at other planets and solar systems. Some scientists have concluded that the invention of the Internet is as important as the invention of the TV. Others say it is as important as the invention of the wheel! Either way, the Web is here to stay. Enjoy your time online, and be sure to make the Web a positive—and fun—influence in your life.

Glossary

Archive. An electronic attic for storing old information, such as articles from an online magazine or questions answered by a homework expert. Web sites put out new information all the time, but they save all the old information in an archive.

Bookmark. A Web browser tool that makes it easy to find sites that you visit often. Also called Favorites in some browsers.

Browser. Software program that reads and displays Web sites. Microsoft Internet Explorer and Netscape Navigator are popular Web browsers.

CD-ROM. A disc that looks just like a music compact disc (CD) but stores computer programs.

Chat. An Internet feature that lets you type messages that appear on a friend's screen as soon as they type them. When several people get together to chat, they're in a "chat room."

Clip Art. Small pieces of artwork that you can use to illustrate Web pages. Clip art pictures used to be on paper, and people "clipped" them out of a book with scissors.

Copyright. A legal rule that says people own what they create. Nobody can download or use copyrighted pictures, sounds, or movies without permission from whomever created them. Make sure a Web site gives you permission to use its pictures before downloading them.

Download. Taking pictures, sounds, programs, or other information off the Internet and putting it on your computer.

E-mail. Electronic mail. This service allows the sending of messages and other files, such as pictures and sound clips, over the Internet.

FAQs. Frequently Asked Questions. FAQs answer the questions people usually have when they first visit a site. Check out FAQs to see what's going on when first arriving at a site.

Favorites. *See* Bookmark.

HTML. HyperText Markup Language. This is one of the main programming codes used to create Web pages.

Hyperlink. Words on a Web site that you click to visit another Web page. Hyperlinks ("links" for short) are usually underlined and a different color than other words on the page.

Icon. A picture you can click that represents something on your computer, such as a program (your Web browser), folder, or function (the trash bin).

Interactive. A Web site or computer program that lets you enter information or control what happens on the screen.

Internet. The network that connects computers around the world. When a computer is connected to the Internet (or Net for short), that computer's user can access information other Internet users have displayed for them to see and read. It's like exploring new places, except the information travels over telephone lines and through a computer.

ISP. Internet Service Provider. This is a company that connects your computer to the Internet through your modem and a phone or cable line.

Java. A programming language that runs little programs on Web pages. Some games you play on a Web page use Java.

Keywords. Words you use to search for information posted on Web sites. You use keywords when working in search engines.

Link. *See* Hyperlink.

Megadirectory. A Web site, similar to a search engine, that helps users find information online. Megadirectories usually list information as topics. These topics lead to other subjects, and so on.

Message Board. A program on a Web site with a form that allows visitors to read and post messages usually about a specific subject.

Modem. A device inside of the computer (or sometimes outside) that lets the computer connect to a telephone line and talk with other computers around the world. A computer using a modem is making a phone call just like people do, except its conversations bring up Web pages and transfer e-mail instead of spoken conversations.

Mouse. A handheld tool used to point to things on a computer screen. Point the arrow on the screen at something and click the button by pressing and releasing it. Most mouses have a right-hand button that provides more functions.

Multimedia. Any information on the computer screen except for plain words, including pictures, sounds, and movies.

Net. *See* Internet.

Password. A secret word people use to get into Web sites that only let in members. When you join some Web clubs, you'll create a password and use it every time you visit the Web site.

RealAudio. A special program you can add to your Web browser in order to listen to recorded sounds and music online. Try out songs on CDs you're thinking of buying or hear sound clips from your favorite movies. RealAudio can be downloaded for free, and it's easy to add to the browser.

RealPlayer. Just like RealAudio, except it also lets you watch movies online.

Search Engine. A Web site, like a megadirectory, that helps users find information. These services look through all of the Web sites that they keep track of to find what you are looking for. A search engine is like the card catalog at the library—it is the best place to start looking for information.

Shockwave. A special program you can add to your Web browser so you can view animations—such as cartoons—and play lots of games. When visiting a site with features that need Shockwave, a message will let you know. You can download Shockwave for free, and it's easy to add to the browser.

Surfing. The word for cruising around the Internet. When people get done working online, they'll say something like, "I've been surfing for two hours."

URL. Uniform Resource Locator. The fancy name for a Web page's address. The address "http://www.pbs.org" is a URL.

User. Computer user. The name for people when they are "using" computers.

Virtual. Internet versions of things found in real life. A virtual postcard isn't a real postcard that you drop in the mail; it's an electronic message and picture that you send over the Net.

Web Page. The name for a document on the Web. Web pages are created in HTML.

Web Site. The name for a collection of Web pages on one topic put up by one person or group.

World Wide Web. A way of viewing the Internet. The World Wide Web (or Web for short) is the group of connected Web pages and sites, featuring animation, photographs, pictures, text, movies, sound, and more. Many Web pages and sites—from all over the world—are linked together (*see* Hyperlink) and can be visited with the touch of a button.

Index